"*Mom Loves the Dogs More* is a poignant and introspective story of family, perseverance, and hope - and that embracing the painful parts of life is the only way we can make space for the joy. Thoughtfully weaving together recollections of the trials and triumphs of her family's many temporary and permanent dog companions, Cindy Ojczyk reminds us that love is an action, not just a feeling." -**Adrian Lott, creator of *Adrian Likes Old Dogs* on Substack and Instagram's @adoptolddogs**

"In these pages, Cindy captures what dogs quietly teach us about devotion, loss, and letting go. Her stories of raising pets and raising children run side by side, offering comfort and courage to anyone standing at the threshold of launching big kids into adulthood." –**Esther Joy Goetz, creator of *Moms of Bigs***

"This book hits so close to home. This is so much more than a 'dog book'. Ojczyk shares the struggles of parents – questioning your choices, your words, your actions. Even though they come from a place of love, it's still easy to wonder, 'Did I do the right thing?' Using the stories of her effort to help foster dogs, she shares the beautiful lessons that helped her also be a good parent – not perfect, not always right, but always trying from the heart. Love this book and all it teaches us, not just about finding a home, but building one. Highly recommend this one - whether you love a kid or a dog, it will speak to your heart." -**Cara Sue Achterberg, author and co-founder of *Who Will Let The Dogs Out***

"A heartfelt memoir about the power of fostering set against shifting family dynamics, that proves just how much it takes to be a good parent to family members on two legs and four. It's a gorgeous testament to the transformative power of love." **—Victoria Schade, author of *Who Rescued Who* and more**

"Tender, candid, and full of grace, *Mom Loves the Dogs More* shows how a family navigates grief and the rough weather of adolescence, then meets the reality of anxiety, depression, and ADHD head-on. Cindy's voice is steady and humane, and the foster dogs are more than a subplot; they're the lifeline that keeps love from unraveling. A healing, hopeful read for anyone who believes dogs help us find our way back to one another." **-Tricia Montgomery, Founder, Moose's March**

"There's so much heartfelt goodness packed into *Mom Loves the Dogs More: A Memoir of Family Rescue*. Author, Cindy Ojczyk mixes the angst and joy of raising two daughters with the stresses and delights of welcoming one canine newcomer after another into their home. And all of the personalities blend so beautifully together, with life lessons learned in every chapter. Cindy captures the unique essence of each family member (both two-legged and four-legged) and bundles them all beautifully in this charming book of enjoyment and life lessons. Every chapter begins with delightful photos of the current canines in the household and is filled with charming humor and vulnerability." **-Dr. Nancy Kay, Veterinarian, author of *Speaking for Spot* and *A Dog Named 647***

"*Mom Loves the Dogs More: A Memoir of Family Rescue*, is full of love, love for dogs, love for children, and love for family. There are bumps along the way, saying goodbye to foster dogs, dealing with mental health, and family drama, but honesty, vulnerability, and love sees the family through. If you're a dog lover or have seen a child leave your nest, you will find yourself in Cindy's story." **—Morgan Baker, author of *Emptying the Nest: Getting Better at Goodbyes*, Professor at Emerson College**

"You don't need to be a dog person to fall under the spell of this remarkable story. As I turned each page, I found myself eagerly anticipating the next furry personality to enter the Ojczyk family's world, knowing that somehow, each creature would arrive bearing the precise wisdom needed for that moment. What emerges is something far more profound than a simple rescue story—it's a testament to the transformative power of unconditional love.

This book gets right to the heart of what it means to love fiercely, whether that's patiently teasing out the needs of a traumatized foster dog or painstakingly puzzling through how to help a struggling child. Ojczyk has crafted a story that will resonate with anyone who has ever felt the weight of a mother's tireless quest to find the key that unlocks her children's healing. Raw, honest, and ultimately hopeful, this is a book about the unexpected places we find grace when our families need it most." **— Marika Paez Wiesen, educator, author, and certified ADHD parenting coach.**

"Cindy Ojczyk's memoir is a lifeline for anyone navigating the emotional labyrinth of parenting teens in crisis. With raw honesty, deep compassion, and a healthy dose of humour, she shares how a parade of rescue dogs became unexpected healers - restoring connection, structure, and hope at a time when everything else seemed to be unraveling. This is not just a story about dogs, and it's not just a story about parenting. It's about resilience, love, and the messy beauty of holding it together when life falls apart. Every page feels like a heart-to-heart with a wise friend who's walked through the fire and found grace on the other side." – **Anke Herrmann, Creator of *Soul Touched by Dogs* award-winning podcast**

"This memoir beautifully reveals how the human–animal bond transforms us, reminding us that the truest gift we can give, whether to a dog on the way to a forever home or a child stepping into the world, is being deeply seen and loved." – **Kristen McClure, MSW, LCSW, ADHD therapist, Author of *ADHD Kids* on Substack**

Mom Loves the Dogs More

A Memoir of Family Rescue

Cindy Ojczyk

Screen Porch Press

ISBN: 979-8-9989597-1-4 (paperback)

ISBN: 979-8-9989597-0-7 (ebook)

Library of Congress Control Number: 2025916971

Book Cover Design by Melissa Williams Design

Author Photo by Jennifer Grace Portraits

Interior Photographs by Cindy Ojczyk

First Edition, 2025.

This is a work of non-fiction. The author has drawn on personal journals, recollections and interpretations of events, and changed some of the names and dates.

This memoir contains passages about mental health and pet loss.

Visit the author's website at www.cindyowrites.com

Parenting is a privilege.

To Joe, who has walked beside me through this journey, we did it! We raised two wonderful people. To those wonderful women, Anna and Mia, your love makes my world go around.

Contents

A Note from Us

A well-worn adage cautions that change is the only constant in life. For a parent, that's a good thing. Time, albeit ticking, affords opportunities to redeem oneself when reality strays far from theory. I committed my family to fostering dogs after surmising I could solve one problem by fixing another. Instead, my experience fostering dogs while parenting teens is best described as a chicken-and-egg analogy: there wasn't one tale told without the other.

While I tried to be true to the memory of events, I found that nothing unfolds in a vacuum. As such, my daughters Anna and Mia reviewed, debated, and adjusted my telling of our story to keep me as close to the truth as our collective memory enabled. A few names and places have been changed to protect the privacy of those connected to events in our story.

SIERRA

Chapter 1

Monday morning of the second week without our beloeved dog Sierra dawned like the movie Groundhog's Day. I was struggling to remain neutral in the sister-war dueling across the kitchen table when my eye caught a flash of gray feathers flapping outside the kitchen window. A chickadee with a caterpillar in its beak flew into a birdhouse to feed its young. I chuckled quietly to myself as I thought of Loree and the irony of the moment. She once joked that if mothers gave birth to teenagers, there'd be no people left in this world; we'd eat our offspring, not feed them, the moment they took their first breath and whined. "I want to eat my kids!" became the joke between us when one of us needed to vent.

What Loree and I really craved was a meter on our phones that would immediately connect us friend to friend when an imaginary arrow hit the red zone from a rise in our fury or panic. The calming voice of a good friend would immediately intervene. Steam vented before a blow-out.

I'd wished for that contraption more than eight years earlier when a younger Anna and Mia sat at the same butcherblock table, united in their first crusade for a dog; one carefully choreographed by my husband, Joe. My beautiful, funny children could easily be pains in the backside with their stubborn persistence. Joe was using it to his advantage, like poking a sleeping bear.

"I think we should get a dog," he casually mentioned during dinner one evening.

"Yeah, Mommy, can we pleeeeeease get a dog?" prodded Mia while Anna added, "Yeah, Mom. Pleeeeeease. We both said, pleeeeeease."

And so it went for days. Waves of pleading and pestering pounding me like a Lake Michigan storm, undermining the stability of the solid-looking dunes. I could sense my adrenaline rising. The steam engine loaded with coal ready to bellow. I hurriedly dialed my phone before the arrow hit the red zone. All I wanted was a bit of sage advice from Loree. She uttered one word, "Petfinder."

"Very funny," I quipped.

"I'm serious," she pushed. "You know it's time you got a dog. There are thousands in need of homes."

I immediately searched Petfinder.com and was sorry. Click after click came eyes pleading for a second chance. Overwhelmed, I clicked X in the upper right corner. Petfinder.com was out of sight. The desire to rescue them out of mind.

But it wasn't out of Joe's mind. He sat in his favorite corner of the brown tweed sectional, left elbow resting on the overstuffed arm, computer on lap, socked feet propped on the solid oak coffee table, large cup of black coffee, splash of skim milk at hand. Page after web page he searched until he was found by Sierra, a smiling Keeshond-mix.

No matter what image Joe clicked next, she always drew him back. With her lion-like mane and dark rings circling her eyes, she could easily have been a littermate to our first love, Snuka.

Anna and Mia were only six and three but eagerly accepted the role of activists in Joe's campaign. In the car, over dinner, while they brushed their teeth, they lobbed bullet point after bullet point on why we should adopt her. And so I caved.

Sierra's troublemaking, however, annoyed the girls. Like a broken record, I would say, "You begged for this dog. Caring for her is the toughest part of loving her." Both girls frequently rolled their eyes as I assigned new chores: bathe the dog, wash the floor, clean the table so she can't lick the plates.

What they didn't register was Sierra's transformation to a companion and confidante because of their efforts. She'd become the greeter when the kids came home from school, offering substantial smiles and genuine affection. It was her paw on a knee or her chin in a lap that gave condolence and reassurance. She'd been their ready friend.

I expected anger and sadness to accompany Sierra's passing. We'd walked down that path of grief two years earlier when their grandfather died. But the tsunami of bickering, back talk, and sparring was much more intense. I knew at any moment either girl's emotions could explode like a beachball forced under water. Sierra's death had magnified an underlying issue. The lens, however, was not yet in focus.

"Hey, Cindy, what time does Max get here?" Joe inquired of our new part-time nanny as he strolled into the kitchen, forcing my thoughts from the chickadee and Loree, Sierra and grief.

"It's almost eight. He should be here soon."

"Mom, I don't want some stupid boy taking care of me," whined Anna, elbow resting on knee, head bent as she painstakingly separated her long, chestnut hair, strand by strand.

"Mom, what if Max is a creep? What do we do then, huh?" Mia contested, accompanied by the same eye roll of her baby blues we'd seen since age two.

"Manny" Max let himself in through the garage door, flashed a pearly white, mischievous grin and yelled, "Anyone home?" He took one look at Anna, equally trim and strong and holding the school record for squats, and challenged, "Bet I can beat you at arm wrestling." He flexed his bicep then extended his hand and firmly shook hers. He turned to Mia, patted his stomach and stated, "I'm hungry! Let's get this party started. I'll teach you how to make the biggest, baddest omelet ever!" Joe looked at me, shrugged his shoulders, and left. I walked to my home office where I released an audible sigh that stirred the ivy cascading from the gray planter.

Max, part comedian, part chameleon, eventually became the only one able to manage the girls' abrasiveness. I was equal parts grateful and jealous as he took on the role of big brother.

"Max, I don't want to ride my bike around the lake with you and Anna," Mia would protest.

"What? You don't want your hair to get messed by the wind?" he'd tease.

"Max, I'm not unloading the dishwasher," challenged Anna.

"I'm sure your mom would be just fine if you skip your chores. In fact, maybe I should do them for you. It looks like your arms fell off while we were talking,"

Max kept their days active and minds off the Sierra void. There were bike races around the lake and weightlifting with Anna. Trips to the mall with Mia and friends. The beach and the candy store for both.

But in the hours when there was no Max and no dog to greet them at the door, they'd pitch, prod, argue, and volley about their own want for a pup.

It wasn't that I didn't want a dog. Oh, how I did. I wanted one to take away the crushing grief that accompanied the longing. I ached for the shared laughter from Sierra's playful antics. I missed her sensitive, reassuring spirit. She'd been the comedienne, the healer, the glue.

But which daughter should we appease? What were the implications of appearing to favor one sister over the other, of choosing Anna's wish for a big, ball-playing dog over Mia's hope for a purse-sized pup she could dress up and carry? What about Joe's wishes for a four-legged companion? How much weight should my vote carry as chief dog walker and pet chore administrator?

Sensing my adrenaline rising, I dialed Loree to discuss the escalating dilemma. She responded coolly, "Why don't you try fostering? I worked with a woman who fosters pregnant cats. Her family cares for the mom and litter until they all find homes. They spend their non-fostering time traveling and doing things they couldn't when they were busy caring for cats."

The idea was intriguing, so I began in earnest to research. I found an article about Second Chance Animal Rescue, a local, all-volunteer, foster-based organization. Their mission was to rescue, care for, and place homeless dogs and cats into loving and responsible homes.

I called a family meeting on the sectional, complete with the expected eye rolls, to share my findings.

"It's obvious we're having difficulty picking one dog to meet the wishes of four people, and I'm not willing to take on the care of multiple dogs. How 'bout we consider fostering rescued dogs? We'd care for one dog, find it a home, then get another. We'd do that until we're ready to quit fostering or until we find a dog to adopt. Seems easy enough to me. What do you think?"

I took their lack of argument as a greenlight to proceed.

Anna and Mia accompanied me to an orientation at the home of Second Chance co-founder Lynda Ahlgren. We sat in brightly colored upholstered chairs in her lower-level family room, a few foster pups in pens nearby. She handed me a folder. To the girls, she gave extra paper and pencils. Page by page, she walked us through the fostering packet, talking of vet checks and grooming, of walking and feeding, of crafting online profiles. She mentioned their seasoned screeners who were both matchmakers and helicopter parents, connecting us with vetted adopters they deemed the right fit. It would be our job to conduct a final interview and decide who adopts whom.

"Many parents tell me they enjoy fostering as an in-home family project," Lynda mentioned. "It helps to develop a spirit of generosity and compassion. It gives families an opportunity to interact with a variety of dog breeds and personalities, helping them to make better decisions when it comes to choosing their own pets."

Turning to Anna and Mia, buoyed by the idea of a dog and sitting taller in their chairs, Lynda stirred the waters, asking, "What type of dog would each of you like?"

Their mouths hung open, but little came out, stymied by the arguments of the previous month. Lynda sensed their unease. "Second Chance rescues mixed-breed animals. I can't guarantee what type of dogs you'll foster, but I bet you'll eventually care for the pup of your dreams."

Both girls began to smile like the Cheshire cat. My mother's-love meter bounced to nearly full.

A parade of dogs in our home without having to choose between sisters.

Busy-work to temper our grief.

A family project from the comfort of home.

Could it get any better than this?!

While Anna and Mia looked over my shoulder, I signed the fostering contract, paying little heed to that nagging issue inflaming the fray—the one that had yet to come into focus.

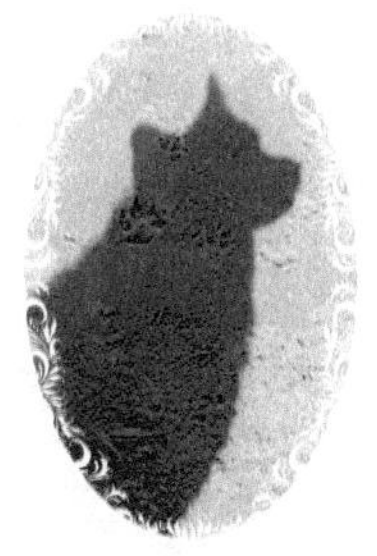

POET

Chapter 2

As the vet laid nine-pound Poet in my arms, he melted like French Silk pie in July. His large marble eyes and limp body pleaded for rest. I tucked him into the blankets in the portable carrier in the car. His quick, quiet snoring while I drove stirred memories of newborns Anna and Mia secured in their car seats for their first rides home. A small crowd of anxious family members and curious neighbors rushed to greet him when I pulled into our driveway.

Mia gently removed Poet from the crate, handling him like a precious gem. He softly licked her face as she lifted him for everyone to see. Fur spilled from Poet's Papillon ears like streamers trailing from the handlebars of a little girl's bike. Tufts of long, white feathery fur flowed down the backs of his legs and tail in marked contrast to his short-cropped body fur. Lopsided black splotches gave him the appearance of a Jersey calf.

The Papillon was named for the fountains of fur flowing from its ears, resembling a butterfly. Poet was as delicate as the insect's wings.

He loved nothing more than to cuddle in the safety of Mia's arms and to snuggle with her under the blankets at night. She cradled him like the pocket dog she'd wished for. His quiet, passive behavior and willingness to do everything asked of him led me to tear down the wall I had erected from my experience housetraining Sierra. Gone was the constant vigilance to ensure Poet was taken outside on a timely basis, the unending reminders to the girls to pick up treasured items from the floor, and the sleepless nights with one ear to the dark waiting for a whimper of unrest.

I was secretly patting myself on the back for a successful beginning to our first foster experience when Poet righted the error of my trusting ways. In the quiet of his Mia cocoon, he transformed. He didn't emerge gracefully like caterpillar into butterfly. Nope! One morning Poet sprinted out from under the quilt as a disagreeable greyhound, racing from room to room, barking as he darted from window to window, yapping at every item he launched like a missile—dog toys, kid toys, socks, shoes. After disrupting the easily accessible items, Poet searched deeper. Laundry baskets were emptied. The kids' possessions, removed from lower shelves and backpacks resting on the floor, scattered. All the while, yellow puddles pooled at the base of walls. Brown packages piled in corners. Up went my wall of vigilance. Into our home came discord as Poet revealed the layers of his complex personality and presented me with foster lesson number one: a rescued dog reveals his true personality in his own time.

The mountain of new chores I administered was greeted with prickly resistance. Mia, still recovering from middle school and Sierra's death, seemed firmly affixed to the safety of the sectional. She had no interest in my definition of walking Poet. Instead, she'd attach a leash to his collar and take him to the backyard for a quick pee. She'd promptly return to her resting place, the cushions still holding her impression. Poet would snuggle tight to her side but sneak away when she was absorbed in other matters. With a bladder still full, he'd empty it on the walls.

Anna became a broken record with a deep scratch, ranting over and over, "It's not fair that Mia got her dog wish first." She was right, but only because no big dogs needed a home when we began to foster. For all her irritation, Anna was dependable. She'd honor the chore list and walk Poet as required. Poet, however, wasn't fond of Anna. He rarely did his business on her watch, choosing the walls inside the house instead.

It was becoming a common occurrence to walk in the door or enter a room and hear "Mom, Poet peed on the wall over there," the teller waving her hand in the direction of the offense, the mess still pooling where wall met floor. The comment was an implication it was my job to take care of it.

"Get off your butts now, and clean this properly," my stiff voice pierced the peace that had existed before I entered. "You girls are old enough to do your chores correctly or to see a need and take care of it." One or more girls would begrudgingly help. The tension between us felt thick and growing.

During the fostering orientation given by Lynda, we learned it's quite common for some rescued dogs to need a year to shed layers of guarded trust before accepting a new house, and its occupants, as home. It took more than six months for Sierra to become "our dog." Poet's rebuff of everyone but Mia was the reminder that relationship-building takes patience until the one-way street reveals a two-lane road.

The on-ramp to Poet's joy was an activity Mia discovered when they were in the backyard. She'd drop his leash when she sensed his energy rising. He would run wide circles, like a greyhound chasing a rabbit at the track. Round and round he'd sprint, flatten his belly to the cool grass, pant for a minute with his too-big tongue dangling to the side, then get up and do it again. He seemed to relish the laughter it brought Mia. In these unguarded times, he let Anna and me watch from the sidelines.

We were cheering a panting Poet on a warm summer's evening when he spotted Joe walking toward us. Fear filled Poet as if Joe was a dog catcher with a lasso. He bolted from our unfenced yard. Anna and Mia lunged at the bouncing leash without luck. We instinctively gave chase, watching Poet occasionally glance back as his little white legs propelled him further up the hill.

"Mom! Anna! Stop chasing Poet," scolded a breathless Mia. "He's scared! You're making it worse. Go home. Let me try to catch him!"

Anna and I dropped back, tears spilling across our cheeks from the great weight of failure. When we reached the edge of the yard, we fell to the grass, our chests fighting to take in air against each sob pushing it out.

Anna began to volley blame. In one breath, "Mom, you shouldn't let him run circles without holding his leash." After another breath, "If Mia got off her butt and spent more time training him, he'd stay in our yard." Then, with a spike, "No one will adopt such a disobedient dog. That is, if we ever get him back!" She stood up, stamped her foot, and turned abruptly to leave.

Joe appeared from the garage while I gaped at Anna, wondering when my thoughtful child had become so disagreeable. Joe had heard Anna's harsh comments. "Knock it off," he demanded, locking eyes. "Poet needs a lot of things, but not your attitude. Neither does your mom. You need to apologize to her now."

Anna began to square her shoulders, plant her feet. A long-ago memory I thought was extinguished flared. A younger Anna was engaged in a hushed verbal brawl with Joe, with a Formica table in a dusty South Dakota restaurant serving as referee. This time, before Anna could provoke a challenge with her father, a rustling in the pine trees caught our attention. We turned in time to see a triumphant Mia carrying a smiling Poet. That is, until he saw the rest of us. He immediately cast a scowl. Anna ran to her room, heavy footsteps stomping up the wood stairs. Mia and Poet retreated to the sectional.

My legs wobbled while I climbed the stairs. Panic pounded in my chest as I retreated to my closet. *What if Mia hadn't caught Poet?* The acres of woods and marsh surrounding our house were filled with fox and coyote and wishful birds of prey. Muck, like quicksand, would've swallowed his trail. *Why did he run from us?* A wave of failure shuddered through me. With head on knees, I let the tears flow.

When my eyes were dry enough to focus, I rifled through the loose papers in the fostering packet I'd grabbed before retreating to the closet. Part of me was searching for answers to help this difficult dog. The other part was wondering if there was an "out" clause in our fostering contract. Could we claim, "Not it," and give him back?

I reread one of the newspaper clippings focused on animal impound facilities and kill-shelters I'd saved in the research side of the folder. Some facilities had an 80% kill rate, sending healthy animals to an early death just to make room for more animals lost, abandoned by people unwilling to commit to their care, or surrendered by others who genuinely can't. If an animal wasn't claimed or adopted, it was sentenced to death. Five days was the typical amount of time an animal was confined to a kennel awaiting her fate. In the event of a natural disaster, like a flood or hurricane, extreme overcrowding could shorten the death row wait to one to two days!

Fostering provided an alternative to death. An unclaimed dog could be released to a rescue agency for placement in a foster home while waiting adoption. The kennel left empty by the released dog would provide space for another dog—and, with it, the possibility of adoption or release to a foster home.

The idea of playing a small role in the rescue cycle appealed to me. Poet was a victim like millions before him. A nameless dog that once had a home, then none. A three-year-old, unaltered male, he'd been abandoned. Not one inquiry was made on his behalf at the animal impound facility where Lynda found him. He'd been there the requisite five days. The next step was death. Our home was his lifeline.

A warm sensation began to rise behind my ribs. My renewed resolve to help Poet swallowed my earlier unease. I called a family meeting. Anna and Joe gathered on the sectional with Mia, Poet sidling closer to Mia as we all appeared. I opened the floor by reading some of the clippings from the folder. I reminded everyone of the difficulties we'd had with Sierra in her first months. I asked for suggestions on how to make Poet a better citizen.

As Mia vowed to commit more time to her walks with Poet, Anna shot out of her seat. "Hold on, I'll be right back," she yelled over her shoulder as she raced to the garage. "I have an idea." She came back with a triumphant smile and a 20-foot lunge line she used for exercising horses. "We can clip this to Poet's collar when he runs circles. We'll be able to catch him if he tries to bolt."

"That won't work," I argued. "The weight of the line will choke him."

Mia and Anna raced out the door with Poet before they could react. As Poet's feet hit the grass, his switch flipped. He immediately ran circles, the heavy, blue fabric of the long lunge line making barely an impediment to his efforts. The girls let out a whoop!

Neighbors Olivia and Annie ran over with their little Yorkie, Rocky. Poet ran faster as clapping and yapping from the onlookers grew louder. When he stopped to rest, all four girls fell to the ground laughing. Poet and Rocky ran between them, licking faces and ears, the lunge line tangling in a heap of girls and tiny dogs.

This renewed sense of commitment and reset of expectations led to several weeks of calm. Anna and Mia walked Poet as needed. Poet had fewer accidents; the girls cleaned up after him if he did. The more circles he ran in the backyard, the calmer he was in the house, and the more he warmed to me and Anna.

"Mom," whispered Mia, her animated hands moving in fast circles, waving me to follow. "You've got to see this." On the sectional, wedged in the pillows between Anna and Joe, was a belly-up Poet, his chest moving in calm slumber. Mia and I deftly slid onto the sectional to join the quiet group of readers and sleepers. Another layer of Poet's distrust had peeled away.

That same weekend, Mia turned twelve. She had asked for a party like every year prior. The only difference was the guest list.

Long-standing elementary school friends and new classmates from middle school were invited.

The initial awkward moments of kids not knowing kids melted into giggles when I yelled, "Start!" to see who, with hands clasped behind backs, could eat the powdered sugar donuts dangling from strings tied to the top bar of the swing set. Girls with white crumbs dotting their faces then began running through the obstacle course stretching from our yard into the neighbor's. A rousing game of red-light, green-light followed by water balloon toss led to growing camaraderie.

As dusk settled and mosquitoes began to feast, the girls gathered around Mia on the screened porch for pizza and cake. A crack of thunder from an approaching storm drove the girls like a swarm of bees from a tight ring around the patio table to the family room. Furniture was pushed aside to make way for the unrolling of twelve sleeping bags within view of the TV. Quiet fell over the tired girls as a movie began. Poet wedged himself next to Mia, letting a few hands pet him in the safety of his Mia-cocoon.

Exhausted from party bustle, I climbed the stairs to bed, glancing one more time at the jumble of girls. A tightening of my chest and unsettledness in my legs quickly blindsided my fatigue. Cell phones I hadn't noticed before were casting blue light on several faces. A few pairs of girls were leaning shoulder to shoulder, giggling. Neither Mia nor Anna had a phone. I couldn't quite place the worry. I wasn't up on cell phone etiquette and was not yet acquainted with the malicious behavior of preteen girls. What I saw seemed benign, but I couldn't help but stare into the darkness of my room, ears straining for discord.

I heard young feet inching quietly up wood stairs. I met Mia halfway. She'd come to tell me one of the girls was leaving. This request was nothing unusual. There'd been the occasional sleepover in the past when Ava left in the middle of the night. I watched as the two friends said an awkward goodbye. Mia tiptoed back to her sleeping bag, shimmied into the zippered fabric and wrapped her arm around a sleeping Poet. I didn't sleep.

I stared into the dark until the evening storm gave way to a bright sunrise. No one rustled until the first pour of batter spread across the sizzling skillet. Young girls in t-shirts and shorts gathered once again around the round table on the porch for pancakes. By 11:00, the house was cleared of kids. Mia retreated to the sectional with her head on a pillow and Poet tucked tight to her chest. I thought her sullenness was a function of fatigue. I tried to ask about the party. I inquired about Ava. Mia flipped over, faced the back cushion, and closed her eyes. Discussion over.

Later in the week, I overheard a conversation justifying my party-night worry. I pressed Mia for details. Gathering information from her was like piecing together a three-dimensional puzzle with no discernible edges. Apparently, two pairs of girls began insulting Ava via text. Soon they had the other cell phone users engaged in their game of silent ridicule. One kid passed a phone to a phone-less Mia so she could read the screen, join the game. Mia became instantly trapped between her desire for inclusion and the need to protect a longtime companion. Whatever decision she made failed to appease the cell phone-wielding friends or their target. Mia's twelfth year began with a painful reckoning: there were piranhas swimming in her school of gentle fish.

I suggested she call Ava. Talk it over. Say sorry if need be. Mia didn't want to and couldn't. Ava had gone on vacation with her family.

A few evenings later, I settled into my chair to craft a profile for Poet's Petfinder page. I was surrounded by chirping crickets and the rustling of wind through the big bluestem outside the screen porch. It was hard to believe we were six weeks into our first fostering experience. Summer was coming to an end. Families would be settling into a new school year. The timing felt right to find the little pocket dog a permanent home.

With warm and truthful words, I painted a picture of a skittish dog with deep loyalties and adoration for a select few. He wasn't fully house-trained but making strides. I added three photos we'd taken of him on a sun-drenched day—his pink tongue dangling, black and white fur a sharp contrast against lush green grass.

I chuckled to myself as I studied the photos of this goofy dog. I knew I would never know the answer to his past but was keenly aware I was writing the opening to his future—and ours; Poet's adoption would be our first foster win. We saved him from an untimely death. His adoption would create space in our home for the next dog released from death row. The victory was palpable. It would be a family triumph after a summer of defeat!

I clicked "save" on my computer. I'd read Poet's profile to the girls in the morning. They would correct my words, editing my writing as they often did when I asked for help. Marilyn, from Second Chance, would post his profile on the Second Chance Petfinder.com pages. I felt certain Poet would find the right home.

The next morning, before I could finish reading the profile to Mia, she began to wail, "You can't take away my new best friend." She snatched Poet from his place by his food bowl and ran to her room, slamming the door behind her. Anna, startled, came running to the kitchen. I read her the profile, believing she'd be receptive. I knew she was anxious for foster dog number two, certain it would be the dog of her dreams.

"I hate you," was all I heard as her angry footsteps thundered on the wood stairs, muffling her expletives. *SLAM* went Mia's door as Anna ran to her sister to commiserate. A nervous hush gathered in the kitchen as the summer air stilled, much like the calm before a tornado.

Against my better judgment and without thought of Loree's calming voice of reason, I roared after my girls, thrusting myself through Mia's door, letting my adrenaline rage. "We aren't keeping Poet. I won't let you renege on our agreement!" After a short, fast breath, my voice rising, I continued, "You listened as Lynda explained the fostering commitment. We agreed to foster six dogs, not keep them! Poet's profile goes on the web today. End of story!" *SLAM* went Mia's door as I left as abruptly as I came.

I thundered down the hall to the shelter of my closet, feeling betrayed. I collapsed with a thud against the wall and slid down to the floor. *We're supposed to be a team of winners, helping dogs skirt untimely deaths. Our task is to find Poet a home, not adopt him into ours. How could we foster more dogs if we commit our care to this one?*

We danced on eggshells throughout the day. The kids holed up in Mia's room, leaving only for a few snacks and a reluctant walk with Poet. My anger turned to deep unease. Not only had my teenage tantrum left me feeling shame, but the girls were unchanged, their anger and sadness paralyzing. Oozing into my heart was the profound reality that Poet's adoption would force my family to face another loss, tearing open the barely healed wound from Sierra's death. I'd assembled a team to play the fostering game but had failed as a coach. I was so focused on scoring a win, I hadn't prepared them for the realities of letting go.

"Should we keep him?"

My question was directed at Joe who'd come home to an unsettled house. He was equally muddled as I. Poet was not the hike-in-the-woods and romp-through-the-snow type dog that Joe wanted, yet he empathized with the girls. He couldn't stand the idea of letting him go. He left the room quickly. "I'm fine with whatever you want to do," he muttered over his shoulder, deferring the decision to me.

Poet wasn't my ideal dog either. He wasn't fond of walking nor overly fond of me. Adopting him would require constant vigilance over house training and continued angst from Anna and Mia over chores. Adopting him would also mean our first attempt at fostering would result in "foster failure." We'd adopt our foster dog rather than find him a home. We would do the very thing Lynda feared: many before us had adopted their foster dog and closed their foster shop. They were no longer a help to Second Chance and the dogs on death row. I didn't want to disappoint Lynda, and I didn't want to think about a dog going to its death because we weren't available to foster. *But I can't manage this needy dog while fostering another*, I thought.

The resolve I tried to beckon was steamrolled by grief from Sierra's death. That night, I quietly completed Poet's adoption papers and wrote a check to Second Chance. I was limp from defeat, uncertain what it meant to our fostering commitment. The girls, on the other hand, cheered in delight to learn Poet's status had been elevated to family pet. Poet was the victory they thought would drain their cup of sorrow.

MARGO

Chapter 3

Poet had been our family dog for just under a month when Lynda called. Stuck in a kennel at animal impound was a large, black retriever-like dog. The microchip listed her as "Margo." The person to whom her microchip was registered refused to return calls. Margo had been dumped. If she wasn't claimed soon, she would face an early end to her three-year-old life.

"Can you foster Margo at the end of the week? I know you'd prefer more time to get Poet settled in, but I don't have any other open homes." I couldn't believe it. *Lynda hadn't given up on me!* With renewed vigor, I said yes. We'd foster Margo until we found her a forever home.

Our experience fostering Poet taught me there are many similarities between bringing home a foster dog and bringing home a baby. Time is at a premium and many things are put on hold during the "get to know you" phase. With a new dog, young or old, a lot of energy is spent going outside, doling out treats, cleaning up accidents, and showering the newcomer with attention.

In the two days between learning about Margo and bringing her home, I nested like an expectant mother, cleaning the house, stocking up on groceries and freezing extra meals. I stopped at the "pet shed" located in the backyard of a Second Chance volunteer, filling my car with an assortment of free food, treats, toys, leashes, cleaning supplies, and an extra-large dog crate. I took Poet to the vet for a Bordetella vaccination to protect him from kennel cough that could accompany Margo from the pound.

When the vet tech led Margo from the back room, my jaw dropped in awe at the confident show dog sauntering my way. Long feathered legs, wavy black fur, regal nose, almond eyes, and a deep chest gave her the look of a purebred flat-coated retriever. Other than a broken tooth removed during her checkup, she was perfect. It made no sense why her previous owner, who'd spent money to spay, microchip, and train her, would dump her on the streets.

Perhaps her former family didn't like Margo's interpretation of nesting. Not more than two seconds after entering our home, Margo spied the sectional, jumped on it, and rolled belly up with hairy tarantula legs stretched end to end. She saw comfort, and she claimed it.

That was, until Poet jumped to the top of the sectional and crashed down. So began the raucous relationship of kid-sized Margo and purse-sized Poet. In minutes, the family room was covered in tufts of fiberfill, punctured squeakers, and the soggy carcasses of unrecognizable toys. Over the carpet and the sectional grew a prickly haze of black and white fur. Shrill yaps, deep woofs, and playful gurgles echoed off the windows in the family room. A rapid realization filled me: bringing home Margo to a house with Poet was not like bringing home baby Mia to meet big sister Anna. All at once our house was filled with two gregarious and playful toddlers!

Amidst the melee, Anna came home from school. She took one look at the big retriever with the friendly eyes and fell in love. Before she slid her backpack off her shoulder, she was down on a knee, rubbing Margo's face, pleading with me, "Oh Mom, she's beautiful. Can we keep her?"

"No, but you can walk her. She seems fond of the leash and appears well trained." Anna hurriedly clipped a leash to Margo's collar. Tall dog and girl left for our meandering road, both wearing grins.

Mia was sitting at the kitchen table with Poet in her lap when Margo bounded through the door. Margo immediately spotted Mia and began to whimper as she ran to greet her. Mia, nose to nose with Margo, cooed excitedly. "What a beautiful girl you are!" Turning to me, she asked simply, "Can we keep her?"

Poet broke the tension by budging his way out of Mia's lap, lunging at Margo, his teeth clamping down on her mane of thick fur. Margo gave a happy bark and swung her head side to side, making a half-hearted attempt to dislodge her attacker. Poet dropped to the ground as Margo ran to the family room, nipping at her ankles as he went. A new game of tug-of-war began with the toy I'd just re-stuffed. Once the fiberfill was removed and shredded, the two friends picked up another toy and began the game anew. Anna and Mia thrust themselves into the dog mix, throwing balls, squeezing squeakers, tugging on the opposite end of a toy.

Into the commotion walked Joe. Margo immediately stopped her play and ran to the door to greet him with tail wagging and hips wiggling. As he stooped to pet her, Margo heaved her body upwards to rest her front paws on his shoulders, locked eyes with Joe, and licked his cheek. "Now this is a dog I could keep," I heard him say through muffled laughter, hinting at foster failure number two.

His immediate fondness for Margo was not a surprise. I'd experienced that "love at first sight" many years earlier. I met Joe while accompanying my boss to a Rocky Mountain resort to give a presentation to a corporate sales team. Joe was the ruggedly handsome bartender at the opening reception, someone my age in a sea of 40-something strangers. We talked. He poured drinks. I gave him a tip, then left with a group who'd invited me to join them in the resort bar. Later, my eyes kept wandering to Joe. He'd since settled onto a bar stool to enjoy a beer at the end of his shift. Some guy in my group (with a name I forgot long ago) watched as my eyes kept drifting to Joe. He soon proclaimed to our party, "I bet Cindy will spend the rest of her life with the bartender on the bar stool!" As if on cue, naturally shy Joe walked to our table and nervously asked if I would join him.

We settled on a first date, hiking above 9,000 feet on a trail that left from the center of town. Over craggy paths, through pine forests and across windswept alpine meadows, we walked and talked, our conversation echoing off rock walls at times. I learned that bartending and whitewater-raft guiding had supported Joe's winter ski habit for five years post-college. He'd grown up in the only county in Michigan without a lake. He never wanted to live where there wasn't water nearby. He once had a dog named JJ—a woods-running, hang-his-head-out-the-window companion.

Months later, our second date consisted of a walk along the eastern shore of Lake Michigan where I lived with my dog, Snuka. Summer had faded to fall, leaving uncluttered miles of beach as tourists returned to their non-vacation lives. Joe listened intently to my story of Snuka, the occasional wave slapping our feet as we absentmindedly followed the undulating shoreline.

Snuka had found me on a sunny spring day during my college senior week. Students with no classes and little to do relaxed on grassy quads, bathing in the sun and tossing Frisbees. As I crossed through the friendly chaos on my way to the cafeteria, I was approached by a wide-eyed, smiling dog. I stopped for a moment to pat his soft head. Moments later, while standing in line for the salad bar, I saw a flash of fur at my feet. The same dog I'd spotted on the quad was wagging his curly tail! I put my tray down and led him out the door. Three hours later, I caught a glimpse of his generous smile reflected in the weight room mirror.

Snuka had no collar. I had no leash. We took our first walk with an extension cord loosely tied around his neck. During the second walk, I upped the distance from one block to two since walking made us happy. By the end of our first month together, we established a three-mile route meandering along a tree-lined river. Yet I still didn't know from where he had come.

I tried placing lost dog ads, calling vet clinics, and working with the local animal control. At some point, an animal control officer told me it was okay to either adopt him or bring him to a shelter; I'd done my due diligence. After a month of searching to find Snuka's old home, he found a new one with me. I bought a real leash and matching collar. I had a tag engraved with his name.

We both smiled generous smiles—until I took him to the vet clinic for his first checkup. Hidden behind his playful tail and lush Keeshond fur was a dog suffering poor health. Heartworm and intestinal worms were sabotaging his body. He was fifteen pounds underweight. The vet estimated Snuka had been scrounging his existence for more than six months.

I was shaken to my core. I'd been trying to provide him a safe home to help heal the wounds of abandonment. Instead, I had to leave him in a confined kennel at the clinic on multiple weekends to endure nauseating arsenic treatment to kill the heartworms. Due to the vet bills, I lost two months' of income and gained a heart full of worry.

The day I was to bring Snuka home from his last arsenic treatment, I took off work. I was looking forward to celebrating a quiet afternoon with him at home. Just before leaving, the vet technician called and said, "Don't come. Something has gone terribly wrong." While Snuka had been fine all weekend, he was vomiting, pacing, and digging at the kennel floor in distress.

My heart fraught with fear, I sat on my front stoop alone and sad, hoping the warm sun would calm me. I was startled out of my sullen mood by the sudden wail of tornado sirens. It wasn't the usual alarm-testing day, so something was amiss. My neighbors stepped out their front doors into the sunshine with equally confused looks. As we began to converse, debris began to rain from the cloudless sky—splintered wood, pink insulation, bits of drywall. The newscaster on the radio informed us that an isolated storm had produced a tornado in a town just southwest of where we stood. Other people's lives were swirling around me when my phone rang. It was the vet's office. Snuka was calm, wearing a smile, and ready to come home. It turned out he'd been reacting with fear to a storm we didn't know was coming. The veterinarian theorized Snuka's lengthy time wandering without shelter made him hypersensitive to changes in weather.

Snuka was also a barometer of people. He knew exactly what his human companions needed, and he delivered—a wide grin, a reassuring paw on a thigh, his chin resting on a lap, miles of walking beaches, roads, and wooded paths as a faithful companion. Snuka immediately bonded with Joe. Joe fell in love with Snuka.

A decade after his death, Snuka's generous, sensitive, and loyal personality was re-embodied in Margo. She was "smarter than a fifth grader," yet she didn't need to be a contestant on a game show to prove her intelligence. She quickly learned our names, position in the family, and the type of spoiling she could expect from each of us. She, like Snuka, measured tension like a barometer, quickly slinking away to the bathroom to avoid it. When Poet got too much attention, Margo would use her big nose to budge her way into the circle. When she sensed sadness, she would rest a reassuring front paw or her chin on a lap.

I soon noticed Margo spending a lot of time on the sectional resting her chin on Mia's lap, Poet tucked tightly to Mia's hip. It was difficult to tell if Margo was seeking reassurance in this new place, or if Mia needed comfort. Seventh grade started for Mia much the same way sixth grade ended—a swirling tumult of struggle—with a new set of changing classes, unfamiliar hallways, wrestling matches with the slim gray locker that was quickly becoming disorganized by the constant badgering from the shrill bell.

Margo was belly-up on the sectional, head resting against Mia's thigh, Poet wedged between Margo and the back cushion, Mia's hand absently stroking his fur when I watched a few tears trickle down her cheeks. I'd walked into the room at the tail end of a hurried conversation between Mia and someone on the phone. My "Mia, what happened?" was quickly met with "Oh, nothing. Sunny brushed by my eyes and I'm reacting to her fur." As I searched the family room for said cat, Mia quickly wiped at her cheeks while dismissing me with a weak grin.

A few days later, a similar event caught my attention. This time I heard, more clearly, a reference to Mia's birthday party. Several conversations later, the theme was still the same. Even with little detail, I gathered that the wounds of the birthday party were still festering.

Mia's reluctance to share the full story of the events that unfolded the night she turned twelve was an aching reminder of the growing divide between us parents and kids as the years progressed. When the girls were in elementary school, it was easy to be in-the-know about friends, teachers, class projects, and school activities. Joe and I had been active volunteers. I taught art. Joe tutored struggling readers. We knew the class disruptors. We could spot problems and mitigate. The kids even turned to us for help.

Middle school and high school teachers requested less assistance from parents, and our older kids had less tolerance for parental engagement. The ever-changing circus of classrooms, classmates, and class subjects made the players and plays difficult to track from home. As our girls turned to their peers, they became less dependent on our insight and less tolerant of our stories. A generation apart, they often claimed we could never understand what it was like to be a teenager!

That's when the real bonus of fostering became evident: it was our family activity and ours alone. No influence from school, friends, other adults. Rescued dogs, like Margo, were dependent on our help.

They needed us to act as a cohesive team in the healing process and the search to find them a forever home. Fostering could be that taut rope to keep us from drifting apart.

As far as theories go, it was solid. But, as the weeks passed with Margo, turmoil bubbled; the rope frayed. Joe and the girls were poking the sleeping bear of trouble. They'd found their campaign mojo from many years past and vigorously fought against me to keep Margo as our second dog. *Second dog? How did we go from a single-dog household to the possibility of two resident dogs while fostering six?!* My answer was a solid no!

Margo had fluid beauty, but she was a dog of little grace—and lots of shedding. She was a "plopper," letting her heft crash to the floor, her fur pouring into a feathery, black puddle. Margo would plop onto a patch of gravel faster than a Ferrari on the Autobahn to scratch an itch. Upon standing, she would shudder from nose to tail, unleashing a cloud of dust and fur, earning her the nickname "Pig Pen" after the disheveled Peanuts character. She was the yin to Poet's yang, letting the spry dog grab at her ears and hang from her fur. Our vacuum cleaner never stopped. Toys and dirt and fur covered every floor and cushion. Two dogs needed walking. One little dog still needed a heap of house training. *What pandemonium would a third dog bring?*

Adopting Margo would also mean another foster failure. As a person who likes to check off boxes of accomplishment, I was resolute about finding her a good home, of securing the win. I sat at my desk and tuned out my family, their pleading, their poking, their whining, and I forced myself to compose Margo's Petfinder profile. I cropped three of her best show-dog-like photos taken on a blue-sky afternoon.

With her flowing beauty captured in pictures and an honest profile of praise and adoration, I was confident Margo would be our easy win.

Many times I tried to send Margo's profile to Marilyn to post on Petfinder. I would sit down to read my words, to check for errors. I would look longingly at the photos of the beautiful dog I often found sleeping with her big, black head resting on Poet's little bed as he slept outstretched in hers. I thought of the gentle soul who measured days by miles, not minutes. She was everyone's wish but my prize—the best of former dogs Snuka and Sierra. I was stalling, avoiding the obvious.

There would be no fostering win with Margo; she'd found the perfect home when she set foot in ours.

BETTY

Chapter 4

We were one month into our life with two foster failures when Lynda asked if we would take in ten-pound Betty. My resolve to make her our first foster win propelled my mouth to utter a quick "Yes." It was through the juggling of fur and toys and floor cleaner and two wet dogs from a rainy November that helped me define my limits on the number of dogs I was willing to call permanent residents. Hell would have to freeze over before I would agree to fail again!

The waiting room temperature seemed to cool dramatically when Betty swaggered in from the back room of Life Care Animal Hospital. With a body shaped like a mini Snuka and fur thick and shimmering like polished onyx, Betty stood erect, scanning the room with sharp eyes and the confidence of a general. The vet knelt beside her, petting her sleek back. "She's part Schipperke—bred for the role of watch dog on barges in Belgium. Her size may be small, but she's mighty." Betty had lost her home, lived a week in a shelter, and underwent surgery but showed no pain or fear.

Margo and Poet embraced their new friend with full gusto. The three musketeers spent their days emptying toy baskets, de-stuffing dog and cat toys, tugging on the end of knotted ropes. When bored, the two little dogs would pester Margo as if she were the kid stuck in the middle of the back seat on a long ride. They would jump at Margo's mane where, for brief moments in time, Margo looked like she'd donned mismatched, tiny dog earrings. To rid herself of the little leeches, she'd shake her head madly, her bark echoing off the windows. Poet and Betty would eventually drop to the floor, replying in a percussion of yips and yaps and *grrr*s while they chased Margo around the sectional. Anna and Mia delighted in their revelry, their giggles barely audible above dog ruckus.

Those fleeting moments of carefree laughter made me pause in appreciation, for there were fewer and fewer cohesive moments among the growing angst. Mia's attitude continued to be worrisome as the school year marched towards December. During parent-teacher conferences we heard about missing assignments, falling grades, and lack of participation in class.

When Joe and I asked Mia to present her side of the story, we got the "nothing" response. "There's nothing to talk about, Mom." "There's nothing wrong at school, Dad."

Our attempts to highlight her shortcomings as a means of motivation (refusal to get together with friends, failure to advocate for herself with teachers, sitting on the sectional rather than doing homework at the kitchen table, blah, blah, blah...) were met with more nothing. "I said nothing's wrong and nothing's what I mean," sighed Mia as her eyes shifted upwards in her signature eye roll. Conversation over.

Joe and I knew better. We'd been teenagers once before. The nothing and the silence were both loaded with a whole lot of something. We just didn't know what. Nor did we know how to engage a despondent Mia.

What I did know was tension was rising between me and Joe. We couldn't agree on what to do with Mia's changing behavior. While I had long been the overseer of kid activities and the writer of chores on the chore board, I began to worry about pushing Mia too hard.

Born when a summer haze softened the edges of a copper sun, she was quieter in physical endeavor than Anna but as social as an Alaskan summer day is long. She'd always been our extrovert and relished the attention paid to her by her friends' mothers. *Would she fall from our nest with resentment and run to a different mother for comfort?* In fear, I changed my approach from dogged discipline to laissez-faire and unsettled Joe in the process. He was ready to instill more discipline, to leverage effort against privilege, dangling less time at the local horse barn as the carrot to increase participation at home and school. *What? Take away horses from Mia?* I was so afraid of the door Mia was quickly closing, I plowed forward without Joe, wedging a giant horse hoof into the opening.

Mia had been participating in the obscure equestrian sport of vaulting, a blend of gymnastics and dance and pairs figure skating with leaps and spins, somersaults and splits and daring dismounts—all on the back of a moving horse. While the sport was celebrated in Europe, it enjoyed only pockets of popularity in the U.S. We knew nothing about it until the day we walked to the stable near our house to pet a friend's horse. Mia and I stood in awe at the group of young girls in leggings and ballerina-like slippers, dusty from head to toe, waiting for their turn. The horse, attached to a lunge line, was being directed by a woman, the lunger, to walk in a circle around her. Another woman, the coach, was giving instructions to each girl as she rode. There was no saddle, only a large black pad on the horse's back and a circular band called a surcingle sitting atop the pad and cinched around its belly, holding the pad firmly to the back of the horse. On top of the band were two handles.

One by one, the girls were given a leg-up so they could sit on the pad. Some were strong enough to swing their legs and kneel, bracing their hands on the handles like a male gymnast against the pommel horse. Some even dared to stand, wobbling against the up and down of the horse's walk. One young woman, whom we quickly learned through whispers was an experienced gymnast, waited in the center of the circle next to the woman with the lunge line. As soon as the horse began to canter the girl moved closer to the horse, running in sync with its hooves. She grabbed the handles and used the upward momentum of the horse's hips to pull herself onto the pad. She sat for a fleeting moment to adjust her balance, then stood as the horse continued to canter around the circle. She began to jump and turn and dance—rider and horse becoming one fluid act of grace.

Mia, mouth open, eyes wide with excitement, was hooked. I was in awe, but hesitant. No helmet. No saddle. Jumping on a moving horse? It all seemed so daring, so dangerous. I was assured by the coach that vaulting was the safest equestrian sport, the low numbers of injuries proving the claim.

Mia's team gathered two times a week. It was a bootstrap operation. Beth, the parent of the gymnast vaulter, coached the girls through their routines of flags, half-mills, swings, leaps, somersaults, flanks, dismounts. Other parents with horse experience took turns coaching the horse to walk, trot, or canter in smooth circles while paying attention to the lunger regardless of the activity by its feet or on its neck and back. I pitched in by moving practice equipment and tidying the barn, keeping arms-length from Mia but within earshot and sight line of her activities. I learned early on with this daredevil sport that I needed to watch Mia's steady progress to train my heartbeat to her abilities.

Logic, however, did not still my beating heart the day Captain walked into the arena. Until that day, I'd only seen Mia and her teammates vault on Blue, a short-legged, patient warmblood with wide withers and hips providing a comfortable base for standing and spinning. Captain, nostrils flaring, ears pricked forward in anticipation, was an 18-hand Shire with gleaming black hair and a white blaze from forelock to nostril. He towered over every horse in the barn.

Each teammate stood along the wall, waiting to sit atop Captain at a walk. When it was Sarah's turn, the coach's daughter with a gymnastics background, she asked the lunger to bring Captain to a canter. Sarah ran beside him, jumping up forcibly to reach the handles. She hoisted herself up to a sitting position on the pad on his back. The explosion of clapping and cheering from the team was followed quickly by a hush. Sarah, holding the handles of the surcingle, pushed with her shoulders while swinging her legs behind, tucked her knees and brought herself to a crouch on Captain's back. Her body began rocking with the up and down of the canter, feeling for the rhythm. In one smooth push of trained muscles, she moved from squat to standing, circling her arms and wrists like a gymnast on a balance beam readying for a tumbling run. Captain continued to canter in a smooth circle. Sarah beamed with accomplishment as the rest of us stood still, barely breathing, to see what would happen next. Sarah jumped down without giving more. She was satisfied with her first attempt.

The lunger slowed Captain to a walk. While the horse gathered his breath, Mia moved to the center of the ring to stand by her. I noticed an imperceptible shift in Mia's demeanor—it was a bit like the resolute confidence I witnessed in Betty the day I met her at Life Care. Thunder began echoing off the arena walls as Captain's hooves, the size of dinner plates, settled into a heavy, rhythmic canter. *Canter? What happened to walk?* My heart pounded as each hoof stamped down, driving dust upwards, shrouding my daughter in mystery. Mia, barely five-feet tall with size-six shoes, ran beside Captain's massive hooves. She leapt with strong legs, arms overhead, to grab the handles. In one death-defying move in sync with Captain's motion, she lifted herself up to a seated position on the pad. A roar came from the band of onlookers and teammates, cheering madly as Mia smoothly rose to her feet and rode Captain around the circle at a stand. I felt my face whiten as the blood left my body, taking oxygen with it.

Through the ever-present dust, I got to witness Mia's joy and see her move in three dimensions. Sometimes she was the sole vaulter atop the horse. Other times strong Mia became the steady base for two other teammates who gracefully turned and climbed and steadied themselves one against the other and the rhythm of the moving horse until the lightest vaulter, 15 or more feet above the soft arena footing, was posing like a flying goddess hood ornament atop a vintage automobile. Vaulting was proof there was passion and perseverance and cooperation in the kid who'd become rooted to the sectional at home. Watching her confidence and bravery helped soften the edges of my frustration. Our "togetherness" was buying me time as I struggled to interpret the growing divide in her personality.

Joe rarely stayed to watch practice. He wasn't fond of smelly horses and horse barns filled with cackling girls and mothers. He was even less thrilled with paying for Mia's horse privilege without a tangible return. Her inertia at home was quickly becoming a thorn in Joe's side. When he'd hound Mia to do the chores I posted on the whiteboard, he was met with, "I'm too tired." He'd counter, "You can't be too tired, you've been laying there all day doing nothing." The more he'd push, the more she'd resist. His impatience often led to yelling. She'd finally give in to what was asked while muttering under her breath, "Dad's stupid." Joe would leave the scene abruptly, knowing that to stay would increase the tension and his anger.

I'd jump into the quarrel, much as he did when Anna yelled at me about Poet. "Mia, you can't treat your dad like that. It's not his problem you aren't doing what was asked. Go get your work done, now."

On occasion, when defiance hovered around her like the billowing soot from a coal-fired furnace, my "I mean it voice" would bellow, "Or vaulting will go away!" threatening to extinguish the very thing I was campaigning on her behalf to keep.

The dogs, however, didn't mind Mia's idleness. When they weren't clamoring over her during play, Margo, Poet, and Betty would drape themselves over her legs and lap, resting, snoring, chasing rabbits in their sleep.

Betty's transition to our home had been so seamless Anna and Mia began pleading with me to keep her. She was undeniably an easy dog, so I had to remind them that caring for three dogs was a lot of work that I was shouldering mostly on my own. As was typical of the two girls when threatened with loss, they quickly resorted to bargaining through hiccups and tears. Their commitments to walk her in the wee hours before school and to forgo sleepovers to care for her on the weekends oozed from the emotional side of their brains. My resistance was a bullseye: I soon became the target of Anna and Mia's anger, both spouting, "I hate you!" and stomping out of the room when I talked about finding Betty a home. I didn't want to keep Betty, yet I hated those pointed arrows deftly piercing my heart.

Joe, seen as stupid one moment, was also Mia's ally. He'd become attached to Betty, the pocket dog that fit comfortably into the crook of his arm like a football. More than once he calculatingly wondered aloud if we should keep her, knowing full well Mia and Anna would immediately chime in, adding strength to his side of the debate. Experienced in the art of foster failure, I feared we were on the brink of number three.

At one point, I deflected their pestering by idly turning pages of a cooking magazine I'd picked up from the coffee table. While scanning recipes for ingredients I had on hand, I recalled a conversation with a colleague from the food industry many years before. It took place on the day I returned to work six months after Anna was born.

My mind was turbulent then from my first daycare "drop." My subconscious wrestled with my intuition, trying to remember the reasons for choosing our daycare provider. *Could she be trusted? Would Anna cry all day? Would the separation create an irreparable rift between me and Anna?* Through my guilt-ridden sobs, I told these thoughts to Jackie, a mother who had recently sent her only daughter to college.

Jackie put her arm around my shoulders and calmly passed along her sage advice earned from raising her daughter and helping her prepare to leave home. She told me life would provide plenty of time for me to build trust in Anna and her ability to care for herself. I would learn to let others come into her life, to teach, to support, to love. "When Anna leaves home, you will cry for the loss of family time. Your once-noisy home will be quiet. You will worry about the challenges Anna will face and the people she will meet. But waiting for you on the other side of the worry and the grief will be a few gifts—the bounty of time, the rediscovery of self, and the peace of knowing you gave her the best you could." Jackie talked further about dates with her husband, newfound hobbies, volunteer work, and reconnection with friends.

Her words were foreign to my new-mother brain, yet the import and depth from which they were spoken left an indelible mark all those years later. They were just what I needed to tune out my badgering family and move forward with Betty's adoption. Three dogs, one cat, one guinea pig, two kids, and one husband oscillating between adversaries and allies had me wishing for the gift of time and one fewer obstacle between us.

I worked on Betty's adoption profile while simultaneously attempting to impart Jackie's great words of wisdom to Anna and Mia. The more I talked, the more unrelenting they became in their quest to make Betty ours. Then one day I realized the error of my ways.

To our young kids, gifts were solid, real, something to get or give. Neither Anna nor Mia was ready to embrace the joy of the intangible gift of time. Placing Betty up for adoption meant nothing to them but loss. I might as well have asked them to return their favorite birthday present to the store. If I wanted the gift of time and the joy of adoption success, I would have to wrap it myself. They would not be the ones to hold a finger over the knot in the ribbon, so I could tie the bow.

Eleven days after Betty came to our home, I sent her profile to Marilyn to post on the Second Chance pages of Petfinder.com. Within hours, I received a call, from Carol, one of Second Chance's veteran phone screeners. She'd spoken with a man whose family was interested in adopting Betty. Carol had "put him through the wringer," as my grandma used to say. She asked tough questions to weed him from the riffraff. She'd even talked with the family's veterinarian where she'd learned of their long, thoughtful history of caring for their family pets. Carol had deemed them viable candidates to adopt Betty. She was passing along the man's contact information so I could do a second interview.

Nervousness set in as I faced Act II of the adoption process, the live screening of a potential adopter from my perspective of living with the dog. I had no clue what to ask these strangers interested in the little black guest of which we still knew so little. *Who was Betty outside of her relationship with Margo and Poet? What would she be like as an only dog? What would make me comfortable letting them take her home?*

I did what I do best when faced with a problem—I dragged my feet, turning to pen and paper to create a list. I carried it with me throughout the day, adding, deleting, editing. I scoured Petfinder to read profiles posted on their site. What did they say about the dogs in their homes, their temperaments, their needs? After dinner, I revised my list, sucked in my anxiety, and dialed the number of Betty's suitor.

As soon as the deep voice of Richard answered the phone, I realized how nervous I'd become. Betty's future was on the line. I had no way to discern if my questions were the right ones to ensure a good fit.

Instead of a lengthy conversation, I invited the stranger to my turf to meet Betty and talk face to face.

My family scattered when the doorbell rang, taking with them a barking Poet and Margo. I lifted a squirming Betty to my arms as Richard, his quiet wife, and equally quiet son and daughter-in-law settled themselves on the sectional. I let them do the talking, letting awkwardness fill the silence, while I scrutinized their faces and body language, searching for comments and behaviors that would signal something for or against the adoption.

I learned they had a fondness for Schipperkes, and Betty had caught their eye. The young married couple rented the upstairs apartment of the parent's house. Four adults would be looking after Betty. Staggered work schedules meant she'd rarely be alone. A secure fenced yard would give her the opportunity to keep watch over the neighborhood. I couldn't have imagined a better scenario to give the tiny commander a second chance at a first-rate life.

Betty left the comfort of my arms to walk over the laps of this family who'd traveled across the city to meet her. She steadied herself on their legs much the same way Mia did when moving to the rhythm of a vaulting horse. I read aloud each line of the adoption contract, the paper guiding me through more tough questions, my eyes and ears gauging the family's responses. By the end, my gut was "feeling it," providing that first opportunity to trust my intuition; there were no red flags tugging at my subconscious. I handed them a pen. They signed the adoption contract and paid the fee. They stood. Betty stood next to them, waiting to walk out the door by their sides. She left our temporary home to live happily ever after in theirs.

It was during our short time with Betty when I first heard others exclaim, "I could never do what you do. I could never foster. I could never let a dog go." I would laugh a little at the comment, knowing we had yet to succeed. When Betty was nestled in the car with four strangers on her way to a home I didn't know, I realized just how hard the letting go could be. It surprised me how quickly I'd bonded with Betty and how deep my desire to nurture and protect her ran. Guilt welled inside me thinking about her first dark night in the scariness of a new home. Letting her go that day felt much like the first day I left baby Anna in the care of a stranger.

A few tears fell across my weak smile as I waved to the family driving away with Betty, already the center of their universe. As soon as I turned the corner on the sidewalk to face the front door, calmness rose within. I had to deal with my family's sadness and anger over their loss. By holding true to my limits, though, we'd finally succeeded at fostering. Our team scored its first win!

As my right foot stepped over the threshold, I thought of Lynda and her words imparted on the day we committed to fostering. She'd been right. Fostering had provided an immersive family experience. The path hadn't always been clear, and some harsh words and resistance muddied the waters, but we did it. We'd become a cog in the rescue wheel helping to move dogs from death row to temporary shelter to forever home. One box on our fostering score card checked. Five boxes to go. Along the way, our willingness to foster connected us to the kindness of strangers willing to take over Betty's care. I knew my family was not ready to embrace the loss, but I was eager to enjoy the intangible gifts of Betty's adoption—one less dog and a bit more time—until the next call from Lynda with another foster request.

SNICKERS
Chapter 5

"MOMMMMM!" shrieked Mia as she and her friend Olivia scuttled from their corner behind the Christmas tree. The two girls, deep in their imaginary world where Christmas ornaments became characters in elaborate plays, were startled to reality when the tree started rocking. I turned my head in time to see Poet bound out from beneath the lower branches, followed closely by Snickers, a ten-month-old Miniature Schnauzer puppy with impish eyes, both dogs short enough to barely disrupt a needle. Big Margo, the bull in the china shop and seven times the size of the little rascals, was in close pursuit of her nimble friends. Her pointy nose suddenly got tangled in a string of lights. Her flowing tail wagged outrageously in delight, scattering ornaments to the floor, and filling the family room with the scent of musty forest and pine resin. Somehow she managed to free herself fast enough to catch the twosome turning the corner of the sectional to dash under the tree again.

"Stop!" I roared. Poet, Snickers, and Margo halted at once as if I'd touched them in a game of freeze tag. "Come on, Anna," I implored loudly, "give me a hand." Anna jumped from the sectional. We quickly corralled the rowdy friends, herding them through the garage to the service door, grabbing coats and mittens as we ran. It was a year of bountiful snow. The door had become a chute from which Anna and Joe had shoveled a thigh-deep, figure-eight raceway within a big oval. We opened the door and let the dogs run directly into the maze. Agile Poet led the pack. Fountains of fur sprouting from his Papillon ears were ironed straight by the wind. Snickers followed closely, nipping Poet's white toes as they kicked up snow. Margo, a monochromatic blur of coal-black fur against a sparkling white background, lumbered behind with a wide smile and thunderous bark.

When they were amply exhausted, we confined the group to the coat room. After matted snow melted and paws dried, the dogs climbed onto the sectional to snuggle up to its occupants, expecting the humans to pay attention to the mischievous companions.

Snickers had been a weary pup when we brought him home from Life Care, cautiously approaching each of us—a methodical reckoning rather than the exuberant all-in we experienced with Margo and Betty. Poet, a lover of play, quickly teased Snickers from his guarded personality. In a matter of days, Snickers was following Poet like a little brother, tossing toys from the baskets, racing from window to window to yell at the squirrels, chasing Poet and Margo around the sectional. Snickers soon wore generous smiles. However, from the bedlam of those budding friendships rose an unwanted digression, and with it, my increasing demands on family members to keep watch over the pair.

Like a toddler who regresses when a sibling is introduced to the family, Poet took Snicker's accidents as an invitation to abandon the skills we'd worked so hard to teach him. On day one when Snickers' anxiety led to peeing on the wall, Poet lifted his leg to mark over Snickers. On day two when Snickers pooped in the corner after breakfast, Poet followed suit. Days three through seven were similar. I pulled the gallon of floor cleaner from the cabinet, the weight much greater from the exasperation that'd seeped in.

To make matters worse, it felt like I was doing the lion's share of the work while my family members' commitment to dogs and chores diminished with the rising spirit of the season; the cozy throws and crackling fireplace called to them from the comfort of the sectional. I would get mad at the kids and Joe for not paying attention to the little dogs. They would get mad at me for getting mad at them. Tensions were rising. Holiday joy was fleeting. As I stood alone at the kitchen sink, hands immersed in warm, sudsy water, watching soft snow swirl under the pine trees, I caught a glimpse of tattered ferns. My mind was whisked back to the previous spring.

During the first warm morning after a colder-than-normal winter, I had cranked open the windows. The clean outdoor air rushed in. With it came an itch for change. We had no spare money to scratch that itch, so I settled on rearranging the family room furniture as a no-cost update. I took apart the sectional and positioned each of the two parts like love seats on opposite sides of the coffee table. The problem was they looked nothing like matching love seats one would see in a design magazine. Each sectional piece was armless on one end with a padded, protruding arm on the other. Imbalanced and awkward, the arrangement made me look like a hack designer, even though I'd recently graduated from interior design school.

Design be damned. The newness felt refreshing, reviving. I enjoyed entering the space in a different manner. That little change altered my mood for the better, until my peace was overtaken by grumbling from kids and Joe.

"The furniture looks awkward. The sectional isn't designed to be separated," scoffed Joe.

"It's too hard to watch TV with my friends and the dogs," complained Mia.

"Mom, the sectional is our together place. Separating it doesn't feel right. Please put it back the way it was," demanded Anna, the "please" only slightly softening Anna's edginess.

They were right. The L-shaped sectional had become the place to hang out, legs draped over legs, watching movies, eating popcorn, reading books. It was where kids and dogs and friends fell asleep during sleepovers, and friends and family crowded to play games during holidays. Separating the sectional was like tearing down a family tradition.

I begrudgingly returned the sectional to its proper configuration, restoring the family peace (and my dignity as a designer). As kids and dogs and Joe piled onto the sectional, I discovered the silent truth about the giant L in the middle of the family room; the unity of the two pieces somehow gave those sitting upon it impunity from shirking chores and obligations. It was as if the sectional had become the safe zone in an ongoing game of tag. Only I wasn't having much fun as the playground lady enforcing the rules, especially with wild child Poet and sidekick Snickers.

At first, I tried to be the teacher, imparting great words of house-training wisdom to Anna and Mia. "Pretend you are a raptor scanning for prey, searching for any signal that might mean the little dogs need to eliminate—a widening stance, a slight lean, the hunch of a back. You must swoop in quickly to redirect their efforts outside. After they go, heap ample praise on them: clap, cheer, pet their heads."

"You want us to cheer?" quipped Anna. "Like, 'Go Team' or 'Give me a P'?"

When Mia finally registered Anna's pee joke, the two bent over laughing, ending my lesson in house training, but not my vigilance. I became the eagle-eye playground lady watching the girls watch the dogs.

"Mia, Anna, get off your butts! Poet and Snickers need to get outside."

"Not now Mom, I'm..." (Insert *reading, doing my homework, watching a movie...*)

"They won't wait for you. Do it now!"

"But..."

"I said now!" My playground-lady roar no match for their complaints, they'd finally give in and get up from their place on the sectional.

With my eyes only able to watch so much, I tried another tactic. After the dogs succeeded in their outside duties, I'd attach an indoor leash to each collar and the looped ends around the wrist of the girls.

"It's like fishing. When the dogs tug on the leash, they're telling you they need something. They either want to play, or they need to go outside. Stop what you're doing. Take them outside. Wait until they go. Give them praise. Then let them play. The routine will help them learn."

It worked for about a day. Somehow the looped end of the leashes mysteriously "slid" off the wrists of the girls, and the little dogs snuck off the sectional to relieve themselves in the house.

"Mia. Anna. Put a leash around your wrist, NOW, or else, there will be consequences!" If I'd had a whistle, its shrill call would have reached the loners skirting the far edges of the playground.

With the threat of personal loss caught in my pulsing tension, both girls acted. In less than a week, Snickers and Poet were responding favorably to our team effort. Even the girls were amazed how effective consistency was for training. With Snickers back on track at last, it was time to find him a home. First up, I needed to write his profile.

Crafting Betty's profile had been effortless. Obedient. Lovable. House-trained. Schipperke. Her breed stood out in a sea of homeless dogs. Snickers? Not so much. He was one of a 100 Schnauzer-like dogs in a 50-mile radius in need of a forever home. I felt great pressure to make him visible in the crowd.

But how? I was a rookie at creating an online profile. And I was bound to the truth: I didn't want an adopter to be surprised or disappointed by Snickers' lively personality and training imperfections. A stream of unimpressive words dotted my computer screen.

It didn't help that I couldn't take a decent picture. I owned what I thought was a suitable camera, but I obviously wasn't a seasoned dog photographer. Outside, I managed to capture a blurry mass that could've been mistaken for the raccoon frequently darting from our compost heap. Photos taken inside made Snickers' perky black eyes become lifeless blobs shadowed by unwieldy fur.

"Mommmmm!" Mia's screeched interrupted my writing. "One of the little dogs pooped behind the Christmas tree!" Branches were swaying and ornaments rattling by the time I turned my head to see Mia scurry from her hidden play spot behind the tree.

Anna muttered, "Gross" and quickly shifted on the sectional as if the little packages had legs and were gunning for her. In the process, she elbowed Margo who stretched her mouth in a great big yawn. A slight squeak escaped. Poet and Snickers, ears tuned for fun, woke immediately, jumped to the floor, and began chasing each other around the sectional, their path leading right to the pile behind the tree!

"Stop!" I bellowed, immediately ending the momentum of their game. While six wide eyes waited for a signal to resume play, Anna ran the cleaning supplies to me. Rather than issuing a sincere thank you for her selfless act, I caught myself muttering a forced thank you. I couldn't get past my exasperation born of the previous weeks' events.

Anna had always been a sharp-brained student with a solid memory and equally reliable work ethics. Yet she wasn't fairing much better in her first semester of high school than Mia was in seventh grade. I had received two calls from one teacher about Anna's cell phone use in the classroom, a call from another teacher about missing assignments, and a third about rumors related to bullying on social media. Joe was quick to take away her new cell phone.

"You'll get it back when we get a better report from school," pressured Joe.

Anna countered, "Those teachers hate me. They're making things up to get me in trouble." Anna turned abruptly and thundered to her room.

Unlike Mia who was simmering in silence through seventh grade, Anna had become a fragile bubble clinging to the wall of a near-boiling pot, constantly threatening to break the surface in an explosive disruption. Joe and I cast glances at each other, wondering from where Anna's rage and irresponsibility stemmed.

Anna had always been an intense and responsible kid. She shouldered her passions with steadfast commitment, letting little get in the way of her goals. When she was seven and Mia five, they attended farm camp with good friends Haley and Ben. Each day of camp on a flat edge of prairie began with riding lessons on ponies barely taller than their helmeted heads. The hours between morning lessons and afternoon fun rides were filled with farm-related crafts and farm chores, like mucking pony stalls, leading sheep to pasture, cleaning bunny cages, caring for the pig. We'd pick up dusty kids with dirt under their fingernails who talked excitedly over each other as they recounted the day.

Smitten by her horse experience, Anna would fill her book bag during each trip to the library with everything horse—horse anatomy, horse training, how to run a stable, show jumping for beginners, proper tack for each style of riding. She memorized page after page, but not words, just images. When the pictures didn't make sense, she'd try to read the words. When she got stuck, we'd read the pages together. She filled three-ring binders with magazine clippings of horse tack, riding tips, and mane- and tail-braiding suggestions.

The following summer, the four friends returned to camp. As veterans, they were made leaders of the new farm kids. They were given "tougher" chores. The same buzz of excitement filled the drive to and from camp and the hours in between. On the final Friday, little kids on short-legged ponies lined the outdoor arena to show off their riding skills and to introduce parents to barnyard friends.

When the horse show was over and camp at its end, Anna began a slow, methodical process of untacking her horse, delaying the moment when she'd no longer be at one with the farm. I became her groom, holding each dusty piece, fighting angry flies. The moment she removed the saddle, where warm sweat mingled with leather and soap, memories of Gravel, my rented horse from so many summers before, flooded my mind. I'd been a little girl circling the wood rails, listening to the rhythmic whop, whop, whop of butt hitting saddle, knees squeezed tight, ankles pressed down in the stirrups.

I listened intently as Anna's mind recalled what she learned from the library books. Not a part of tack or pony was excluded as she worked from nose to tail, instructing me on grooming, showing me how to care for the saddle. When her pony was back in the paddock and tack returned to its proper location, she cleaned the riding equipment forgotten by other campers, a strong obligation to leave the barn in the order she'd found it that morning. We worked side by side as Mia entertained Joe with the farm pig and bunnies.

Soon after, Joe and I leveraged riding lessons against the chore board, and Anna took the bait. For years she'd faithfully complete her work, exchanging a week of hard work at home for a day's worth of grooming, tacking, and riding her lesson pony. The lesson we paid for took place at a well-managed stable ten miles north of home. The stable's owner, Susan, had rules. Those rules were concise, clearly written, and posted on walls in every barn. Susan expected, and demanded, kids, parents, and trainers to follow those rules. Anna thrived in Susan's black-and-white world where Susan gave second chances, but not thirds. She wasn't warm and fuzzy, but she was fair. She took no crap from fast-talking kids of money-wielding parents. One had to prove one's abilities to earn privileges at Susan's stable. Nothing was free, quick, or easy.

At Susan's barn Anna learned to jump fences. The process of taking her horse over an obstacle while remaining safely upright in the saddle demanded patience and perseverance. Perfect for Anna. The sixty-minute group lesson was divided into forty-five minutes of flat work, each rider proving she could do what was asked by the trainer. If the riders proved they were focused and the horses properly exercised to manage their energy, the group would be allowed to jump. All week long, Anna would dream about those glorious fifteen minutes to take flight. The weeks when the other students didn't live up to the trainer's expectations and jumping was postponed, Anna was a wreck of anxiety, lobbing blame at the lesson disruptors.

A boarding barn of mostly adult horse owners and very few kids was an easy drive from our home. There were no posted rules. The stable's only lesson trainer, Melissa, was an independent contractor who spent her time between three barns to make ends meet. When Anna offered to be Melissa's assistant in exchange for a lesson at the end of her shift, Melissa jumped at the chance to reduce the strain on her already-packed days. She also dangled a carrot in front of Anna: work and train hard through the winter, and she would take Anna to jumping shows the following summer.

Adult boarders soon noticed Anna's keen horsemanship, athleticism, and commitment to safety. She was asked by several to exercise their horses throughout the week. Within six months of her twelfth birthday, Anna was riding horses four days a week. Joe and I only paid for one.

Dark, cold winter days passed quickly for Anna as she worked every Sunday without fail. She committed to memory each riding lesson. She read every book she could find to make herself a better rider. When mud replaced snow and barn swallows returned to the rafters, Anna's excitement about the approaching summer show season blossomed with the longer days of sun. Melissa, however, nipped the bud before it started to bloom. There would be no shows for Anna that summer. According to Melissa, while Anna had worked hard, she still had more to learn before jumping a borrowed horse in an unfamiliar arena. In the name of safety, Anna needed to wait another year before donning a show coat and breeches. End of story. No discussion about effort and reward.

To temper Anna's disappointment, Melissa invited Mia and her friend Ava to work with Anna each Sunday in exchange for a lesson. Anna continued to help Melissa's lesson kids while Mia and Ava were given cleaning rags and paint brushes. Wooden objects like storage lockers, arena walls, and split rail fences were renewed by two young girls heady with responsibility and the sweet tobacco aroma of old manure. One day of work turned to five as the three girls worked for Melissa and exercised other people's horses. They ate lunch and took breaks at the picnic table under a shade tree overlooking a rolling pasture filled with mares. Barn cats lounged on their resting laps. No one received a dollar in exchange for her work. Some might call it child labor. They called it heaven.

The start of school brought an abrupt change to their daily horse-fix, but not to their commitment. Friday night through Sunday afternoon was filled in much the same manner as summer. Anna's steadfast commitment to her summer show dream never waned, even as Melissa took on more free labor, casting her promises too wide to contain. It wasn't long before Melissa's Jimmy Buffet-laid-back demeanor turned sour like last year's decomposing leaves under the weight of a new autumn. She began to shorten each girl's private lesson time. She then forced them into a group lesson by threatening to take away all lessons. She even started sneaking away from the barn when her paid lessons ended, leaving the girls without any reward for their work. The girls began to grumble loudly.

One glorious spring Saturday when the expansive barn doors had been cast open to a warmer wind, I brought Sierra to the barn with me to bring the kids an extra snack. Dust was dancing in the sun as we walked by pastures filled with placid horses tearing off bits of new grass. Suddenly, Sierra's ears pricked forward, straining. Her legs pulling against the leash forced my legs into motion before my brain registered Melissa screaming at Anna, "I don't care if Amy was bothering you. I expect you to tell Amy to get back to work."

"I was trying to tell her to get back to work," Anna quickly countered.

"Don't sass me. I saw you talk to her."

"I wasn't sassing you. I did talk to her, to tell her to get back to work!" exclaimed Anna, voice rising, a simmering bubble expanding. "Amy wouldn't listen. She kept going on about some boy." Off in a dark corner never dried by the sun, Amy swished the tines of her rake through the arena footing, pretending to look busy.

"I don't care what she said. You were supposed to mind yourself and get your work done, not talk to her," snapped Melissa, stomping off like an angry bull.

Anna, frustration rising, words spilling, continued, "She told me I wasn't her boss and she didn't need to listen to me. What am I supposed to do if she doesn't mind you?" Then, in one final stick-up-for-herself moment, she belted out, "It's not fair that you are accusing me of doing something wrong when you were right there watching Amy do wrong."

"Life's not fair, Anna. You might as well learn that now," snorted Melissa as she pushed her shoulders back, nose pointed to the roof, and turned abruptly to leave. As she did, she turned into my path and Sierra's angry barking. With my heart pounding against my ribs, threatening to punch through with rage, I belted out, "How could you put this blame on such a hard-working, honest kid? She's done everything you've asked of her and done it well."

"She's the smartest one in this barn. I have higher expectations of her," retorted Melissa.

"What does that mean? Those two girls do the same work for the same reward. Why would you not expect the same from Amy?" I fired back

Glaring at me with dark eyes and a quivering finger pointed at my chin, Melissa rebutted, "I don't have to tell you why I do what I do." Her eyes wide and cheeks flaming red, she spouted, "I'm done with you AND her," she screamed, thrusting a crooked finger at Anna for emphasis. "There will be no summer shows this summer. By talking to Amy, you proved you're not mature enough to trust." Angry dust spouted from beneath Melissa's weathered boots as she turned to leave.

"You can't go back on your word," I countered. "You've been promising for more than a year to take Anna to summer shows. Your exact words said to Anna in front of me were, 'Show up, work hard, and you'll be rewarded.'"

"Too bad what I said. Life's not fair."

We watched as she sprinted to her battered pickup and drove away, weaving like a drunk. Just like that, Anna's unwavering commitment to a gentleman's handshake was ruined by two disruptors. As I turned to wrap Anna in a hug, to hold her up against the great weight of disappointment, I noticed the stark contrast between her red, tear-stained face and the baby blue ball cap perched on her thick mane of chestnut hair. Embroidered on the front panel was a smiling brown horse head and the words "Life Is Good." Up to that moment in time, Anna had a strong belief in that truth. I had an equally strong hope Melissa was going to come through. We cried into each other's shoulders. Anna from dashed hope. Me from the reality that I could not protect Anna from a bully like Melissa.

Anna spent the following week sullen and angry, yet determined. Words penned with thick ink from her heavy hand filled an old spiral notebook with pros and cons of the other riding stables within driving distance. She made phone calls and did internet searches. From the scratch marks, Xs, and words scribbled in the columns making sense only to Anna, she decided to return to her former stable. The path to show jumping would take longer but the promise of reward was far more dependable.

Anna's struggles, however, did not end with her return to the iconic red barn with black and white rules. High school proved to be more of a difficult circus to manage than middle school. Her troublemaking left me flustered and confused. *Why was she becoming the one thing she despised, the class disruptor?*

Those were the thoughts clouding my mind when Anna stepped into the moment of crisis with Poet and Snickers and the stinky piles behind the Christmas tree. Anna knew what needed to be done and took charge, grabbing the cleaning bucket before she was asked. It was a deed that didn't go unnoticed, but one I only half-heartedly recognized. I couldn't seem to control the vein of pulsing tension throbbing below the surface of our relationship, and it bugged me.

Yet with her help, I was in and out of the corner and we were herding dogs to the garage with the precision of an Indy pit crew. On the way I grabbed my camera, passing off the photographer role to Anna.

The three dogs were lunging at the service door ready to bolt into the raceway dug into the deep snow. Anna ran ahead of them, positioning herself at the top of the figure-eight. I could hear the shutter snapping as she took shot after shot of animated Snickers in pursuit of nimble Poet, racing around the tight turns. Margo, as always, was two steps behind.

When the dogs slowed and we grew cold, we led them to the coat room so their snowy fur could thaw and dry. Anna and I rushed to the computer to download the pictures. "I have a feeling these will be good," she said, her voice hopeful.

The images were in focus, but Snickers' frown made him look like the guilty raccoon being chased from the compost heap. Anna slunk down in her chair until her chin rested on her forearms resting on the desk, her feet kicking the leg in frustration. As was typical of Anna when her anxiety rose, she began to fidget. One hand wandered. She began idly pressing buttons on my computer, absently clicking on the

Petfinder web link on my favorites bar. In no time, we were surfing the profiles of other rescued dogs, noting the way photos or words grabbed our attention. Together, we constructed a new profile.

"Don't let this sad face fool you. Snickers is one happy little Miniature Schnauzer pup that walks with a bounce and races wildly through snow. He's an inquisitive and fast learner responding well to positive reinforcement. He's well on his way to being house-trained."

We cropped the best photos and used photo editing tricks to brighten his face. Together we pressed the enter button and sent the profile to Marilyn at Second Chance. In no time, she had his story on the web.

A few days before my first Petco Adoption event, a woman named Loretta phoned. She'd seen Snickers' profile posted on Petfinder. He'd drawn her in. Loretta had been given my number by our Second Chance screener to ask more questions of me.

I had questions for her, too. Screening was my chance to calm the anxiety that had surfaced at the thought of letting Snickers go. He was still a pup. His house training wasn't complete. *Did Loretta have the patience for a pup and the accidents that can happen during transition and training? How long would she be away from home when she worked? He needed lots of exercise. Would she walk him? Did she have a fenced yard? When was the last time she checked it for holes and gaps curious pups can paw through?*

I learned Loretta worked from home. Under her desk and at her feet had been the family's dog, a Miniature Schnauzer she raised from a puppy and cared for until he died of old age. She had a seventeen-year-old son equally excited about getting a new dog, only he didn't know she was looking for one. She planned to meet me at the adoption event, son in tow. This would be a surprise for him.

Loretta agreed to meet me at the Petco store in Roseville, Minnesota. Second Chance was hosting its monthly meet-and-greet so the community could meet the dogs and cats available for adoption. I was alone when I entered the store with Snickers. The girls and Joe wanted nothing to do with the letting go part of fostering.

I waited for Loretta in the circle of Second Chance volunteers, sharing the same hope our dogs would find good homes that day. During my first adoption event, I met a husband and wife attending adoption day with their fifty-fourth foster dog! A middle-aged man held the leash of an elderly shepherd, hoping to find an adopter willing to give an old dog a new beginning. An older woman and two friends struggled to keep three foster puppies from pestering two intolerant adult dogs. A young mom juggled the leashes of two curious foster dogs while her two young daughters amused the circle of adults.

I was engrossed in monitoring Snickers, who was curiously sniffing every dog from head to tail, when I noticed a very tall teenager lean over to pet him. Then I noticed a woman I thought must be Loretta. *They'd shown up!* Even better was the wide smile growing on Loretta's son's face when he learned Snickers was available for adoption, and he and his mom were there to bring him home. I handed Snickers' leash to the son while Loretta and I talked. We watched as the tall young man melted in the charms of a calf-high pup that begged him to play. They ran down the aisles. He threw balls to Snickers. He picked out a new leash and a few toys. All the while, Snickers kept his eyes glued on the son, watching his every move, indifferent to the circle of barking at the adoption event.

By the end of my first Petco Adoption Day, Snickers had found his forever home. The people and their stories surrounding me in those three hours increased my resolve to help the Second Chance community. I left knowing our family's small success would help Second Chance achieve something bigger.

Two days later, I wiped the last completed chore off the chore board and removed my playground-lady whistle. I nestled into the sectional with Poet and Margo while Joe encouraged smoldering embers to life in the fireplace. I pulled the cell phone from my pocket and dialed Loretta. It was time to learn how Snickers and his new family were faring.

"He's wonderful!" The high-pitched joy in her voice gave away her delight. "He's already claimed two favorite sleeping spots, in the new bed under my desk and curled in the arms of my son." They were thrilled with their new pet. I was relieved he'd found a good home.

Anna, Mia, and Joe, who'd left me alone to handle Snicker's adoption, began to wedge themselves between me, Poet, and Margo on the large, upholstered L. With fleece blankets tucked tightly around laps and the soft glow of Christmas lights tempering my frustration over Anna's confusing behavior, I shared Loretta's news. My family might not like the letting go part of fostering, but they were reveling in team victory number two, a gift we were able to unwrap early that holiday season!

As I put my arms around Anna and Mia to draw them close, my eyes caught a glimpse of the gingerbread barn we'd baked from homemade dough and decorated the weekend before. Adorned in colorful candies and dripping icing, it was originally centered on the kitchen table where I later found Poet and Snickers standing and licking gumdrops. I quickly relocated the barn to the top of the refrigerator. It was a joyful reminder of another family tradition and the little moments of togetherness that matter. For the time being, life was good.

62

SHELBY

Chapter 6

The anger in Lynda's voice was all I needed to know that the situation before us was dire. The owner of a puppy mill in north-central Minnesota had euthanized one thousand dogs in her quest to downsize her "designer puppy" breeding business. My eyes shut tight against Lynda's words, holding back the image of the woman, a helper, perhaps a veterinarian, injecting each dog into silence, or worse, shooting them because it was cheaper.

A rescue agency in Duluth got wind of the cruelty and negotiated with the woman to end the killings. Rescue agencies and shelters around the state rallied in the depths of a January freeze to pitch in with hauling and housing the remaining 200 dogs. A Second Chance volunteer with a large delivery van was driving back from Duluth with 22 dogs for our agency. Anna, Mia, and I and a few volunteers hurriedly staged the large wraparound porch of a Victorian home in St. Paul with dog food, treats, training pads, leashes, and bowls hauled from the pet shed. Our goal was to have the supplies in place so we could quickly move dogs from the van into the warm cars of waiting foster folks lined front-end to back-bumper along the snowy street.

The somewhat festive mood from a gathering of people on a mission was quickly dampened when the van arrived. We were greeted by the stench of new vomit and old feces from filthy, fearful, uprooted dogs. One by one, the little carriers holding cowering dogs were brought to the porch. A gloved hand would carefully remove each straining dog so it could be identified and noted on a chart. Each was assigned a name, put back in the carrier, and taken to a waiting car.

Almost all were small females around the age of four that'd spent their entire lives producing litter after litter of puppies for the pet trade market, while confined to tiny crates stacked one on top of the other warehouse style, like factory-farm chickens. In fact, dogs in breeding facilities with more than four breeding females fall under the category of livestock per federal government regulations. Put simply: The same entity to whom I pay taxes labels companion animals as livestock. The regulation has minimal requirements for veterinary care and nutrition. Dogs and puppies from puppy mills do not live with blankets or beds to soften the space between wire and skin. There is no exercise for physical and mental health and no socialization with humans or other dogs.

"I can't believe there are people who think this cruelty is an acceptable way to treat companion animals. All this for money," I steamed through clenched teeth to Anna and Mia, equally wide-eyed and upset. Making matters worse was the knowledge that people willingly paid top dollar for her Schnoodles and Bichypoos and mini-Labradoodles, mixed breeds once labeled as mutts now elevated to designer dogs through marketing spin. It made me wonder if buyers knew, or cared, about the mother dog or their new family pet's deplorable upbringings.

"Mom, it'll be all right," whispered Mia, watching my anger brewing. "There's nothing more we can do but our part. At least these dogs will get a chance to sit on a lap."

Who is this kid acting mature in my place? Her display of wisdom was a stark contrast to the evening before when we exchanged words over her lack of motivation.

"Mia, you need to change things up a bit," my voice abrasive. "Seventh grade is passing you by as you sit on your butt on the sectional. Call a friend. Get out of the house."

"Mom, Michelle is a cheerleader now. She's too busy. Haley is away this weekend at a big dance competition. Olivia is at the same event. Besides, I don't feel good. I'm too tired," countered Mia from her nest of blankets.

"Hey, Mia," a muffled Anna called from the coat room as she wrapped a scarf around her face. "Come out with me and shovel. We'll make a fort at the top of the driveway."

"No thanks. It's too cold. Maybe I'll join you when the fort is finished."

"Come on, Mia. Anna could use a partner and you could use some fresh air," I said, my voice rising with frustration. "If you aren't going to play with your sister and your other friends aren't available, what about calling Ava? You haven't been together since summer. Talk to her. Work through your troubles. You could do art projects with the new watercolor paints I bought."

Mia's face drained of color as quickly as a mood ring on an ungloved finger. Time did not heal all wounds, not even those created accidentally at birthday parties.

"Beth is holding conditioning sessions for vaulting at her home this week," I offered, softening my voice to counter her pain.

"I don't want to go. My ankle still hurts from last time," Mia said loud enough to shut the door on my discussion. She turned her head to the back cushion and pulled the covers over her head.

I turned to the kitchen as a vine of incompetence strangled my throat, its tendrils digging into my heart, seeding new worries. *It's been over a semester since her self-imposed isolation, and I haven't made headway. How will her extroverted nature survive such loneliness glued to the sectional?* I felt like the unlucky Candyland game player stuck in the Molasses Swamp, pleading with the stack of colorful cards to help me join the others rushing towards the Candy Castle.

I felt the soft nudge of Anna's elbow, stirring me from my thoughts. "Mom, there are only three dogs left in the van. Lynda wants to know which dog we'd like to take home."

I took a deep breath. The frustration of the night before mixing with my anger of the day was like cold water running out of the hot water tap. I wanted to be the strong parent to wash away the grittiness of human callousness. Yet it was their goodness attempting to stoke my fire.

"You've been so helpful. You two choose." A weak offering was all I could offer.

Newly named, nine-pound Shelby in a light blue carrier was coming home with us. As I buckled my seatbelt and the outside chaos subsided, my edge softened. Our focus now was on caring for one dog, not twenty-two. While the kids gagged from the stench rising from the crate buckled between them, I formulated my plan for Shelby's recovery.

First up was a much-needed bath. One bath quickly turned into three as we fought the buildup of matted feces. Once toweled dry and showered with human touch, we saw a glimmer of shine in her hollow eyes, years of neglect swirling down the drain. A doe-eyed poodle mix with a hint of apricot emerged from the tangles.

That first night, knowing Shelby was used to falling asleep to the sound of a thousand breathing dogs, I dared not leave her alone. I stuffed myself into a sleeping bag and nestled next to her crate with Margo by my side. Sleep was sporadic for our little group as I whispered encouragement into the dark walls of my office.

The morning dawned frigid and gray, but I was determined to get Shelby into the household routine. I took her outside with Margo and Poet, where she danced from foot to foot with wide eyes of panic. I took her in my arms while the dogs finished their business in the snow. Once inside, she tried to walk. Years without exercise in the confinement of a crate left Shelby unable to navigate a straight line. It was then I noticed the sparseness of fur on her left side. Nervous energy or skin irritation must have led to constant licking.

We set up a nice home for Shelby in my office using a pet fence so she could move from crate to a training pad to soft bed outside her crate as she grew comfortable with her surroundings. I continued to work at my desk. The girls would sit in the chair by the window and talk to Shelby in soft tones. As our familiarity with each other grew, she spent less time in the crate and more time on the bed. She became less fearful, letting us pet her head. On occasion, she'd raise a paw to our hands, requesting a longer scratch.

We spent many days cleaning her home, as it took a while for Shelby to get the hang of using the potty pad. When she did, we rubbed the pad in the snow to transfer her scent outside. Little by little, small victories were ours as her natural instincts to mark the snow replaced her fear of being outside.

After two weeks of forward movement, I drove her to Life Care. She needed to be spayed and given a thorough vet check. Normally, a dog would receive medical care and grooming before coming to our home, but the overwhelming need to get twenty-two dogs housed quickly rerouted the routine. Shelby's teeth were so rotted, twelve had to be pulled. Two days later, I brought home a sore and trembling dog. We had to start from square one with trust and healing.

I noticed Shelby turn a corner in her mental and physical recovery one morning before walking Margo. I typically left her behind on my twice-daily walks because she was not strong enough nor had a thick enough coat to tolerate the cold. That changed when Shelby began to vocalize her disapproval, waking up the household, including Poet, who'd been asleep in a ball under the covers at Mia's feet.

I was in a quandary about what to do when I noticed a cloth messenger bag hanging from a coatroom peg. I swaddled Shelby like a newborn in a thick fleece blanket, stuffed her into the bag with only nose and eyes peeking through the flap, and slung her over my shoulder. She rode like this two times a day for several weeks, excited to be going with me and Margo rather than being left behind.

One day, everything changed. "Come on, Shelby," I muttered in frustration as I tried to settle her now ten-pound body into the bag.

She stiffened her legs like a toddler in a tantrum. She made it clear she was not getting in the bag. From that day forward, she ran to the back door and waited patiently to be put into a winter coat so she could walk beside us. At first our walks were short and cumbersome as I switched between letting her walk and carrying her in my arms. As one block turned into two miles, strong muscles enabled her to walk a confident, straight line.

At home, Shelby favored Mia's dependable position on the sectional in place of her fenced home in my office. After long walks, she'd snuggle tight to Mia's hip, opposite Poet, for a deep, restful sleep. I was thankful Shelby could trust Mia for this much-needed solace, but Mia's codependence on relaxing dogs had become maddening.

"Mia! Anna and Annie are in the backyard making a snow family. Go out and join them," I demanded.

"I don't feel like it. It's too cold. I have a headache. Besides, Anna's been so bossy lately I don't want to be near her," responded Mia with as much enthusiasm as Eeyore on a gloomy day.

So went our sparring, me stating all the reasons she should be outside. Mia countering with a million excuses to stay put. I wanted to take her by the shoulders and shake her fiercely. I wanted somehow to loosen the lid, to let her spirit free. Joe, equally frustrated, was no more able to swing Mia's pendulum than I was.

A heated discussion between me and Joe over each other's lack of ability to motivate Mia pushed me over the edge. Not the "I want a divorce" edge but the "I'm going to spend money we don't have to get to the bottom of this" edge.

Money was a difficult subject between me and Joe. He worked full-time; I worked part-time. We weren't lacking in necessities. In fact, the much-used sectional sat in the middle of the family room constructed of beautiful wood posts and beams. Luck had been ours many years before when we bought the architect-designed home off the foreclosure market. We felt like royalty to afford such a warm and welcoming home on a hill with wood-plank ceilings and big windows surrounded by pine forests and thick marshes of chattering frogs. Its cheap price and extended time on the market should have raised a red flag.

Our luck had lasted one week. While a monsoon pounded the exterior, water gushed into the window wells like a fire hydrant being flushed, the pressure forcing water to cascade over the interior ledges like Niagara Falls. The kids' toys floated on rising water in the basement. Unpacked boxes swelled until cardboard collapsed and contents spilled. We soon learned a foreclosed home has no responsible party but the current occupant.

The basement flood was the harbinger of many costly home interventions to come for our five-year-old home: two bathroom remodels to rid them of mold, wall insulation to keep pipes from freezing, new windows to replace those that had imploded from bad seals, and regrading of landscaping at the foundation to keep snakes out of the basement. Our home was the proverbial money pit. There was no shortage of plates spinning and balls juggling as we attempted to juggle our young family's needs with our young house.

Mia's continued lack of ambition became the first ball that dropped, necessitating a financial commitment to intervention. Our prodding, pleading, and withholding of privileges were not successful. We needed help. The only place I could think to go was Mia's family physician. She gave Mia an extensive physical, took multiple vials of blood and administered a ten-question mental health test. Mia was prescribed over-the-counter vitamin D supplements—no shock to us, given that her lack of physical activity meant she rarely saw the sun. She was also referred to a children's mental health specialist for a "neuropsychological evaluation."

It was just me and Joe during our first visit with Dr. Bonnie at Children's Hospital. Dr. Bonnie, with her kind face, youthful blond hairstyle and forgiving demeanor, was the quintessential psychologist one would imagine in a feel-good movie. Her office was tidy but packed. Books, games, and fidget toys were within reach of the two cushioned seats. Lush, green ivy cascaded from the ledges of two large windows.

Dr. Bonnie's probing was unobtrusive. She cataloged our concerns and observations, inquired about our marriage and work, dove deep into Mia's relationships with us, her sister, her friends, and teachers, and read through the medical report from her physician. She thoughtfully laid out the plan for Mia's assessment, pausing to ask questions, waiting to be sure we understood. She sent us home with several behavioral questionnaires to complete. Others were sent to Mia's teachers. No assumptions were made on a diagnosis. "Let's see what can be learned from all the different sources of input before making any conclusions," were her parting words.

Mia and I ventured downtown for two full mornings of assessment over a two-week period. She was led through a series of computer games, math quizzes, reading tests, and hearing and visual exams. She completed self-reporting questionnaires to assess symptoms of anxiety and depression. She was asked about sleep. Dr. Bonnie was looking for clues to Mia's fine motor speed and coordination, memory retention, ability to sustain attention, impulsivity under varying conditions, and her mental wellness.

After Mia's second testing session, she and I went to lunch at her favorite downtown restaurant where she could dip broken pieces of crusty Italian bread into fragrant tomato sauce. She told me Dr. Bonnie asked her if she understood why she was being tested. Mia admitted to me she did not but thanked me for feeling "less heavy." We finished in silence, until Mia begged me to let her skip the rest of the school day. It was already 1:30 in the afternoon. "Why not," I agreed.

We went home to three eager dogs, hooked them to leashes, and walked them around the block. When we returned, Poet, wound tight like a top, ran to the toy box in my office, found the small, knotted rope and dropped it at Shelby's feet. She stepped back, eyeing it like a hiker inspects a stick that looks like a snake. Poet nudged it closer to her with his little black nose, marble eyes gleaming, tailing wagging. He picked it up and shook it, letting out a little, "*Grrrrr.*" Margo let out a big "Woof." When Margo's bark stopped vibrating off the windows, Shelby gently grabbed the rope's other end and tugged. Poet gently tugged back. Shelby, startled by the tension, dropped the rope. Poet dropped his end, waiting patiently until she had the courage to pick up hers. In a matter of minutes, Poet had Shelby engaged in the first game of her new dog life.

A few days later, I received a phone call from Mia while I was at work. Barely able to contain her excitement, she shouted, "Mom, Shelby's playing with the Santa toy, tossing it in the air and growling as it falls. She's playing by herself!"

I immediately attributed that stroke of good fortune to Poet. For all his shortcomings, fear of male visitors, and continued reluctance with house training, he was the all-time best host. His leadership shone around every new dog that came through our door. He would nudge them with his nose, drop toys at their feet, and bark short, happy snips encouraging them to play. Margo, always in proximity to Poet, would bark encouragement, too. This pack of dog happiness was what Shelby needed to shed the darkness of her past. When she did, in its place was a beautiful, playful dog. Thanks to Poet, it was time to find Shelby a forever home.

The thought of letting Shelby go, however, was crippling. I'd never spent so much time rehabilitating a dog, nor had I experienced such joy in the result. I worried that I wouldn't be able to find the right owner to care for her recovery the way I did...until I met Sharon. She was searching for the right dog to help her tiny Maltese recover from the death of her husband.

Sharon locked souls with Shelby when she saw her pictures on Petfinder.com. In a great stroke of fortune, I discovered Sharon lived just two miles from me. Shelby, Mia, and I spent a week of afternoons visiting Sharon, Maltese Molly, and Sharon's extended family, including two grandchildren who went to school with Anna and Mia. It was the slow transition I needed in order to find comfort in letting Shelby go. It also gave Sharon and Molly time to get used to a new dog in their home. One sunny Sunday, I closed the door of Sharon's house, leaving Shelby behind in the good hands of a lot of loving people.

With the success of Shelby's adoption boosting my spirits, Joe and I drove to St. Paul to meet with Dr. Bonnie. All the questionnaires were returned. Every test analyzed. It was time to hear the conclusions Dr. Bonnie drew about Mia.

We learned quickly the seventeen pages of single-space, eleven-point font with the word "Confidential" in bold across the top summarized the beginning of a long journey. Single words, like standardized, percentile, fluency, and paired words, like processing speed, scaled scores, and executive function, peppered the pages.

All those words supported the executive summary "...consistent with Attention-Deficit/Hyperactivity Disorder: Predominantly inattentive type (ADHD)...trouble staying focused and attentive...difficult for her to complete work consistently in a timely manner...and to refrain from responding in an impulsive manner...mild anxiety that is typically expressed as somatic or physiological complaints (such as headaches...body aches...tired...)."

Yes! That's it! The lens had come into focus. There was a reason for Mia's fatigue, headaches, and physical ailments. Like finding the final piece to make the frame of a puzzle, I shuddered with glee as problem was linked to cause. My brain, however, became a racecourse of thoughts with no smooth hand-offs in the relay. Batons were dropping as I stumbled in search of the right lane. My own feet zigging instead of zagging.

Joe was equally silent. I assumed he'd moved from mulling to stewing, contemplating what the words meant and would come to mean.

Ever-patient Dr. Bonnie let us stare at the pages in silence until she knew we were ready to listen. She carefully explained each section, pausing as before, to let things sink in, to ask questions.

Words spilled from my mouth, tripping over each other to be first in line. "Mia saw the doctor every year for a wellness check. How did we miss this? Why now? Is ADHD genetic? Is it curable? What does this mean for her future?"

Dr. Bonnie told us to imagine adolescence as a time when fifty percent of a child's brain is unwired so it can be rewired. The unwiring makes way for all the new connections a young person will need to become an independent adult, to navigate a life separate of parents. The brain growth and new connections make life chaotic for kids for years.

"Mia, who is intelligent and extroverted, probably had strong coping skills and enough behavior consistent with kids around her you didn't notice anything out of the ordinary until puberty. Even then, many of her behaviors were like kids her age. My guess is that Mia's excessive idleness, isolation, and changes in academic performance raised the red flags." With a long pause to ensure we were listening, she emphasized, "It's great you took action when you became worried. Her diagnosis provides a path to intervention."

A brief shot of warmth from Dr. Bonnie's pat on the back coursed through my blood. The knot in my stomach loosened slightly. Then, as if two sumo wrestlers were playing tug of war, tension seized my shoulder blades. A throb developed in my right temple. Mia did not have strep. No one-and-done course of antibiotics would cure her. There were no casts, splints, or braces for support. She had mental health disorders, requiring a whole lot of trial and error to point her back towards something resembling normal.

Keeping her on a steady path would require me and Joe to reach beyond the boundaries of our home for help. Our private selves were uncomfortable with the new role of vocal advocate. Dr. Bonnie also cautioned us to expect change over time: what may work for years may one day cease to help. Hormones, sickness, excess stress, and growth were just some of the obstacles that could render a good path void.

Trial and error and more help from others would be necessary to find the next solution, the new road.

The most critical five pages in the report were those outlining the "recommendations" for home and school. It was suggested we start with a return visit to her physician to discuss the benefits and risks of putting Mia on a trial of medication to manage the physiological symptoms of ADHD. We could also explore the idea of using melatonin for sleep. Counseling was suggested as an option to help Mia build coping strategies she could use throughout life.

School options were many, varied, self-contained, or reliant on others. To start, it was suggested we share Dr. Bonnie's report with Mia's teachers and school counselor. We were encouraged to ask about special services, including distraction-free environments for test taking, extended time to complete tests and assignments without penalty, and reduced work volume emphasizing quality over quantity. *Ask overstressed teachers to accommodate our child's needs? Oh, fudge.*

Our car ride home was so silent a proverbial pin could drop in our car in St. Paul and people over the river in Minneapolis could hear it. We were stunned by the diagnosis and the overwhelming list of things to do.

"What are your thoughts?"

"I don't know."

"What do you think about medication?"

"I don't know."

"What should we try first?"

"I don't know."

That torturous exchange—at times me asking Joe, then Joe asking me—was just one of many conversations to come.

Mia's doctor suggested starting with the lowest dose of Ritalin, a common ADHD medication. We were to keep a journal to note changes and issues. The plan was to meet frequently to discuss results.

Mia's middle school counselor was delightfully gracious. She offered to meet weekly with Mia during Friday study period; together they would organize Mia's locker and read through assignments to ensure work was being completed and turned in on time. The counselor suggested we purchase a single-ring binder with multiple subject sections and built-in folders, so all Mia's schoolwork could be contained in one place instead of the "one binder and matching folder per class" system used by her teachers. "Some kids thrive with a color-coded homework and filing system. Others, like Mia, get overwhelmed by the process. No need to create stress if none is needed," she said. The counselor began meeting with Mia's teachers to disseminate the suggested support options. Later we learned all her teachers had agreed to let Mia take tests in the quiet of the counselor's office. It appeared my worry was for naught.

Eight weeks later, Mia was on a stable path. She returned to vaulting with enthusiasm. She started hanging out with friends. She was completing her homework and turning it in. She'd take Poet to the backyard to run circles or hook him to the leash to walk with me and Margo. Along the way, she'd share stories from school. She even suggested we take an afternoon to visit Shelby and Sharon. Sharon's grandson, Jameson, told Mia on the bus that Shelby was "doing great." Mia wanted to see for herself.

Shelby greeted us at Sharon's door with a wagging tail and wide grin. Framing her vibrant eyes was a lush coat of apricot curls. She ran circles around our feet as we settled ourselves on the floor. She immediately jumped from one lap to another, licking our cheeks in greeting. It was a brief gesture of enthusiasm but not a signal she wanted to come home. She immediately jumped on the couch and firmly planted herself next to Sharon. She was home!

Mia and I floated out the door of Sharon's house uplifted by adoption success number three. The diligent and patient work of our village helped to create a happy chapter in Shelby's story, rather than a quick and dismal end.

The same could be said for Mia's story; seventh grade was ending much better than it'd begun. As I let out a long-awaited sigh of relief, I reflected on the empathetic and knowledgeable village we were able to gather around Mia. Many patient individuals helped us turn the page to a happy chapter in her story, pointing Mia back towards her once-extroverted self. Joe and I, not yet comfortable in our new roles as vocal advocates, were glad to leave behind the Molasses Swamp. The path ahead, at least for now, aimed straight at the Candy Castle.

RASCAL

Chapter 7

I doubt the girls were thinking of kid games and Candy Castles the day we told them they had to haul dirt. Joe and I were beat. He and I'd spent a difficult week cleaning the yard after the last piece of heavy machinery was secured to a trailer and hauled away, leaving behind a replacement drain field for the young septic system that'd failed. Most of our driveway had been pulverized, displaced, or scattered down the road by muddy wheels of massive dump trucks and trailers carrying field stones, backhoes, bulldozers, and rich black dirt. Plants we'd dug from the garden had wilted in their temporary buckets and needed replanting. The back door, the side door, the service door, the walls, and windows on the back of the house were all splattered in stinky, sticky, gray clay.

No sooner had we tidied the yard when the rains came. Pounding, pouring deluge. The mound that once sported a beautiful layer of rich soil to nurture the seeds we hoped would grow into grass was washed clean to its clay core. Out came another company with yet another dump truck and yards and yards of soil—piled at the end of our battered driveway.

"Max, how'd you like to make a few easy bucks," joshed Joe, hoping to soften the edges of a tough job enough to entice Max.

"Sure, sure," he quickly answered. "Tell me what to do, boss. When do I start?"

Anna and Mia weren't thrilled to find they'd been assigned to Max's team. Each began to petition why she should be excused. As was typical, the banter began like a quick poke in the Pillsbury Doughboy's belly. When each realized their soft approach wasn't working, they pulled Mohammed Ali punches.

"Mom, it's too hot," they'd bellow.

"Mom, my friends don't have to do stupid stuff like this," they'd whine.

"Mom, you could be put in jail for child labor," they'd threaten.

Monday morning Joe left for work. I directed Anna and Mia's efforts for the day, showing them how to conserve energy by taking turns shoveling dirt into the wheelbarrow, pushing the wheelbarrow up the mound, and spreading dirt. The process would be theirs to manage the next day with Max. I wanted to be sure they had it right. Grumbling and heat plagued the work. By the time Max arrived the next morning, both girls were in a foul mood. His cheerful smile, gentle ribbing, and hearty laugh, "C'mon you babies. What's your problem? This will be easy," did not bring a smile.

After reviewing with them the tasks that needed to be done, I settled into the peacefulness of my air-conditioned car and left their thick gray cloud behind. I was glad to pass the dirty work to the younger crowd while equally curious to see what would be accomplished in my absence.

As I drove back over our busted driveway, I stopped short. Before me was an updated chain-gang scene from the movie *O Brother, Where Art Thou?* Anna, Mia, and Max were singing rap songs in unison as they shoveled dirt into their own wheelbarrows, pushed them up the hill in a single-file line, then spread dirt. *Three wheelbarrows? I'd left them with one. Where did they get two more?* Poet, once white with black spots, now all black, trailed the long lunge line through the loose soil. Margo, the lone white star on her black chest now coated to match, looked at one with the dirt as she ran up and down, barking.

Just great! Now the dogs need a bath. I could feel tension rising through my spine, my cheeks tightening. I wanted to scream, "What were you thinking?" and would've if it weren't for Max.

"Hey, boss lady. How was your day? Me and the girls've been doin' just fine." Throwing his head back, he laughed the short series of chuckles we came to know as his signature.

Anna and Mia rolled their eyes, trying to make it look like they'd had a torturous day. I tried to not look pissed. The dogs were a mess, but the dirt mound at the end of the driveway had been greatly reduced. I owed it to them to be happy.

"Where did you get the extra wheelbarrows?" I asked, my voice rising with curiosity, picking words I could make sincere.

"Max went home and borrowed one from his dad. Jane let us borrow hers," exclaimed Mia, beaming with resourcefulness.

"With three wheelbarrows, we raced each other to fill and dump 'em," added an excited Anna. "Hey, Max. Let's go get that ice cream you promised us. Loser!" She gave Max a teasing punch to the shoulder.

"No way, man. I beat your sorry butts up the hill!" bantered Max.

Twenty-four hours earlier the girls were ready to mutiny. Had it been my job to lead the day, it would've been disastrous. Max, however, found the key to guiding his crew through the maelstrom! It was a challenge conquered, and neither Joe nor I did the work. My former colleague Jackie's lesson of letting go to let others lead wasn't lost on me that day.

The weather finally cooperated. The grass grew green and lush. Within weeks Poet was back to racing circles in the backyard, lunge line trailing, nipping at Margo's ears, using her like a trampoline when she'd lie down. From Margo was a steady stream of woofs, yaps and *grrr*s as she rubbed her face and wriggled her back in the soft, young blades.

With the big drain field project complete and the dirt tucked under soft grass, I resumed my efforts to convert Poet to a "good citizen"—a term Loree used to define a dog with good behavior. Poet was food motivated, making it easy to teach him "stay" and "come" in the house. At issue? He lost all interest in treats and training when outside. His ears were cute Papillon, but his short-cropped fur and unyielding fixation on squirrels, rabbits, and virtually anything that moved pointed directly to terrier.

Undeterred, I worked with him often, convinced his stubbornness could be cured by patience, consistency, and Margo's good influence. She found great pleasure in being a pleaser and enjoyed every enthusiastic word, vigorous rub of her belly, and crunch of a small treat. On occasion, Poet would let his eyes wander to Margo, following her moves. On those days, I felt like a champion trainer, both dogs' eyes on me, attentive, watching for hand signals, responding when asked, chomping on treats when successful.

One beautiful summer evening, the kind I wished could be bottled and uncorked when winter cold seeped into short, gray days, I took Poet outside with Margo. He'd been exhibiting good citizenry of late. I unhooked the lunge line. He ran circles until Margo was wound up and trailing him. As she closed in, Poet doubled back and ran for her ears, grasping her thick, long fur, tugging until she barked. Margo tossed her head, throwing Poet in the air. He shook his head vigorously when he landed, sat back on his haunches, then leapt at her again. Margo laid down, letting Poet jump over and on her while she rolled and wiggled with a grin.

Both dogs ran to the garage to drink from the large metal pasta pot now serving as a water dish. I knelt to gather the training treats that had fallen from the bag, and curled the long lunge line into a tidy circle. As I stood, I caught the tip of Margo's black tail rounding the corner on the outside of the garage, heading for the front yard.

"Stop" I shrieked. I dropped my things and ran, fear rising like water flooding from a breached dam. Margo knew not to cross the normally quiet street. Poet did not. At the edge of our yard, Margo and our neighbor's dog pranced and whined, staring anxiously at their little buddy curled in the middle of the empty road. There was no blood nor tire mark on his white fur. Yet the fear in his eyes and rapid breathing spoke volumes of trauma. I let out a blood-curdling, "Noooooo!" while frantically scooping him into my arms. My head swung left and right. Not a tailpipe in sight. Not a sound. *Who would hit a dog and run?*

Anna, horrified by my outburst, ran from her room, crashing into me at the base of the stairs as I pushed Margo into the house. I demanded she get in the back seat of the car, handing her Poet, now bundled in a towel. I drove furiously to the animal emergency hospital, the steering wheel rattling from speed and nerves, vomit threatening to push past my throat.

A vet tech met us at the door and rushed Poet inside. Anna let out a string of expletives as she stomped through the parking lot, first hands on head, then hands on knees, steadying herself to keep from throwing up. She reeled away from any attempt I made to comfort her and went to the farthest end of the parking lot to dial her phone. I was on my phone crying to Loree when Max drove up. Without a word, Anna shut me out of her grief when she slammed the door to Max's car. No goodbye. No "I'll call you later." Just gone. I cried harder into the phone.

The awful moments of the night continued to tally. I drove to Mia's friend's house, interrupting their sleepover. I broke the news her "best friend" had died under my watch. Poet's body was at the vet clinic. She couldn't hold him to say goodbye. The shock was abrupt. Her grief was heavy. I gathered a stiff child into my arms and drove her home where she slammed the door in my face and wailed into her pillow. Only Joe was allowed into her sorrow.

I was left to my own mourning, guilt, and the loneliness of a house without Poet. Margo, overcome with great unease, sought reassurance from me. I had nothing to give her except the tears I cried into her fur.

Two weeks later, we walked a great expanse of beach along Lake Michigan, trying to find "family" in our vacation. Every summer prior, we'd nestle ourselves into sleeping bags in tents pitched among the lake's great dunes. The last trip with unending rain, puddles like ponds at our campsite, and continuously wet clothes and shoes had me looking for alternate lodging. My cousin Susie came to our aid. She offered us her small cottage one mile from the beach.

By day, we'd hike with Margo up the steep, sandy dunes, then race to the water's edge, letting bits of happiness escape from the tough armor we'd built around our grief. No one said a word about Poet, perhaps afraid to say his name aloud and drive Margo back to her funk. We swam in the waves, lounged in chairs, and read with toes tucked into sand. To any casual observer, we looked fine.

One night, we built a fire in the grill at the picnic area and ate dinner while the sun descended the sky. We noticed a hush among the crowd. Everyone had turned towards a lone bugler, playing taps on the wraparound porch of the pavilion. The last bits of red were swallowed by the shimmering lake, pulling melancholy notes below the horizon. A crack sheered through my heart. Profound sadness threatened to escape. I turned quickly to check on my family. Joe and Mia, still facing west, were frozen in place. Anna, however, was gone.

Mia bolted to the bathrooms to check for her there. Fueled by adrenaline, I sprinted down the darkening beach, wondering how one finds a kid who wants to hide deep inside her pain. Three-foot dune grasses and heavily wooded bluffs stretched for miles north, south, and east. To the west was Chicago—more than fifty miles away by water. No one lingering in the dusk had seen a distraught teenage girl.

Joe drove the car back to the cottage while Mia and I peered through open windows into the deep forest lining the trail back to the tiny beach town. I hated that Anna could be hiding behind any of the massive tree trunks, letting us go as we passed. I pictured her crouching behind a tree, eyes glaring at me with contempt.

Anna and I'd taken a long walk earlier in the day to a more secluded area of shoreline. I was lost in the rhythmic whoosh of gentle waves washing through the coarse sand as I scoured the beach for sparkling, wet beach glass. Just as I crouched to salvage a piece of blue, the crown jewel of color, Anna let into me, "Why do you keep telling people I killed Poet?" Her stiff body leaning into the anger, fists clenched.

"What?" I stood up to face her so I could hear more clearly what I couldn't believe I thought she said.

"You keep telling people I killed Poet. Everyone hates me. Everyone blames me for his death," she stammered, turning abruptly to run in the direction of our footprints.

"I don't tell people that," I shouted, throwing my words across the growing divide as I ran to catch her. Try as I might, sadness spilled into my lungs, replacing the air I needed to keep my legs moving. I sank to the wet sand, gasping, my tears lost to the lake with each wave.

A born director from childhood, Anna began to tell me and Joe what to do as soon as she could stand in her little play kitchen and wave a wooden spoon. Donning her homemade chef hat, she would dole out roles. I was usually Donna, Joe's sister. Joe was Tom, Donna's husband. Anna was their son, Jake. Together we would make imaginary feasts, drive cars and school buses to the grocery store, stop at the post office to mail letters, and pretend to call her grandparents on the plastic telephone.

When Anna got older, she would gather her best friend, Annie, along with Mia and Mia's friends to play horse barn and vet clinic. She created show-jumping rings, so the girls could ride stick ponies through the courses and win ribbons they'd make at the craft table. An "E" for exceptional student, she worked hard at school to earn a weekly horseback riding lesson and the opportunity to groom a real horse.

Anna was persistent and passionate and mostly predictable. She saw life in black and white and had a nearly photographic memory. I thought law would've been a good profession for her; she thrived on arguments backed by facts.

Lately, however, she seemed like the wooden tiles in our Scrabble box, turned this way and that, waiting for someone else to manipulate the letters into coherent words and connections. It didn't make sense why she believed I thought she killed Poet. If anyone was to blame, it was me. If he'd been on the lunge line, I would have caught him before he ran to the front yard. Yet I wasn't the one who killed him. He'd been hit by a car. The facts were as solid as could be.

Anna wasn't thinking in black and white. That alone scared the crap out of me. She had run away from me earlier in the day and ran from all of us that night. With Max more than 600 miles away, I worried her pain ran so deep she'd drive away with a stranger.

Mia and I called the local police to ask what to do. We learned time would have to tick by before we could file a missing person's report. Joe was gone, too, driving slowly down neighboring streets, the activity of looking for Anna helping to pacify his anxiety. Margo paced in the cottage, antsy, our anxiety fueling hers. Mia and I sat on the porch, waiting, talking in hushed tones. We moved inside and tried to watch a movie, our eyes moving to the picture window whenever a car drove by.

Shortly before midnight, bright lights washed the darkness from the family room as Joe drove our car onto the little driveway. Mia and I bolted for the door. Anna was home! A flood of contradictions washed over me as I rushed forward. I was relieved to find her safe. The urge to hug her, hold her, and cry fought against the desire to scream at her, ground her, pack the car, and leave for home. Instead, I gave Anna a brief, deep hug, offered a sandwich, and let her be. Frankly, I had no idea what the emotionally intelligent thing to do was. Neither did Joe, so we gave into exhaustion and did nothing.

When the sun hit the sand, we packed the car and returned to the beach. We took long walks, read books, made a sandcastle, all while avoiding the proverbial elephant now lying on our beach mat. Few words passed between us other than to ask for sunscreen, look at each other's beach glass collections, or to wonder out loud what was left in the cooler. I wanted to ask Anna about running away. I wanted to know what we could do to help. *How does one talk to a kid on the edge without pushing her to flight?*

The remaining few days of the trip looked quite similar: the ever-present elephant, flipping over to tan, refused to leave. By week's end, the elephant had lost enough weight to buckle into the back seat of the car with the girls and Margo for the long trip home.

Sunny the cat was happy to see us return, but the sadness still plaguing our trip made itself at home as we unpacked the bags. Margo sulked, nose resting next to Poet's favorite toy box. The girls retreated to their rooms. Mia packed Poet's clothes in a small blue suitcase with red trim and shoved it under her bed. Days later, the girls and I piled into the car for a trip to the mall. Preparing for school was a welcome distraction.

I would've given up fostering after Poet's death, except that Margo needed a playmate. I was banking on the passage of time and the strength of our connection to get Anna and Mia through their loss and to repair our relationship. But I couldn't sway Margo. As much as I tried to play with her, walk her, reassure her, I was no substitute for her four-legged friend. She couldn't be budged from her sadness. No matter what I did to encourage a spark of life in Margo, she'd counter by laying her head on Poet's little bed. She'd shuffle listlessly through her walks. She'd curl around the toilet rather than play with the girls. After watching Margo mourn Poet for two months, we all—as a family—agreed to try fostering again.

My heart was pounding and hands shaking as I opened the door to the Life Care vet clinic. Just walking into their waiting room challenged my fragile confidence. I felt like a farce. Poet had been the real host, welcoming, encouraging, nudging each foster dog to shed its fear. Tears were rimming my eyes when the vet tech led Rascal from the back room. The long-legged, very skinny, mini black labradoodle with close-shaved fur looked at me with a gigantic grin, his rat-like tail flipping back and forth like windshield wipers during a summer downpour. As I bent over to pet him, he leapt upwards with the force of all four legs and landed in my arms. He licked my face as I laughed hysterically at this clown.

I talked incessantly to Rascal as I drove him home—partly to calm my nerves, partly to reassure him I would do my best to help him heal. No guarantees were promised, just a best effort. I knew little about Rascal and less of his needs. He'd been captured by animal impound somewhere in the city of St. Paul. He was three, neutered, and very underweight. Messages left by animal control to the phone numbers on his microchip went unreturned. He'd been dumped.

Rascal bounded through our door, past Margo, and made a beeline for the toy box. In no time, stuffing was flying. Squeakers lay abandoned on the floor. The once-full box emptied. His unbridled joy stirred the depths of Margo's depression, rousing her playful spirit. She began to bark loudly, her ample tail swishing back and forth, creating a breeze in the still air.

"Mom! Make them shut up," huffed Anna from the sectional.

"Mom! I can't hear the TV," whined Mia, pulling the throw over her head, flopping to the cushions in a show of irritation.

Margo ignored their outbursts. She grabbed a toy and tossed it into the air. I caught a glimpse of her guarded smile just before she nudged Rascal. Soon, Large Marge began to chase Nimble Rascal through the tight turns of our house until they spotted the end of a knotted rope peeking from under the sectional. All-black Margo with a white star on her chest picked up the end of the rope, urging all-black Rascal with a star on his chest in tug-of-war. Flat-coated retriever pulled against the curly-haired labradoodle—two wide smiles between clenched teeth.

In that brief encounter, my unease eased. Anna and Mia, however, were not amused. Their eyes cast daggers in our direction, giving Rascal a chilly reception on a warm September afternoon.

We learned quickly Rascal was a noisy dog, keeping vigilant watch over the animals and humans moving about our neighborhood. Rarely did he sleep, preferring instead to chew on bones and toys with one eye focused outside. Shrill barks pierced the quiet whenever squirrels, rabbits, an occasional turkey, and garbage trucks passed by his favorite window. Margo often accompanied Rascal's sharp cries with her own deep woofs, the loudness further amplified as the sound bounced off the glass. I could barely hear the kids scream, "Mom-mmmm, make them stop!"

The fact that Rascal lived up to his name meant we had to be more vigilant imposing rules and following through on chores. Our teenage daughters already had a love-hate relationship with me and Joe because of the small white board listing their daily responsibilities in colorful marker. The board had been in service since Anna was in second grade, leaning against the same Douglas Fir post abutting the countertop in the kitchen. They knew the chore board was helping them to become better citizens. That didn't mean they liked it.

Because of Rascal, the chore lists were longer. Garbage cans needed frequent emptying. Otherwise, a mischievous Rascal would tip them over to get at the contents. He'd climb the chairs to eat from plates left on the table. Toys needed to be stashed in toy boxes and lids closed. We found dolls with mangled arms, stuffed animals missing eyes, and half-eaten plastic play food extracted from the play kitchen stored in the basement. At times, the house looked like an exhumed graveyard. On more than one occasion, I heard the kids mutter, "I hate you."

For all the headaches Rascal caused, though, the kids took great pleasure in telling stories of his antics and misdeeds. They found it cute when he pawed at them for attention or snuck onto their laps to snuggle. He accompanied me one day to meet Mia at the school bus stop. Rascal, lunging against the leash, yipped and yapped with uncontrolled excitement when he spotted her in the line of kids. She was about to stoop to pet his head when he jumped with all four legs, landing in her arms. Laughter spread through Mia like sun filling a dark room when curtains are thrown open. She became the instant cool kid as the others waited in line to have Rascal jump into their arms. From that day forward, he greeted both Anna and Mia at the back door, jumping into their embrace like a circus dog to lick their faces.

My once-leisurely walks with Margo became race-walk competitions. Small Rascal walked with intent, tugging at the leash, pulling big Margo and me faster down the road. We walked many miles, much to Margo's pleasure. Our favorite off-leash hiking loop with rolling hills and open prairie was perfect for a stop-and-go dog like Rascal who paused to investigate interesting smells, then bounded after us with abandon to take the lead. When Rascal and Margo raced down the hills, the soft curls of fur on Rascal's bouncing ears curved sharply upwards, giving his head the appearance of a nun's headpiece from the back. At any moment I thought he might take flight.

On a warm evening with a hint of smoldering fire stoked by crisp leaves lingering in the air, I sat before my computer to compose Rascal's profile. The house was quiet. So were Margo and Rascal, lying next to each other on the cool floor. The oscillating fan occasionally stirred their fur. In Rascal, I saw the perfect dog for an active adult. Give him the right toys and bones and his busyness could be contained. He was good with other dogs, cats, kids, and men—qualities that would make him appeal to more families. As a house-trained dog, he would certainly rise to the top on Petfinder.com.

Our elderly cat, Sunny, walked in front of the dogs. The contrast of white ghost against two black shadows drew my eyes again to the slumbering friends. Neither Anna nor Mia were begging to keep Rascal. Margo certainly couldn't ask. The ease with which she let Rascal melt her grief, however, said it all. Just like the night I signed Poet's adoption papers to spare Mia and Anna from loss, I signed Rascal's adoption contract to end Margo's grief. The remaining chapters of Rascal's loud and busy life would be written with ours. There'd be no check added to the fourth box of our fostering contract checklist. It would have to wait, along with my relationship with Anna.

APRIL

Chapter 8

I was leaning against the counter at Life Care while the vet tech went to retrieve April from the back room. A memory of enthusiastic Rascal leaping into my arms like a circus dog gave me a hearty chuckle and a yearning for another spirited foster dog. That wish was quickly extinguished when a listless dog shuffled behind the vet tech. The silver Shih Tzu, with closely cropped fur and broad shoulders, stopped at my feet, and cautiously peered around my ankles. She looked past me with paralyzed eyes, barely able to keep her chin from dusting the floor. April had no response to my high-pitched attempts at encouragement.

The same could be said over the following weeks. Very little of anything we tried ignited her spirit. No amount of peanut butter, hamburger, scrambled eggs, or tuna got a response. She ate without joy. She went on walks with Margo and Rascal with no spring in her step. She snuggled next to Mia, Anna, and Joe with what seemed like a burning need for quiet and comfort. April was a good little dog. No accidents in the house. No budging the other dogs. No barking. Her body was alive, but her spirit wasn't.

April did have one peculiar habit. April could beat anyone in a stare-down contest. I would position myself opposite her and look deeply into her glossy black eyes. She would gaze intensely into mine as if searching my soul. Minutes would go by without her breath stirring the silence. The only movement was her little pink tongue slipping past her lips to hang just above her chin. I indulged her in these games daily. Oddly enough, she warmed to me. Soon, I was receiving soft kisses.

I turned the corner to the kitchen one afternoon and found Joe frozen in a crouched position like an offensive lineman waiting for the snap. Opposite Joe was April, motionless, eyes fixed on Joe's, her pink tongue dangling. My presence did nothing to break their concentration. A few minutes passed, and Joe cried "uncle," caving to her doggedness. He patted April's head and handed her a treat. She welcomed him into her trust. He, too, was soon on the receiving end of her friendly little kisses.

Try as they might to have a stare-down contest with April, Anna and Mia gave in quickly. Their lack of patience was no match for April's determination. She was the victor in all the challenges yet rewarded them for their participation—kisses on their cheeks and guarded smiles when they walked in the door.

April's slow progress in shedding her layers bugged me, so I reached out to Lynda to see if she could provide more information about April's history. I knew Lynda had rescued April from animal impound the day she was scheduled to be euthanized. Her five days had been spent cowering in her kennel, uninterested in engaging with workers or visitors. Without intervention, she wouldn't live to see another meal. Lynda, equally concerned about April's well-being, offered to call animal impound to see if there was something in her records that'd been missed.

Nothing more was written in April's records. A part-time intake worker, however, overheard Lynda's call to the director. She told the director that April had been surrendered by a middle-aged woman who agreed to watch two dogs while a co-worker went on vacation. The co-worker bought a one-way ticket and never returned. The woman with a short-term offer ended up with two dogs she had no intention of keeping forever. When she realized she had been duped, she brought the dogs to the shelter. April's young buddy, possibly her pup, was adopted quickly, leaving older April behind. That was it. We had no more clues to help this troubled girl.

When Mia was in fifth grade, her class made a town. Each kid was given a milk carton to fashion into a house. All the houses were placed on two 4'x8' pieces of plywood set end-to-end. Over the course of a semester, yards, roads, sidewalks, parks, lakes, businesses, hospitals, and schools were added until a multi-layered town rose from the smooth wood. Students "graduated" from high school, got "married," raised "families," got "jobs," and "volunteered." They learned about banking and insurance and paying bills. When discretionary income allowed, some kids added solar-powered hot tubs and purchased RVs for travel. They discovered how people follow different paths through life, that various influences such as education, career choice, family size, personal desires can impact outcomes. Their efforts yielded a vibrant town of unique homes, businesses, and recreational opportunities.

Alongside the "things," an abundance of conversation and help-fulness grew.

One common thread throughout the neighborhoods was the telephone line connecting home to home and business. While cell phones were already commonplace, and one student had built a cell phone tower in her yard, the students said the telephone line was necessary. The teacher quoted the kids as saying, "A community needs to communicate to grow well and be happy."

I was stroking April's soft fur as the memory of Mia's fifth-grade town converged with the teachings of Dr. Temple Grandin. I learned of Dr. Grandin's work while doing research on ADHD and mental health after Mia's diagnosis. As a prominent scientist with autism, Dr. Grandin gained a following by applying her insights from a lifetime living with autism to advance the humane treatment of food production animals. Her many years of research and experimentation were communicated via research papers, academic lectures, and boots-on-the-ground efforts. She helped livestock farmers, food manufacturers, and executives of global restaurant chains understand how animals have emotion systems in their brains much the same as humans. They can't communicate in our human manner to tell us what they are experiencing, but they do communicate—if we pay attention. Grandin believed that knowing what drives positive emotions and reduces negative ones can improve mental well-being and the physical health of confined animals. Grandin connected the dots for others, transforming animal welfare from a touchy-feely, do-good waste of time to a business imperative. Livestock welfare and good mental health became a means to improved business outcomes.

Dr. Grandin also wrote *Animals Make Us Human*, the book I bought for a buck at the local library on the way to the beach the day after Anna's runaway incident. The goal of Grandin's book was to help people understand what animals need to thrive and be happy in human settings such as homes and hobby farms. Her writings don't teach people how to "talk" to animals in a Dr. Doolittle sort of way, but rather to observe behavior, to understand what's considered natural and abnormal, to share and compare to create a more complete picture.

She suggested ways to change personal actions or physical surroundings to help one's pet. According to Temple Grandin, happier animals with fewer behavioral issues result in better person-pet relationships. Yellow highlighter mixed with sand as I sat at the beach and moved through the book, hoping to use Dr. Grandin's insight with our foster dogs. It was the dog-eared pages near the beginning, those in the chapter titled "What Do Animals Need" that kept pulling me back month after month. I wondered if they might offer clues to help Anna with her reoccurring struggles.

We started fostering April during Anna's first semester of sophomore year in high school. Not much had improved in my relationship with Anna since our summer beach vacation; we couldn't seem to lose the elephant that'd followed us home. Anna's behavior was on a steady decline with increased static in our lines of communication. Joe and I continued to walk on eggshells, fearing Anna would run again. We were receiving phone calls from teachers and the school counselor for offenses such as texting during class, throwing pencils during exams, and truancy during math class. She'd asked for a bathroom pass on several occasions and never returned, opting instead to sit idly in an empty classroom, lift weights in the weight room, or chat with the school nurse.

"Anna, what were you thinking?" My voice rose, fuming against the frustration deep within. "Where'd you get the idea it was okay to leave class?"

"I wasn't thinking anything. I was bored and left," Anna replied in a nonchalant manner, the same Anna who used to complain about class troublemakers.

I felt my legs stiffening, protesting, like Shelby when I tried to stuff her into the messenger bag. I knew I was on the verge of losing my temper.

"Get the dogs out now," I demanded, pointing my finger in the direction of the door. "We'll talk about this later when your dad is home. There'll be consequences for this behavior."

Anna scowled but walked the dogs as asked, probably relieved to be free from my exasperation. My tension notched down an inch as soon as she was gone. Into that inch of relief oozed fear and confusion. I couldn't wait to have her bad attitude out of the house, yet I leaned into the security of knowing she'd return with the dogs.

Joe came home from his retail management job after Anna had gone to sleep. He was equally frustrated by her truancy but admitted to great relief that she had never left school grounds. To teach her a lesson about privilege and respect, we grounded her for two weeks. Horseback-riding lessons were put on hold. Anna flailed her arms, stomped her feet, and slammed the door of her room in response.

I came home from work a few days later to find Mia cowering on the sectional with Rascal and April tucked tight to her hip, chins down, eyes barely looking at me. Margo was wrapped around the toilet in the bathroom, serving as my barometer for brewing trouble.

I sprinted up the stairs, crashing into the screams rushing from Anna's room. As I threw open her door, breath drained from my lungs like water through a hair-clogged drain. Several fist-sized holes punctuated the walls. Drywall bits and dust powdered the floor where a math test with a big "F" was circled in red. I wasn't sure if I should stay or run.

"God, I hate that teacher. She's out to get me. I know she wants me to fail," thrashed Anna, face swollen from tears. Well-trained muscles wound tight, ready to swing again. "I tried to talk to her after class. She told me to figure it out myself." A short pause while she wound up again. "I went to her because I couldn't figure it out. She wouldn't even give me the time of day, just turned her face to her papers and shooed me away."

I looked at the paper again. Only half the questions were answered.

"Want to see something worse? Look at my science test." Her voice rose again as she flung the paper at me with another "F" circled in red. "I studied what she told us to study. I read the chapters. I tried. Stupid teacher asked about things she didn't teach!" Pounding her fists on the wall, she continued wailing, "Are we supposed to read her mind? How could we prepare? It isn't fair."

"Knock it off, Anna," I shouted, my bluster countering her bluster, hoping my volume would outweigh her height and might. "This may be your room, but this is my house. You don't get to abuse it. Sit down and cool off."

I glanced at the windows as a wave of panic rose. *Thank God, the windows are closed!* Our exchange had been kept inside our walls. In a slightly quieter voice I demanded, "I want you downstairs in thirty minutes to help set the table for dinner. We'll talk about school later." I turned sharply on my heels, leaving the room with some authority before my knocking knees gave away my fear.

Little did Anna know her math and science teachers had called me earlier that day. She didn't just fail a test in each class. She was failing each class. Failing! Our "E for exceptional" student was acting like a screw being driven below the surface of sheetrock with an errant piece of hair caught in its thread, twisting tighter until there was little left to unwind from its grasp.

"What's going on with Anna, Mom?" asked Mia as I struggled to find footing on the stairs.

"I don't know, Mia. Stop worrying about your sister and focus on yourself." My voice was quivering as I lashed out at Mia. "You were asked to get your chores done before practice. I see no progress. You're still sitting on your butt." Hollering extra loud for emphasis I added, "Get up now and do your work."

I leashed up Rascal, Margo, and April and hurried them outside, seeking comfort from fall leaves rustling across the road, hoping to still the turmoil in my mind before my mouth erupted further into even more regrettable comments.

Unwelcome thoughts flooded my brain. *Failing classes. Running away. Punching walls. Could Anna be on her way to flunking high school? Will she be "that" kid, the one with her name making headlines, harnessing her anger to her fists?*

My knees gave way to the heaviness of my thoughts. Anna had always been at the top in her class and a stand-out athlete. It was easy to rave about her accomplishments. But now... *What will people think about Anna failing high school? What will people think of me as a parent if she hurts someone else?* Shame washed over me as I slumped to the gravel shoulder. Rascal and April began vying for a place on my lap. A neighbor's car slowed. A head stretched across the passenger seat to ask if I needed help.

"No thanks. I had to tie my shoe," I quickly lied, flicking my hand, waving her away, doing the same thing Mia did to me after the frustration of her twelfth birthday party.

In Grandin's book *Animals Make us Human*, Grandin states, "Frustration is a mild form of rage that is sparked by mental restraint when you can't do something you're trying to do." I realized that I was frustrated because I couldn't control Anna's decision-making and behavior. I couldn't seem to turn the wheel to steer her back on course.

Anna, however, was beyond frustration. Her behavior was anything but mild. Punching walls. Truancy. Running away. She was in rage, defined by Grandin as a response to physical restraint. My mind raced wildly, jumping to conclusions. *Is someone abusing Anna?*

Later that night, the two of us lay beside each other in her dark, quiet room where we couldn't see the wall damage from her earlier frenzy. April snored softly between us. I finally steeled my courage to ask if someone had hurt her.

"God, Mom. Don't be so stupid. I'd beat up anyone who'd try to mess with me." That quick confidence in her physical abilities calmed my concern about physical abuse. She wasn't lying about it. *But what is causing her to act so violently without prompt?*

I felt a dim tremor moving across the bed. The silence was broken by quiet tears and small hiccups as Anna tried to hold back the flood. "Mom, I don't know who I am anymore. I don't look like me. I don't act like me." With a deep breath followed by growing sobs, she continued, "I see what I want, but I can't get it. I can't move in the direction I know I should. Instead, I do what I shouldn't. Something is happening inside me, and I can't control it." Neither could Joe nor I. We all felt helpless as we watched an avalanche of changes bowl over Anna, burying her self-confidence and restraint.

One change we'd been working to correct was the onset of painful, purple cystic acne that had overtaken Anna's once-porcelain cheeks and jawline. This wasn't run-of-the-mill teenage acne, the kind cured by $29 kits offered on TV. We'd been working for more than a year with her dermatologist and doctor, methodically experimenting with medications. Every benign drug had been tested. No luck. We were now standing on the cusp of last resort as we prepared her physically and mentally to begin Accutane treatments.

Almost guaranteed to work, the powerful drug would require monthly blood testing to ensure her kidneys weren't failing. Anna would have to complete monthly pregnancy tests to prove she wasn't pregnant; the drug "would" cause birth defects, not "might" cause birth defects. Every meeting would require a mental health evaluation; Accutane was a drug associated with teen depression and suicide. Accutane could cure her acne but could lead to the end of her life. I sucked in my breath just thinking about the risks. We'd been through many discussions already. Nothing was going to stop Anna from the chance to look in the mirror once again without contempt.

Joe was still awake when I finally returned to our bedroom. Eerie shadows cast by dim moonlight through tall pines danced across the walls. We contemplated the events of the day, of the past few months, of Poet and Sierra's deaths, of Anna developing a troublemaking switch easily flipped on but not easily shut down by chores and punishments.

"I've always said Anna struggles in math," insisted Joe. "She stumbles on basic multiplication. She fights through every homework assignment. You've run out of ways to weave horses into every word problem to keep her interested. Let her move to an easier class. You need to let go of the dream of her attending college. Your pressure is making it hard for her."

"Anna's excelled in every math class she's taken," I argued. "It makes no sense why she's failing now. It seems wrong to give up."

"Why can't you see that math is her Achilles' heel? Keeping her in this class is making her stressed. You need to give her permission to drop it. Let her take something else," Joe countered.

I couldn't allow myself to agree with Joe's level of reasoning. Anna dreamed of being a veterinarian. Colleges with pre-vet programs required high-level math. Letting her off the hook now seemed counterproductive to her goals.

We argued back and forth as the wind whistled and the earth moved towards dawn. The only solution we agreed upon was for me to call an acquaintance of Joe's who happened to be a family therapist.

Dr. Steve was not taking new patients but recommended two things: first, arrange a meeting with Dr. Bonnie to determine if Anna had a medical issue in need of intervention, and, secondly, stop worrying about college. "There are plenty of colleges and tech schools in this country in need of students to fill their classes. Unless Anna has a strong desire to go to a specific school, let her take ownership of her path. Stop defining it for her," he said. I sucked in my breath, readying myself to interject, but Dr. Steve did not provide an opening. "Your role in high school is to be a support system, not a helicopter parent nor a dictator. Anna needs opportunity to make choices and own the consequences. She's off track now, but her history has proved she's capable. Support her recovery, then step away."

Like a sailboat without a keel in a sideways gale, I'd been rammed. Sputtering and flailing, I struggled for days to reconcile Steve's suggestions with my vision for Anna's path. Letting go was both terrifying and liberating.

Anna met with Dr. Bonnie for two days of intensive testing, repeating the process her sister had recently completed. Former and current teachers, coaches, and I completed questionnaires, assessing her abilities, emotions, functioning. Anna sat at the computer taking a variety of tests.

The 18-page report summarized how Anna "demonstrated relative strengths in her ability to solve problems and reason using words and language but struggled more with tasks involving perceptual and spatial reasoning and nonverbal skills...the relative weakness in visual-perceptual skills may be contributing to her current math difficulties...compounding these are symptoms consistent with a diagnosis of Attention Deficit Hyperactivity Disorder (ADHD): Combined Type."

Like Mia, Anna had ADHD and a growing difficulty with focus and initiation. Unlike Mia, her rising frustration and anxiety were symptoms of a growing problem with "executive function," or the ability to see the big picture of a problem, formulate steps to solve it, then follow through. "Students with this type of profile have a tendency to lose emotional control... Anna would benefit from clinical intervention."

We finally had a reason for Anna's rage, one born of physiological changes occurring at a critical point in mental and physical development. She was a good kid caught in a tough situation. It was no wonder she wanted to rage and run. Re-charting her course would be our mission, even if it meant a whole lot of trial and error to get back on track.

We began with the bird in hand. Anna's doctor initiated a course of Zoloft to moderate her mood during the beginning months of the Accutane acne treatment. She then started Anna on a regime of Ritalin to regulate her attention. Within two weeks of combining Ritalin and Zoloft, Anna began to make strides. I came home from work to find Anna doing her homework without prompt and without agitation. She radiated a sliver of excitement from the success.

A week later, Joe and I sat in a stuffy, windowless room at the high school with a cast of characters we both described as "the mean administrators." They were stereotypical actors from a coming-of-age big-screen movie. Hair pulled tight in crisp buns. Lips pursed against the pressure. These women, with nary a kind greeting or smile, were hell-bent on reducing Anna to special education classes to keep her teachers from making accommodations. "Too much work in an already overstressed public school environment," was their reasoning. Joe, stifling his anger and swallowing the words he wished he could say, calmly, but pointedly replied, "Nonsense. You are not putting a kid capable of A-work in remedial classes. You'll kill her spirit and her future."

Anna's high school guidance counselor, sporting an open-collared golf shirt under a slightly rumpled blazer, took over. "I agree with Mr. Ojczyk. Let me talk with Anna's teachers and intervene on her behalf.

Moving Anna to special ed will change how every kid sees her and how she sees herself. There's no reason to put her self-confidence at risk to save a few teachers from work they signed on to do." He took a short breath and continued, "Here's what else I'll do. I'll make a standing appointment to meet with Anna every Friday to help her review her weekend homework, help her organize her locker, and review class syllabuses. I'll also set aside a place for her to take tests without classroom distraction. We'll evaluate the need to keep doing it based on how she responds to the effort and her medication." With his words, I felt a flicker of hope.

"I also suggest we move Anna to a different math class." The flame extinguished. Sensing my shift, he reminded me he was a high school guidance counselor and knew which math class was college-appropriate, yet more aligned with her abilities. When we conveyed the class change to Anna, the release of pressure was audible. Joe and Dr. Steve had been right.

As Anna began to rebound, Joe and I grappled over the issue of reward. We'd both been raised on the 'carrot or stick' principle; we didn't get something for nothing. We'd taken away Anna's horseback riding due to poor school performance and attitude. She was lobbying for it back.

"Joe, I feel like we should let Anna ride again. She's been working hard at the things we've asked of her." I'd always been a disciplinarian, like Joe, but something now felt wrong with our all-or-nothing approach.

"No. She has to pay the consequences of her actions if she's going to learn a lesson. She can't punch walls and flail her arms when life gets hard. She has time left to serve," was all Joe countered before walking away.

Anna's psychologist, Dr. Jeff, a new addition to our arsenal of solutions in our ADHD toolbox, suggested Joe and I meet with him to work through the struggles we were encountering as the parents of two teens with ADHD and anxiety. During our first hour-long session we learned two things. First, horseback riding had more value than the privilege we'd prescribed. For a kid with ADHD it provided a positive avenue for the release of excess energy associated with the hyperactive "H" in ADHD; Anna needed a harmless way of releasing steam. Secondly, the strong bond of kid and horse was a confidence booster for someone like Anna who'd lost so much in a short amount of time. Taking away what we saw as a "privilege" was more harmful than helpful.

Secretly, I felt relieved. The stress of withholding horses was eating away at my relationship with Anna. She'd been doing her homework at the kitchen table but then holed up in her room the rest of the time. I hated her isolation and worried deeper troubles were brewing. Yet, I knew Joe was not thrilled to give Anna a privilege not earned.

A week later, we attended another session with Jeff, this time as a family of four. In the safety of Jeff's office, Mia confessed to her growing wariness of Anna's strength, of the times Anna squared her shoulders, inflating her chest, making herself even taller and imposing. Mia feared being an easy target for Anna's rage.

Wow! It never occurred to me Mia could be in harm's way. Another level of worry was added to my growing anxiety.

In that same counseling session, Anna confessed to eavesdropping on a conversation I'd had with Loree shortly after Poet's death. She heard me recounting our frantic drive to animal emergency. Anna thought I was blaming her for Poet's death. I couldn't believe Anna and I'd spent months dancing around such a huge elephant of misunderstanding.

Anna also talked about Michigan. Through large gasps of breath and long hiccups from crying, we parsed together a story of a kid traumatized by Poet's fight against death and her feeling of helplessness in the back seat of the car. A kid who had no control over her impulses when the sad melody of taps washed over the hushed beach crowd. She ran because she didn't know how else to get away from the tight confinement of grief. Neither Joe nor Mia nor I stirred, except to dab at the tears spilling into our laps.

Soon after, we let Anna return to her beloved four-legged Theo at the stable twenty minutes north of home. The confident "born director" who'd been buried under the confusion of adolescence and ADHD started to reappear. A few months after beginning Accutane treatment, her skin was clearing. Anna was beginning to thrive. April still was not.

Lynda suggested putting April's profile on the web. It was obvious she needed time to heal. It was best to find a forever home with a guardian who could help her continue to heal than to hope all the healing would happen with us. Crafting an honest story would be the key to matching April's needs with the right adopter.

But—what to say?

Snickers had been a happy puppy with a sad, old-man face. His photographs weren't much, but his exuberance was easily told through story. April was a middle-aged, guarded dog with an unflattering haircut that made her look more boy dog than girl. Had I been able to gather her fur into a tiny sprout on her head like many Shih Tzus on the internet, I could have given her image a bit of feminine flair.

Instead, I wrote a story about a quiet little companion with a sweet disposition and a quirky obsession with stare-down contests. A dog that warms quickly to men and women, enjoys a good belly scratch, and gives soft kisses.

Debbie and Ron lost their beloved Shih Tzu a few weeks before sad April entered our life. Their princess had been showered with attention and spoiled with a dresser of drawers stuffed with homemade dog coats carefully crafted by Debbie. The lowest drawer of the dresser was lined with blankets. It was left open for the little dog to take a nap. Debbie, with a body worn down by years as a nurse, was looking for a quiet companion to keep her company while Ron went to work.

As I opened our door to welcome Debbie and Ron inside, wisps of sweet campfire from my neighbor's fire pit begin filling the house with the smell of late fall. The girls were next door roasting marshmallows, deliberately avoiding a possible foster loss. Little April, hiding behind my ankles, gave a quick sniff of the air, then peered upwards with curious, yet cautious, dark eyes. She refused to budge from the safety of my legs, so I picked her up and settled her on my lap at the kitchen table.

Ron sat opposite April, immediately locking eyes in a stare-down contest across the butcher block surface. Neither Ron nor April stirred while Debbie and I talked. After a few minutes, Ron stood up, his large frame looming above us, and he gently picked up April, settling her onto his lap as he sat opposite Debbie. April stared intently into Debbie's eyes, her little pink tongue slipping past her lips to dangle gently. No words were needed as April searched her soul. In those moments of silent communication, the contract was sealed. April became their newest family member.

The months following April's adoption were quite enjoyable for me. Every week or so, Debbie and Ron would call, taking turns telling me stories about April. I heard about their efforts to pull her out her sadness: the short walks, the reassuring naps, little scraps of chicken. Debbie described in detail the soft blankets and colorful coats she crafted for her new princess. I also learned about their personal travels, Ron's passion for Buddy Holly music, and the shenanigans of his mostly sixty-year-old band members. Our long phone conversations gave me hope; April was in the good hands of two people who cared about her welfare and knew of its importance to me. I was certain she would eventually find peace.

Just before Christmas, Ron and Debbie called, their voices giddy like school kids, ready to burst with a secret. In unison, I heard, "Surprise! April's a momma." Speechless, my mind raced through the details of April, positive she'd been spayed. *Other than an immaculate conception, how could she have given birth?* Sensing my confusion, they announced their adoption of a kitten, fondly known as "April's baby." As soon as the kitten entered their home, April immediately took over her care, hovering near her while she ate, grooming her after, snuggling with her at naptime. Within a matter of days, April's sadness melted to reveal a spirited, loving mother no longer searching for what she'd lost. Ron and Debbie had found it. They, like Temple Grandin, knew the importance of observing and searching and communicating until one discovers what matters most.

In celebration of April's happiness and our foster success number four, Anna and I challenged each other to a stare-down contest. She surprised me with her patience and won. Mia slid onto the sectional, budging me out of my seat. After a few tense moments where neither girl stirred, I swooped in to tickle their sides. "Mommmmm, stop it," they giggled as Margo and Rascal jumped into the melee, licking their cheeks, and nudging their hands with wet noses. Neither girl was out of the weeds since her ADHD diagnosis, yet our efforts to find dependable new paths had been illuminated by generous professionals who, like Dr. Grandin, believed fostering positive emotions was the key to mental health. Now, if only I could remember where I put that key.

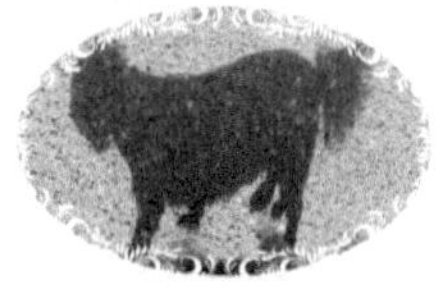

LIZZIE

Chapter 9

"Get this damn dog out of my house. Now!" blasted the woman on the other end of the line. "I can't have this destructive dog in my home. The wood floors! The curtains! The carpets! They must go. Everything has to be replaced because of this damn dog." Like flame from a fire-breathing dragon, her voice exploded in intensity as she continued, "Either you do something this instant, or I will find a way to get rid of her!" My silent response was: *What the heck? How could Lizzie, ten pounds of meekness and the light of this woman's life become the target of such malice in such a short time?*

Older dogs in need of a new home can be cursed. The number of people desiring a puppy far outweighs those willing to take in a dog with a shorter lifespan. Letting go is hard and few people are willing to do it sooner rather than later. I thought eight-year-old Lizzie's path would be different. She came to us with a known history, making it easier to write her profile and find a match. Lizzie was one of several pets from a small breeder of favorable reputation who once fostered for Second Chance. The breeder's health was failing quickly. She asked Second Chance to help her find loving homes for her dogs.

Lizzie was a Löwchen, a rare breed of royal lineage dating back to the mid-15th Century. Her Bichon-like resemblance and compact size was the perfect fit for a pre-screened adopter on the Second Chance waiting list, a retired woman with a drawer-full of dog coats and hand-sewn pillows to pamper any pet through a Midwest winter. Her Bichon had died. She was in search of another small, white, female dog to fit the wardrobe. The Second Chance screener received a rave review from the woman's veterinarian, reporting a glowing record of animal care and a fine reputation for her work in canine massage. Most importantly, the adopter was confident she could help older Lizzie break through her house-training struggles.

"Lizzie, c'mon girl, you've got to go," I'd whisper into the night, into the daylight, into the dusk, without success. No matter what I did, no matter how much time I gave her outside, our new foster dog just wouldn't go. She'd cower at the end of the leash, her head as far from me as possible, just her eyes peaking back.

"Lynda, I'm worried about Lizzie. What should I do?"

"Don't worry now, but call me if she hasn't gone for two days. Some dogs need time to get comfortable in their surroundings. Something must be really bugging her," she mused as her voice trailed off.

Nearly forty-eight hours after coming to our home, Lizzie finally peed in the yard. I called Lynda to tell her of Lizzie's small success. Lynda, however, had grown concerned that it had taken Lizzie that long to relieve herself. She called the vet at Life Care who reviewed Lizzie's chart. Nothing indicated a possible urinary tract infection or other medical issue.

Lynda called Lizzie's previous owner. She learned that Lizzie and her eight dog companions had lived in a dedicated dog room attached to the woman's home with individual crates and a dog door enabling them to go outside on their terms. The dogs had never been formally house trained nor had they been on a leash or taken anywhere outside her home. No walks on concrete sidewalks or asphalt roads. No excited car rides to a dog park. Lizzie had lived eight years in a small, sheltered world. Now outside of it, she was paralyzed by fear.

That information did not deter the adopter on our waiting list with the handmade dog wardrobe. She'd been through the house training of many dogs before. Her husband had already shoveled a wide path through the deep Lake Superior snow to a dedicated dog area just for Lizzie. The husband and wife were retired "with all the time in the world to coax Lizzie out of her shell."

Ten days after Lizzie came to our house, she was heading "home." The adopting couple lived three hours from me. We agreed to meet at a park halfway between. Lizzie trembled in my arms when she met the couple, shying away from the man. The woman took immediate control of the situation, sat down in the back seat of her car, and gingerly lifted Lizzie onto her lap as if she were handling a fine piece of china, cooing to her in hushed tones. She began to apply gentle massage techniques to Lizzie's back and legs, inching her fingers in small, rhythmic circles towards her shoulders as Lizzie relaxed into the touch. The tension in my shoulders released.

The woman carefully placed a calm Lizzie into the portable carrier secured in the back seat. As the car drove away with two smiling adults, my waving hand began to shake. As if on cue from an imaginary conductor, every part of my body began to spasm. I hurried to my car, sinking into the seat as big sobs released. The windows began to fog in the bitter November cold. For reasons unknown, I sat for an hour paralyzed and perplexed, until confident I could start the engine and drive safely home.

The explanation for my unusual reaction came a few days later while lounging on the sectional in the post-foster dog calm with Rascal and Margo dozing next to me. Into my relaxed mind oozed the apprehension about the adopter that I'd shoved to its recesses. Bits and pieces of remembered conversations prior to Lizzie's adoption began to knit themselves together. Through the flash of pointed needles twisting and pulling at the truth, out came the questions I wanted to ask, but didn't. I'd given greater value to Lynda's experience and that of our seasoned screeners than to my observations and intuition. I'd buried my fear of being wrong and took Lizzie's well-being with it.

At first, I brushed off my reaction like a mere speck of white dust on a black sweater. *How could I possibly think anything was wrong?* The adopters were given a green light by our team. Lizzie had leaned into the massage and gone willingly into the crate in the back seat of the adopters' car. The forty-eight-hour checkup was as syrupy as a Disney movie, with the retired couple gushing over their "sweet princess." The longer I sat with my unease, the more the white speck on black sweater grew into a stain of bleach unable to be flicked away. Needing reassurance that Lizzie was well and my intuition wrong, I dialed the adopters' home. Instead of responding with the calm voice from conversations past, the woman snapped like a dry twig under the weight of a twelve-point buck.

She was spitting obscenities at me at rock-concert volume over an accident Lizzie had had in the living room. Lizzie was not adhering to the "scheduled" outside time. She hadn't peed or pooped since she left my home. When nature finally called, the door wasn't open, so Lizzie used the floor. The adopter was livid. She had no patience for a dog that "took liberties" in her home. Lizzie could no longer be trusted. She wanted her "gone now, or else!"

The woman's thundering behavior attracted the attention of her husband. He quickly took control of the phone. Through profuse apologies he confessed of his wife's recent diagnosis of dementia and onset of erratic behavior. He assured me Lizzie was safe, then asked if he could give her back.

The husband drove three hours to my house. Alone. As I took a trembling Lizzie from the portable crate, tears streamed down his cheeks with the heaviness of his wife's newly diagnosed disease. He wanted a dog as much as she did and realized her new reality made that impossible. I held Lizzie tight as she trembled wildly, hoping the husband had someone he could turn to for comfort.

Lizzie's return was just one of the week's browbeatings. I grew up in a rural area on the edge of suburbia with a sensible education in personal security. When I went for a walk or run, I was taught to turn into a neighbor's driveway and walk right into their house if I feared for my safety. At the mall, I used the bathrooms in the department stores said to be safer alternatives than the mall restrooms typically located at the end of long, dim hallways. The myriad of people comprising college campus security became my friends after many nights escorting me from library to dorm.

Nothing, however, prepared me for the verbally abusive bully with a pedigreed background and upper-class home. I was a residential interior designer then working for homeowners Jim and Mary on what I thought was a dream job, the ultimate kitchen remodel for my portfolio. The couple was sparing little expense: custom cabinets with artisan-designed glass inserts, rare stone countertops, contemporary crystal chandeliers.

They seemed nice enough, respecting my time during meetings and completing their homework to prepare. That is, until Mary showed up during a final approval session without Jim. It wasn't unusual to me as Jim was an executive at a prominent business. In fact, I was impressed he'd made it to our meetings at all. Mary seemed agitated, checking her watch, looking over her shoulder, barely engaging in conversation. After ten minutes of uncomfortable chitchat and growing unease, I asked if something was wrong. Tears welled in her eyes and her voice choked on fear as she divulged a secret; Jim was so opposed to the project that he had become threatening. "This is my hard-earned money paying for your project. One little mistake and you'll pay dearly," were his final words before storming to his car. Tears fell onto Mary's shaking hands clasped in her lap as she asked for a guarantee we'd neither encounter, nor create problems during remodeling. Mary lived in a twenty-year-old home. I couldn't give her that guarantee.

I should have untangled myself from their web of dysfunction. But I didn't. My design vision had already begun to unfold into reality. I could clearly see the final photograph as a centerpiece of my design portfolio. Demolition had begun. Cabinets were ordered. The glass artist had delivered her first beautiful renderings. Mary had come to the meeting to cancel the project but couldn't. She was as drawn to its possibility as I.

All went well for quite some time. Jim rarely appeared on site. When he did, it was usually with his head down, quiet. Demolition uncovered a few hurdles, but Jim handled the change orders and payment quickly and without challenge. Mary was a hit with the contractors, making them coffee in the morning and bringing treats and sodas in the afternoon.

Everyone was looking forward to the date on the calendar with the big red star: countertop installation day. It meant the worst of the demolition and construction challenges were over. The plumber was scheduled to follow. It was a milestone on the project timeline to be celebrated. Feeling victorious, I left the jobsite as the workers were wiping away the last bit of errant caulk from the seams of the gleaming countertop. One more giant piece to the puzzle had been set in place. The picture I'd created with Mary in digital reality was coming true, and it was stunning.

I returned to my office to make a few sales calls; my experience taught me that the best time to sell something was when I was feeling successful. I was adding a new client meeting to my calendar when my phone rang. Jim's number popped onto my screen, immediately taking me back to the day's earlier events. I was so eager to hear the accolades from him that I was totally thrown off guard by his verbal slaying. He'd gone home early from work to inspect the countertops. Finding the seams unacceptable, he kicked everyone off the jobsite, then called to inform me just how angry he was.

Numb, I sat there taking punch after punch as he swore at me, called me inept, and damned every beautiful thing that'd been done. He couldn't see my tears, and I couldn't steel my courage. I let him bellow until his sails were empty. I should have calmly said, "I understand you are upset, but that doesn't give you the right to talk to me this way," exactly what I hoped the girls would do in the face of a bully. Then I wondered if I ever gave them those words and the permission to use them. In the world of fight or flight, I'd done neither. I cowered like Lizzie in the shadow of her bully.

Worse yet, it wasn't the first time that week when I was at a loss for words and unable to lift my forearms to block a punch. I'd been at a design event with a few acquaintances when I shared my story about Anna and Mia's diagnoses of ADHD. In a brazen display of judgment, one person told me the girls' ADHD was my fault; God was punishing my children for my sins. Another woman in the group who volunteered in her child's elementary school classroom claimed all the teachers believed ADHD was a fake ailment perpetuated by money-grubbing doctors to medicate difficult kids. Puffing out her chest with self-importance, she accused me of being "like every disinterested parent sending an out-of-control kid to school to force the teachers to babysit." Not knowing how to reply, I didn't. I'd taken a risk talking about ADHD. Instead of welcome arms and open hearts, I got sucker punched. With nothing to counter their attacks, I sat silent.

While Jim was throwing his punches, I had an image of a ring announcer hollering to the crowd through a gleaming chrome microphone, forefinger thrust into the air: "Remember, folks. The client is always right." *Isn't that what the sales training classes and books preached?* Yet, I couldn't recall any instruction on how to respond to a man hell-bent on bullying a woman. With my nose to the mat and no energy for piledrivers or backbreakers, I gathered what composure I could muster and met the countertop contractor at Jim's house. We needed a fix, and fast.

Jim didn't show. He should have. He'd been right to complain, just not the way he did. The rare stone turned out to be too heavy for the approved supports. As the supports sagged under the weight of the stone, the perfect seams separated while the day progressed. By the time Jim got home, the seams were noticeable, as was a slight downward tilt to the plane. The contractor immediately removed the pieces. Two days later, a wood craftsman installed four bigger custom supports. The countertop was replaced with a scowling Jim present to approve them.

The countertop installer tried to apologize to Jim, taking responsibility for approving my design and not knowing the stone well enough to know the type of support it would need. Jim told him to stop defending "that bitch of a designer." As the installer opened his mouth to speak for me, Jim spun on his heels with his nose in the air and abruptly left the kitchen. The last I saw of the executive in the designer suit and power tie was his middle finger trailing his body as he rounded the doorway to the garage. The rest of the work was completed quickly and quietly by a deflated crew. A few months later, Mary steeled her courage and left Jim.

I thought about Mary as I stroked Lizzie's fur, wondering if Mary's marriage had always been toxic or if Jim had changed over time. *Is this what unattended ADHD looks like in an adult?* I hadn't a clue, but Jim's erratic behavior seemed to match that of Anna's behavior prior to her diagnosis and intervention.

The more I thought about Jim and his reaction to the countertop, a fog began to cloud my brain, obscuring the image I had of Anna growing into a happy veterinarian. *Would Anna be like Jim or Lizzie's first adopter? Will others walk on eggshells or distance themselves from her fury?* Anna's medication and counseling were tempering her mood and behavior swings. Dr. Bonnie, however, cautioned there could come a time when effectiveness would wane. We'd need new strategies to keep her hyperactive behavior under control. *Maybe Jim's medication was no longer working?* It was all conjecture playing games in my mind.

Adding to my heavy heart was Lizzie's heightened distrust. I stopped thinking about the win of adoption and settled solely for the comfort of routine instead. For the next three weeks, Lizzie was just another dog in the house, taking walks with me, playing her version of catch with Anna, and snuggling under the covers with Mia. The relaxed pace gave us a chance to get to know her better.

Like Anna, Lizzie was an introvert. A few solid, dependable people in her circle was all she needed. Lizzie warmed to women but had a deep fear of men. Joe was determined to break her of that fear. I often found him sitting with his back against the refrigerator, tossing dog treats to Lizzie, attempting to earn her trust. Despite his best efforts, theirs was a tenuous relationship.

Lizzie had spent her first eight years freely moving in and out of her crate amongst eight dog friends, so I thought putting her in a crate when we were gone would provide comfort. Nope. That smart, observant dog learned Rascal and Margo had free reign of the house; she wanted the privilege as well. Like a protesting Shelby with the messenger bag, Lizzie was all stiff legs and thrashing head when I tried to put her in the crate. If I asked her to go inside on her own, she ran to another room.

The only tactic I had to counteract her protests was peanut butter training. She responded eagerly. Three dogs would sit with hind ends trembling in the kitchen while one of us would stand at the counter smearing peanut butter into the hollows of empty Kongs or bones.

Three dogs would race to Lizzie's crate where her treat would be placed inside, luring her like a feral cat into a live trap. She'd nudge big Margo and swift Rascal, sometimes giving a little nip on the way, to get to her treat. A few days of this solid routine, and Lizzie claimed the crate as home.

When Lizzie began to smile on a regular basis, run to the door for a walk, and budge her way past Rascal to sit on my lap, I knew it was time to look for her next home. She'd moved from a place of fear to one of "seeking"—defined by Dr. Grandin as the pleasure of looking forward to something.

I posted Lizzie's profile on Petfinder.com, hung up posters in grocery stores, and did my usual social media blast. In less than a week, I got a response. Carol, a soft-spoken widow with a heart brimming with patience, fell in love with Lizzie and her insecurities.

Carol lived in a quiet house on a tiny lake with a bench near the shore where she liked to watch the birds. She imagined herself sitting there with Lizzie. Framing her side yard was a secure fence where Lizzie could hide in the fern garden to keep a watchful eye on the chipmunks and birds.

I said goodbye to Lizzie after enjoying a cup of tea at Carol's dining room table, warmed by a small crackling fire. A striped cat named Mack, curled on the buffet, kept a wary eye on Lizzie. There were no red flags signaling mental instability. I felt no tension or trouble. Lizzie wasn't sure about Carol and Mack, but Carol seemed undaunted by Lizzie's past and the task of making friends with a cautious companion.

As I drove home, I reflected on the need for Joe and me to be similar advocates for Anna and Mia, to be willing to learn, to trust our intuition, and to give second chances while navigating the challenges of ADHD. I'd have to be better at modeling self-advocacy while learning to deflect people with too much self-importance. Even though adolescence was supposed to be a time to loosen our parental reins, we'd need to remain covert dance partners in their marathons, balancing stamina, and exuding grace. For two people whose last big dance had been at their wedding decades before, there'd be a lot of stepping on toes before we'd win any awards.

ANNIE

Chapter 10

Annie was a pink tongue in a sea of toasted marshmallow softness and a whole lot of happy the day I met her at Life Care. Her stout body and stubby legs reminded me of the jolly Welsh Corgi at Mia's vaulting stable who ran to meet every car with a broad smile. The slight curl to Annie's fur hinted at poodle. Her perky, folded ears appeared to be golden lab. Only a DNA test could get us closer to the truth. It didn't matter. Like all those before her, her lineage would remain shrouded in mystery and serve as an easy conversation starter, much like our Midwestern weather.

Cheerful Annie, with a spring in her step, walked assuredly to my car, large marble eyes glancing up at me, tongue dangling lazily, as if we were best friends. She wiggled her butt, uttered a soft grunt, and plopped her stoutness onto the back seat. I settled myself behind the wheel and placed her adoption folder in the passenger seat. Next stop: the pet shed to stock up on food and toys. I moved the shifter into reverse. As I turned my head to check the parking lot, Slurp! A big kiss from Annie was planted firmly on my cheek. "Oh, Annie. You're silly," I exclaimed as she beamed. *You'll be an easy win in our game of adoption! Sweet win number six!*

Annie pushed past the door from garage to home and nudged her nose from Margo to Rascal. She followed Rascal's lead and ran with him to the toy box, scattering everything, yet playing with nothing. She trotted to Margo. Slurp! Another big kiss doled out to a new friend. I leashed all three and began our first walk as a team. Halfway around the block, Annie stretched and arched her neck like a giraffe trying to nibble grass and backed out of her collar, darting swiftly across the road. With a big slurp, she planted a kiss on a very surprised neighbor kid. Annie slunk to the ground like a widening puddle as the girl vigorously rubbed her belly.

Annie's affection was charming. Her lack of house-training skills was not. It was the one thing about Annie that had me befuddled. She'd pad along eagerly with Margo and Rascal, amusing herself for miles, nosing about in the weeds, her golden bottom wiggling like Winnie-the-Pooh when stuck in the doorway to Rabbit's House. She'd smile brightly at every passerby. Yet, despite her outdoor eagerness, she preferred completing her dog business inside.

Her behavior didn't add up with the story Lynda had relayed to me, which came from the notes read to Lynda by the shelter worker where Annie was surrendered. On her paperwork was a line written by her previous owner stating she was a "house-trained" dog.

My trust in the words "house-trained" and my lack of vigilance as a result meant a whole lot of work to clean puddles by the back door and piles in the basement. I became hypervigilant, watching Annie's every move. If I saw any small gesture that suggested her need to go, we were out the porch door and into the dog run in a flash. Most times, she would look at me with her innocent grin and trot back in.

The dog run was my creative solution to my family's continued angst over dog duty. It wasn't that they were unwilling to help; I was told it was not always easy to live up to my high expectations. Walking three dogs around our quarter-mile loop peppered with distractions made for complaining, frustrated, and sometimes leash-tangled family members.

My "high" expectations were also crafted from two years at the front line of cleanup duty. I'd learned early that newly spayed and neutered dogs needed to urinate more frequently. The anxiety of a new home and trauma of abandonment often led to additional accidents. Even so, a dog given plenty of exercise and time to explore was often a better citizen. Better citizenry meant less work for me and my family. Each time I tried to make the case, or—as the kids would say—"nag," I was met with resistance. Sometimes I even heard, "Weren't you the one who suggested we foster?"—implying I should shoulder the burden of responsibilities.

We were all lounging on the screened porch in the encroaching dusk of a lazy summer evening when discussion turned to my birthday. As soon as Anna asked what I would like as a gift, an image of wire fencing and metal posts adjoining the screened porch immediately popped into my mind. My request was met with a loud groan of disapproval that competed with the bedtime chirps of the robins. How could I make such an impersonal birthday request? (They knew so little about the joy that comes to a mother who doesn't have to barter or nag!)

I imagined the dog run making it easier for the kids and Joe to get the dogs outside without need of shoes and leashes. In the warmer months, they could sit in the porch and read a book while the dogs lounged in the fenced-in shade. During a blizzard, the fenced run would provide an opportunity to get the dogs outside quickly and safely. It would unburden us from some of our responsibilities. It would set us up for success.

My girls are dog-crazy, but horses are their first true love. Soon after the last post was pounded into the ground, we dubbed the dog run the "paddock." It would be as close as Anna and Mia would get to their own pasture of equines. In celebration, they opened the door from the screen porch to the paddock. Like a herd of horses leaving the stable for a tasty bale of hay, Annie, Rascal, and Margo trotted right in. Margo peed in a corner then promptly plopped down in the shade. Rascal meticulously marked every metal post. Annie looked at me and grinned.

The following day, the door to the screened porch was open. A gust of wind blew a section of newspaper from the kitchen table to the floor. Annie's short legs trotted to the papers where she squatted over them and left a puddle. *What? That's odd.* I replaced the soiled papers with a clean stack. A few hours later, I noticed a yellow ring drying on the paper. I cleaned the mess, layered more papers, and added a few to the basement floor. Annie obliged by leaving puddles upstairs and piles down below. She was "house-trained" all right—trained to go in the house! On papers! On the floor! Like a puppy! With this new information, I started rubbing the soiled papers in the paddock to give Annie a familiar smell outside. Little by little she began using the paddock for its purpose, inching ever closer to the primary goal I set for foster dog adoption, the mastery of house training, or, at least, a solid movement in that direction.

As I celebrated my success getting Annie on track with my goal, I was blindsided by a call from one of Mia's vaulting coaches. During the previous night's team meeting, Mia refused to set goals for the season while the other girls sat and made lists. "Why set a goal I can't achieve? I'd rather spare myself failure," were the words spoken by Mia and conveyed to me by her worried coach, Laura. Into the emptiness of the phone call's ending was the same ooze of heaviness I'd felt when I compared my design client Jim's hysterical behavior with Anna's. *Was Laura's concern an omen of Mia's struggles ahead?*

I was perplexed. Ritalin and counseling were helping Mia to make day-to-day progress at school. She attended vaulting with enthusiasm, participating in hot, dusty practices with the zeal of the other girls. Her repertoire of advanced vaulting skills was expanding; standing on the back of a cantering horse had become "boring." High jumps with quarter turns, split-legged leaps with pointed toes, somersaults onto the horse's neck, and rebounds by quickly jumping off and on again were practiced over and over until polished for an upcoming competition. *All this accomplishment without goals?* It made no sense, especially to a mother who thrived on to-do lists crossed off at day's end.

A few weeks after Laura's phone call, Mia, her vaulting-buddy Lexi, and I took a cheap bus from the Twin Cities to Chicago, leaving a smiling Annie in the care of Anna and Joe. We transferred our gear from bus to my parent's car, so I could drive the remainder of the trip to Lexington, Kentucky. While I fixed my attention on an audiobook and watched the terrain shift from thick fields of corn and beans to forested hills and a lush river valley, Mia and Lexi schemed from the back seat. They practiced applying heavy competition makeup and fake eyelashes. They brushed and pulled and sculpted each other's hair into a myriad of tight up-dos. "Cindy, what do you think of this look on Mia?" "Mom, doesn't Lexi's hair look cute in two side buns?" I'd quickly glance their way before bobby pins were removed and another style attempted.

They giggled about ribbons around their necks and medals of gold. I'd hear the rustling of stiff nylon as they unzipped garment bags to stare longingly at their competition costumes: matching, long-sleeved, royal blue unitards with white vaulting slippers for team events and flashier skating costumes and black slippers for individual competitions. Songs were sung with zeal, until we reached the hallowed gates of the famed Kentucky Horse Park.

A hush filled the car as I reluctantly shut off the audiobook two chapters from the conclusion while my two passengers shrank in the sprawl of crisp, white fencing and manicured lawns. "Turn the car around. Take us home. We don't deserve to be here," they cried together as tears streamed across rouge-stained cheeks. False eyelashes, like caterpillars, crept along dripping mascara lines. Chip bags and candy wrappers crinkled as the two friends slunk down to the floor. Their sobs gently vibrated off my seat.

I turned the car around past the big sign and parked on the grassy shoulder. As I rolled down the windows, the bay of distant horses and the comforting smell of manure flowed in. From the floor, and through their tears, I heard about Mia and Lexi's fears: of being unprepared and ridiculed, of not meeting their coach's expectations, of vaulters with more experience, money, and flashier costumes.

"I can see why you're worried," I said to the rearview mirror. "Let me tell you a story to help you feel less afraid." I paused a long moment to add a bit of dramatic flair. "Remember the large arena at the Midwest Horse Expo with its soft footing, warm lighting, and seats up to the rafters? You two were on the horse cantering in the center of the arena. There was a horse off to each side, walking in a circle opposite the cantering horse. Near each of the horses was a team of girls and a lunger. While the announcer read a script over the booming audio system and soft music played beside his voice, you and your teammates, in period costumes, took turns demonstrating the history of vaulting from the time of Roman warriors to a modern-day equestrian sport. Into the center, onto the horses, one at a time, sometimes three at a time, for fifteen minutes, you and your team wowed the audience by standing, twirling, leaping."

I continued as Mia and Lexi fixed their minds on the memory and climbed back onto the back seat. "The arena was packed, not with just the usual few parents with cell phones in the air. More than 5,000 people filled those seats!" I said, my voice rising with the same energy I had while watching the girls. "Beth knew you were scared. She had you lock arms with your teammates before entering the arena. Into your circle she yelled a fiery pep talk, then got you chanting, 'Step, step, step.' As your voices lifted up to meet hers, she led your team, knees lifting in unison, as you marched single file into raucous, welcoming applause. When the music began, you performed as if you were back at the barn. Calm. Collected. One beautifully choreographed routine!"

The rearview mirror reflected smiles.

I continued, "Now tell me how you'd feel if I started the car and left for home now? If you never felt the whoosh of soft footing from the Kentucky Horse Park arena below your slippers?"

"Honestly, I'd feel relieved," confessed Lexi.

"I'd be able to breathe," conceded Mia.

The car was quiet as the young equestrians contemplated their choices.

Eventually, the two best friends locked eyes across the empty middle seat and then exclaimed together, "Disappointed!" and "We'd be disappointed if we left now. Maybe we should stay and try."

"Then let's go investigate," I said. "See the barns and the horses. Meet up with your teammates. Practice. If you still feel compelled to leave, we will."

I drove slowly past countless pristine barns, covered competition arenas adorned with filigree iron work, outdoor show jumping venues with brightly painted fences, trimmed hedges, cascading flowers, and a seemingly endless number of elegant horses, riders, and grooms. I sensed a tightness in my chest as I remembered my childhood rental horse, Gravel, and a riding competition at some well-heeled stable many miles from the comfort of my rural lesson barn. There wasn't time now to indulge my clouded memory. The twisting road had led us to a vast metal building with stall upon stall of glistening horses cooled by whirling fans.

We met our team under our Northern Lakes Vaulters sign swinging gently above the entrance to two joined stalls, our home for the next few days. Vaulting surcingles, extra pads, mirrors, and hooks for garment bags littered the already-cramped quarters. The familiar smell of horse sweat and the chatter of kids drew Mia and Lexi down the aisle to the excitement. No sooner had we arrived when the girls shed their fears to meet new friends, donned their practice unitards, and left me in the aisle to explore the vast grounds alone.

Three days later, we packed sweaty, dusty costumes and smelly vaulting slippers into the car, adorned the back seat with numerous ribbons, and set our direction northwest to Chicago. Mia and Lexi, pleased with their performances, immediately closed their eyes, bodies relaxing into pillows fitted tight into the corners, dirty feet propped on the back edge of the center console. I left the audiobook on pause, eavesdropping on bits of contented conversation between two friends who had conquered a challenge. From the rearview mirror I saw faint smiles push against tired cheeks. They bantered about plans for next year's competition. Their voices trailed off as miles distanced us from the horse park, but not before I heard Mia utter, "My goal for next year is to be a silver-level vaulter." Lexi whispered, "Me, too." As they went quiet, my smile lit up the rearview mirror and a knot of tension relaxed in my shoulder blades. *Mia did have goals, after all!*

"We're home!" Mia yelled in a high-pitched voice from the back door. Toenails clicking on wood floor exploded the quiet as Annie, Margo, and Rascal bound over each other to greet us. Annie lavished us with kisses. Rascal bounced into open arms like a circus dog. Happy whines and gurgles came from Margo as she wiggled her hips and heaved her blackness to plant front feet on shoulders. Joe and Anna said a quick hello before departing quickly. Annie had been good but not perfect, meaning theirs had been a week of extra work.

I immediately noticed the dent in the cushion at the top of the sectional, formed from a solid week of Annie perching like a hawk looking for prey. She'd become comfortable in our home, even while I was away. It was time she moved to a forever family before she became too dependent on our home as hers. I decided to test the waters of the internet to see how Annie's slower-than-normal journey to good citizenry would be received on Petfinder. I put together a truthful profile, included some darling photos, and sent her story to Marilyn to post. Annie had her own web page in time for a Petco Adoption event.

The ever-friendly Annie was the belle of the Petco ball. Like a relaxed Mia at her vaulting competition, Annie proved a consummate extrovert, confidently mingling with the Second Chance volunteers and cornucopia of dogs. Every visitor was drawn to her charm and ample smile. Much attention was lavished upon her. The three hours of the adoption event passed quickly, yet no one showed interest in Annie. I was ready to pack her bag when a family with two young children appeared.

They came at the end of the event hoping to have a quiet opportunity to meet the dog that had drawn them in on Petfinder. While the parents, Amanda and Derek, worried aloud their kids were too young to treat a dog with respect, little Clara knelt beside Annie and gently linked her arms around Annie's neck. Clara's strawberry blonde hair melted into Annie's. Kid and dog became one. On their faces were two wide grins. With that positive sign, the parents scheduled a home visit.

I drove to a quiet neighborhood in St. Paul with Annie, nose out the window and joyful tail wagging like a metronome. As soon as I opened the gate to their little backyard, she bounded up the steps like it was home. I talked with the adults while Clara, dressed in a shimmering blue princess costume, sat at a wooden desk just right for a kindergartner, coloring a picture and cooing to Annie.

From a rustling paper bag, she snuck Annie treats, believing no one noticed as Annie chomped and slurped. She dressed the ever-patient

Annie in a matching blue princess costume and tiara. Annie soaked in the attention with the grin of the Cheshire cat.

Clara's brother, Campbell, wanted to show Annie the park. A very happy Annie was flanked by two skipping children as the adults walked through the neighborhood. Just as I was explaining Annie's reluctance to do her business outside, Annie walked to the edge of the sidewalk, peed in the grass, and made me a liar. Three blocks later she did it again. All at once it occurred to me: our blacktopped neighborhood with winding roads rimmed by woods must have smelled differently than her concrete sidewalk memory. She must have been a city girl!

Three days later, I called Amanda to follow up on Annie's adoption. Amanda passed the phone to a gleeful Campbell and Clara. Through high-pitched squeals of two young kids, I learned how Annie went to summer camp to meet their friends and explore the playground. Clara and Campbell rattled off the names of all the dogs Annie had met on their walks. I even heard how Annie got to snuggle with the kids under the ceiling fan of the sleeping porch during hot summer nights. They thanked me over and over for making Annie such a good dog. I thanked them over and over for giving Annie a good home. I hung up the phone wearing my own Annie-grin.

We'd done it! Annie's adoption marked the sixth checked box. We'd finally met the terms of our fostering contract. Together we'd accomplished a major goal! In celebration, I called Anna, Mia, and Joe to the sectional, each nudging Margo or Rascal for space. As we looked at the photos of our adoption successes—Betty, Snickers, Shelby, April, Lizzie, and the ever-smiling Annie, I couldn't help but be proud of the work we'd done. We'd given those dogs a second chance. Along the way, we'd grown as a family and developed a collective spirit of generosity and compassion.

I stood up to finish packing the cooler for an afternoon of family geocaching and picnicking at a state park along the St. Croix River. My mind had moved to the marshmallows and bars of chocolate we'd need for s'mores. My right foot was about to step up from family room to kitchen when I heard two girls inquire, "When can we foster again?"

"Don't tempt me," I teased. "I might say yes if Lynda needs help."

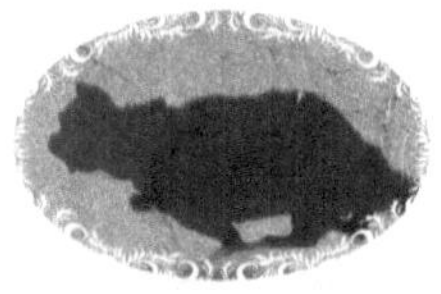

ODIE THE FOX

Chapter 11

That yes came quicker than I thought when Lynda called two months after Annie's adoption. Gray-tipped ears, dark ringed eyes, and a black button nose stood in contrast to Odie's stark white coat. He looked like an arctic fox in seasonal transition. He was hardy and playful. In fact, he was one of the first foster dogs that enjoyed playing with Joe. Many before him had an aversion to Joe despite his best efforts. We don't really know why but guess some dogs might have been abused by a man or lived in a house run by a woman. Odie, a ten-pound blend of this and that, had the spirit of a ball-loving retriever through and through. His eyes were constantly watching us, waiting for someone to engage. His legs, like Tigger's, were always ready to pounce. He didn't mind who threw the toy. If it was fuzzy and flying, he would chase after it, bring it back, and eagerly wait, tail wagging, to do it again. Odie, like Rascal, was easily entertained with toys.

Rascal, however, was not entertained by Odie. Odie was the first male foster to come through our doors since Rascal became king of the throne. Gobs of stretchy, stringy drool started flowing from Rascal's mouth the moment I let all three dogs into the paddock. It wasn't long before a flip of his head made the drool flop over his nose and dangle past his lips like a St. Bernard. Shortly thereafter, the mounting began. Rascal pursued Odie, trying to show him who was boss. Odie mounted Rascal not wanting to be outdone. Both were covered in drool and panting. Since neither was doing what I put them in the paddock to do, I leashed the three and took them on a walk. After a bit of jockeying for position, Rascal took the lead on his slightly longer leash. Once secure as the chief of his outdoor domain, his drooling and mounting ceased.

As the drama eased, allowing room for thought to enter my brain, a distant memory flashed across the IMAX screen of my mind. At the front of a beige-painted room cast in prison- gray from cheap fluorescent lighting stood the Early Childhood Family Education instructor. She held a colorful wood model of a strand of DNA. Her pointed finger gently pushed one side of the coil to set it spinning slowly. The other arm raised it to eye level. "Your life with two kids will be like this spinning DNA. Each strand represents the path of one kid." She stopped it suddenly, and softness like warm bathwater, washed through her voice. "Look here. At this one point in time, the red dot of the left strand, representing child one, is in line with the orange dot on the right strand, representing child two. Alignment. Harmony. Calm. No fighting. Warm, fuzzy love wrapping you in a big bear hug." She pushed the strand of DNA until it began spinning, her voice rising, tension growing like the tightening of a guitar string. "Nudge the helix and the strands twist. To your still eye, the dots appear to move independent of each other. Unalignment. Agitation. One kid in a time out for pushing, biting, taunting the other. Your nerves in fray. You want to scream, 'That's it. I'm done!'"

I turned to Joe and saw the same resignation darkening his eyes that I felt within. Mia was only six months old, and already Anna was asking to send her back. Joe and I grew up with siblings. Each of us born near the middle of our packs. We knew the anguish of never being the only child and felt a sympathy for Anna's loss. And, our loss, too. For somewhere deep down we both harbored the same crazy hope our family would be different, free of strife, with two siblings living in harmony. We also knew that was a dream. The unraveling of it so early in our young family, however, was disconcerting.

"Not all is lost," continued the teacher, her hand stopping the double helix, knowing more parents than just Joe and I were struggling. "Look, you're back in harmony. Red and orange on the same plane. A moment to recharge, embrace, be thankful." An audible sigh bubbled through the room of young parents. "Life with two children will be exhausting and challenging but deeply rewarding. When the dots align, love will pour."

Fast-forward to Anna's junior year. Odie was safely in his crate, lured inside by a peanut butter Kong. Margo and Rascal were lounging on their soft beds, working at their treats. Anna, Mia, and their friend Lily were running behind the wagon of straw bales on which Joe and I were riding. Loud laughter was punctuated by "Wait, my shoe is stuck!" from a screaming Mia. More giggles from the girls as each one propped up Mia while she tried to retrieve her white tennis shoe gripped tightly by sucking mud. "Ewwwww!" she screeched as she put clean sock into dirty shoe and scrambled after the tractor.

The girls arrived at the pumpkin patch like three mud wrestlers who'd lost the match. After instructions from Farmer Paul on how many pumpkins they could take (as many as they could carry back to the farm), mud no longer mattered. The three friends stood in place long enough for gears to turn in their minds, scheming. As they huddled in discussion, the tractor began emptying rapidly of kids and parents filling the pumpkin patch. "Let's go!" yelled Anna, and the three leapt over rows two at a time to the other side of the field.

Joe and I walked slowly through the browning vines, rolling the orange orbs this way and that. Bugs and worms scattered while earthly smells from decaying matter rose to meet our noses. My prize, a perfect sphere for a wide, candle-lit smile. Joe, a suppressed artist, inspected each, weighed feature against feature, finally selecting two oblong, watermelon-shaped fruit. I couldn't wait to see what would emerge from spoon and knife. We placed our pumpkins on the tractor, now only for parents and their pumpkins and the trip back to the farm, and we started out for the other side of the field, clippers in hand to see what the girls had discovered.

A single-file row of pumpkins already picked from the vine were lined up from smallest—where two could fit in the palm of one's hand—to largest, as big as a bushel basket. Each girl was so lost in the thrill of the hunt and the idea of "as many," they forgot about the "carrying" part. When I mentioned that little detail, they looked at us in unison, exclaiming, "You can help us carry them!"

Two dots on the double helix of siblings had aligned, wrapping a warm bear-hug of love around our shoulders in a misty farm field framed by crimson maples on the river bluff. How could we deny their joy? Joe and I rolled the largest pumpkin onto my spare sweatshirt, using the sleeves as ropes to carry it between us. The girls followed our lead, tying knots in sleeves, slinging the knots over their necks, and filling their makeshift bags.

Laden with treasures like pirates after a raid, we slogged through puddles, splattering more mud while the tractor of waving parents passed us on the way to the barn. We piled the pumpkins by the wheel of the car, then lined up with the others for the shared potluck feast signaling the end of the farm season.

Joe had barely thrown the car into park in the garage before he flipped off his shoes and ran inside to grab a pile of towels. Once back, he hid behind the workbench stool, quickly stripped to his underwear, tied a towel around his waist, then ran to the shower. When the coast was clear, the girls undressed, leaving piles of stiff jeans and sweatshirts heaped by the door. I grabbed three leashes and three eager dogs for our evening walk around the neighborhood. Wet grass and pavement turned them into a dirty mess of dripping undercarriages requiring multiple towels to wipe them reasonably clean. I opened the door from the garage to see sock prints cross the floor and move side by side up the stairs like ancient human footprints found in a volcanic mud flow in East Africa.

I stripped wet socks from my feet and padded over their footprints to the shower. Warm water softened the edges of laundry frustration, letting the glow of the farm and two girls aligned on the helix settle into my memory. Once showered and dried and a whole lot cleaner, I went to the garage with renewed energy, ready to tackle the mound.

Much to my surprise, it had disappeared. And then, I heard it: the faint swishing of the washing machine a story above.

My pace quickened as I took the wood stairs two by two, three dogs in tow. Odie and Rascal were sparring with each other and letting out *grrr*s at my heels. As I approached Anna's bedroom, muffled discussion met my ears. There they sat, two fresh-faced sisters wearing well-worn sweatpants and hoodies. Long wet hair twisted into towels. Newspaper on top of an old sheet to protect the carpet below. Tiny pumpkins surrounded by a sea of colorful markers. They'd already begun crafting faces on the bright orange canvas.

"Mom, come sit with us. You can decorate these if you want." The girls chattered eagerly in unison while each offered a tiny pumpkin to me. I settled my back against Anna's bed as they enthusiastically added, "By the way, we started the laundry, so you won't have to!" Never had the sudsy sound of heavy swishing been more poetic than that moment when two dots aligned on the sibling DNA. I closed my eyes briefly to bottle the moment.

The next morning, the continued tension between Odie and Rascal broke the spell. My hand itched to rub the magic bottle, to be granted a wish to end the mounting, the drooling, and my nagging of kids who had suddenly lost the urge to help. With no wizardry coming to my rescue, I had to summon my inner patience, of which the outside world saw as abundant while my inner team complained was sorely lacking.

I kept the boys separated as often as possible or walked them long miles to redirect their energy. I wrote detailed chore lists and time requirements on the white board, pushing the girls until the jobs were done. I made sure Rascal had first chance to sit beside me on the sectional. Two weeks later, Odie took the hint and resigned himself as second-in-command to Rascal, usurping Margo in her position.

That same sort of king-of-the-hill jostling followed by silent resignation seemed to chase Joe and me through our relationship, starting as early as our first year of dating and the classic first fight. He had generously offered to help me as I embarked on a large-scale remodeling project. My small food-based business was moving into a 100-year-old bank building in a derelict part of town; my two business partners and I were eager to contribute to the downtown revitalization and to take advantage of the tax breaks of an enterprise zone. Our landlord, excited to have a tenant, let us do the demolition and reconstruction to reduce our rent. Donning hard hat and work boots, Joe helped as we tore down sheetrock, exposing peach-hued brick walls topped with elaborate crown molding. We removed cheap plywood over the marble entry and lightly sanded the wall-to-wall solid maple floors stretching to the bank vault. When repairs to the base structure were complete, we began to assemble the components to make the space work for our needs.

The bank building was situated on a hill. The front entrance was at street level. Tenants parked in back, one flight below street level. Entering the kitchen from the parking lot meant a walk up a long flight of metal stairs to a door set in a brick wall that couldn't be moved. I laid out the kitchen cabinets as best I could, positioning the refrigerator to maximize the workflow of the kitchen. The only drawback to my plan was the relationship between the kitchen door and refrigerator wall. Every person walking through the kitchen door would look right into the space between the refrigerator and the wall behind it—and it bugged me.

The refrigerator wall, like the door wall, could not be moved. It was part of the two-foot-thick brick wall system forming the bank vault. A large upper cabinet hung above the refrigerator. To the right were more upper and base cabinets capped with a long countertop. We hung sturdy wallpaper between the upper and lower cabinets for an easy-to-clean surface, extending it twelve inches behind the refrigerator. This approach made it seem as if the wall behind the refrigerator was papered when looking at it from the center of the kitchen.

Every time I entered the back door, the interior designer I was later to become was drawn to that seam behind the refrigerator where the wallpaper from the right met the painted wall to the left. I wanted to pull out our wallpapering tools, move the refrigerator, and hang wallpaper to cover the full space behind the refrigerator. Joe and my partners, who had put remodeling behind them after arduous months, were not bothered in the least. They refused to be convinced the small design element mattered.

So began the fight that almost ended my relationship with Joe. We argued and postured and positioned about who was right. We did not drool, but we both got angry when the other wouldn't concede the throne. After months of carefully working to resolve issues, we had no compromise left.

Like boxers committing fouls in a ring, we went to opposite corners. Joe holed up in his attic apartment a block from the beach. I took many quiet walks on that same beach with Snuka, unwilling to walk north in Joe's direction.

We remained distant for many weeks until the dots on the strands of DNA aligned and a desire for each other pulled us together. We can't recall who called whom. We can't even remember if we put wallpaper behind the refrigerator. Somehow, we moved past the fight and committed ourselves to a lifetime together.

Reflecting on that memory made me wonder if Odie had silently conceded to Rascal in the same way we Joe and I had, leaving thoughts and needs unspoken. The peace that had developed between the two dogs, however, made me think dogs were better equipped to broker differences and move on with easy acceptance. In fact, Odie quickly shed his entanglement with Rascal to seed a new storm with the rest of us.

Lynda's response to my frustration over this new development was to review Odie's case file at animal control to see if anything had been overlooked. Odie had been surrendered by a middle-aged woman who'd lost her job and her home near the end of the 2008 recession. She described Odie as house-trained, which he was, and well-mannered, which he'd been. After his dethroning, though, he become a yowler and a howler, voicing his disagreement every time we left the house. Lynda guessed the tantrums were a product of newly formed separation anxiety from the stress of abandonment, his five days at the animal shelter, finding himself in a new home with unfamiliar smells and faces, and human affection shared between five animals. If it'd been me in his situation, I'd howl, too.

To help him, we embarked on peanut butter training. At first, Odie had absolutely no interest in the sticky treat left inside the hard rubber chew toy we put inside his crate. Margo and Rascal, however, danced impatiently from foot to foot and licked their lips while we prepared their treats in the kitchen. They would race to my office and whimper in anticipation as we doled them out—Rascal's first, set on the footrest of his favorite red chair by the window, while Margo's was placed on her big tan bed on the floor. We put Odie's in his crate, forcing him to choose between his fear of our leaving and our goal to get him willingly in the crate. Margo and Rascal, food-crazy opportunists, took advantage of Odie's hesitation. They realized quickly they could finish their treats and pounce on the uneaten one in Odie's crate. Peer pressure finally drove Odie to step inside. Soon, he secured his place in the kitchen lineup, wiggling his bottom, licking his lips, and racing the other dogs to my office. He may have howled after we left, but at least we could leave without hearing it.

Anna and Mia, on the other hand, began their own howling. "Mom, can we keep him?" became a constant cry in our home. The girls were aligned on the DNA but not in the happy way a parent hopes. Odie was a keeper. He was the type of pocket dog Mia liked to coddle, not a perfect replacement for Poet but pretty darn close. While Anna was still in love with long-walk Margo, our retriever was not a ball-chasing dog. Odie was. Anna enjoyed his enthusiasm for play and willingness to engage. His good citizenry also meant the kids and Joe could meet my dog-care expectations with minimal effort.

I knew I had to get him adopted quickly. The firmer I said, "No," the louder they screamed, "I hate you," and retreated to their rooms. The bam of wooden door slamming against wood trim and the click of metal latch to metal plate might just as well been a mallet striking a timpani drum. Those three little words hurt bad, arousing a nagging fear I was driving my girls away. *How hard can it be to have three resident dogs?* When I began bargaining with myself, I knew I was moving towards trouble, not just because I'd be giving in to their bullying, but doing so would continue a pattern of poor communication and response. As I sat with my back against the wall, head in hand, a new worry emerged. *How could I expect my kids to communicate effectively if I did not model it well?*

Thankfully, there was a professional in the ring we'd come to trust. I arranged for a family counseling session with Anna and Mia's counselor, Dr. Jeff, to help us broker a peace. We stuffed ourselves shoulder to shoulder on the leather couch of his shared counseling space. Dr. Jeff acted as referee and coach, intercepting fouls, redirecting emotion, and pulling out conversation from those who retreated into quiet resignation. Before our hour ended, we arrived at a mutual conclusion to find Odie a new home.

I'd like to say I felt a sense of relief after our therapy session. What I mainly felt was unease. While my fingers typed Odie's profile for his Petfinder page, a tight lump pressed against my throat. *Were the kids and Joe truly comfortable with the agreement? Could they accept his adoption and move on without contempt for me? Could I accept their unease in exchange for the peace I'd receive from his adoption?* That's when I knew what I would wish for if I only had one wish from a genie in a bottle: to have Dr. Jeff's voice of reason coaching me through tough decisions and conversations until I could trust the process of compromise.

A young professional woman was searching for an apartment-appropriate pet when she came across Odie's picture on the web. For Katelyn, it was love at first sight. She passed muster with our screeners and called me on the phone to learn more about him. I instantly liked that she worked from home, believing it would be helpful to cure Odie of his separation anxiety.

Katelyn had a few reservations about Odie, though. To keep herself from falling under his spell, she brought her mother with her to meet him; her mom would be her voice of reason, reminding her not to rush into a decision. I admired Katelyn for her honesty and willingness to share her vulnerability with me.

After Katelyn and Odie's first game of fetch, her fire was stoked. She desperately wanted to take home the playful fox waiting at her feet to throw the toy again. She would have written a check and clipped a new leash to his collar if not for her mother waving a red flag from my butcher-block table.

"I'm glad you connected with Odie, Katelyn," said the mother. "But we agreed. Today's meeting was just that—a meeting. Your plan was to walk away so you'd have time to reflect on what a commitment would mean." Resigned to her own logic, Katelyn and her mom petted Odie on the head and walked to the opposite corner of the ring to cool off. I returned to a quiet day. My family had scattered at the thought of losing Odie.

Towards early evening, my phone rang. I rushed to answer it, eagerly wondering about Katelyn's decision. On the other end of the line, however, was the older voice of a recently retired woman. Her beloved Bichon had died. Lovestruck when she saw Odie's picture. She was hoping to meet him that night.

Two people interested in the same dog posed a new twist to our fostering story. *Now what to do?* I knew firsthand how powerful "love at first sight" was. I hated to disappoint either woman.

I told the older lady that Odie already had a suitor, letting her know if I didn't hear from Katelyn by noon the next day, she could meet Odie. Disappointment shadowed her voice as she said goodbye, tearing into my desire to please.

The hours ticked by. My family reassembled around the kitchen table to crank balls of dough through the pasta maker, forming thin sheets we topped with cheese. Dinner would be hand-crafted ravioli to accompany homemade pasta sauce. It was my secret weapon to draw the girls from their rooms.

Engrossed in something other than adoption, we were startled when the phone rang. Tripping over dogs scattered under the table, I rushed to answer the call. It was Katelyn. In her high-pitched excitement, she told me Odie was the one.

I drove Odie to Katelyn's apartment at the start of the week, getting tangled in a construction detour and arriving thirty minutes late. Katelyn was deep into a work meeting in her home office. She let us in and returned to the call. Odie and I did what came naturally to him; we played fetch and tug-of-war with toys I'd brought from home. He explored the open rooms of Katelyn's apartment nose to end, connecting with his new environment. I was excited to see a winding path leading to an outdoor mall and coffee shop; I could easily picture Katelyn and Odie walking to meet friends.

By the time Katelyn completed her call, Odie was moving about comfortably in the apartment. He switched focus from me and began playing fetch with her. He sat eagerly for treats. Giddy with glee, she signed the adoption papers. I left her apartment equally full of joy.

I was eager for our follow-up call, to hear how the next chapter in his book began. It wasn't the rosy prose I'd crafted in my head. Katelyn was struggling to close the chapter on Odie's separation anxiety. It appeared that, without the encouragement of Margo and Rascal, peanut butter was no longer soothing Odie's worries. He was back to howling when she left.

Katelyn could have been overwhelmed, disappointed, and angry with her decision to adopt him. Instead, her rational approach to problem-solving overrode her emotions. She had already enlisted the help of a dog trainer to address Odie's separation anxiety. Her faith was strong she could help her little dog mixed with this and that, and move happily to the next chapter in his life, to become a secure king even when he ruled alone.

I couldn't wait to tell my team Katelyn and Odie were on a good path. We'd achieved another win for our record books! Anna, Mia, and Joe, however, scattered to separate corners of the ring, not in the mood for my happiness. There would be no celebration. No Gatorade buckets poured over my head. Instead, each sought solitude in their loss. I was observing the unspoken communication of my team much the same way Temple Grandin observed and interpreted the unspoken communications of animals. No one told me they needed time to heal. This time, I gave it to them.

Days passed before curiosity pushed their grief aside. During dinner of grilled vegetables brushed with pesto on toasted focaccia, my family opened the door and let me back in. They were eager to hear about my conversations with Katelyn and stories of Odie. His success became their success, and the excitement mounted. It wasn't long before Mia and Anna, laughing in unison, asked, "When can we foster again?"

There were no words to utter. Instead I cast an incredulous stare. *You can't be serious! After all the "I hate yous and rebuffs, you want to do this again? Fine. I'll call your bluff. We'll see what happens when I agree to foster again.*

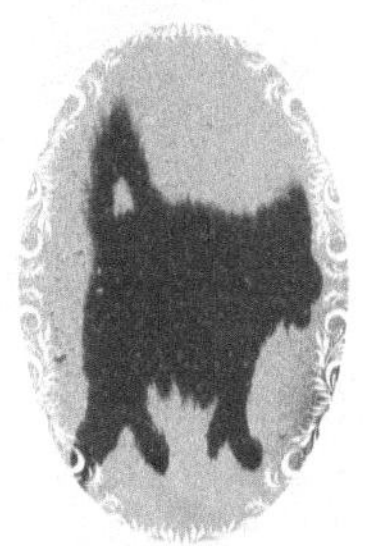

CROSBY

Chapter 12

When I was a young girl, I accompanied my mom to the vet clinic with Brandy, our bull-headed Airedale Terrier. Brandy tolerated our constant attempts to soften her stubborn demeanor, but she never subscribed to mine or my brothers' wish for a ball-loving, people-pleasing, snuggle-beside-you dog. On the clinic wall in a breed identification poster, I saw a dog I imagined would gladly live up to my expectations: the lamb-like Bedlington Terrier with its cropped coat of curly white fur, approachable eyes, and black marble nose which resembled the many smiley-faced stuffed animals on my bed. *Surely this sweet-looking dog would enjoy my doting attention!* I resolved someday to get my lamb.

Mousy clouds hung tight to the horizon the October day I left home to pick up our new foster dog from Life Care. Joe had reluctantly agreed to foster after intercepting Lynda's plea on the answering machine. The shelters were overrun with dogs dumped before winter. We were the only foster home in the Second Chance family without one.

Crosby, a three-year-old Bichon mix, had just been neutered, groomed, and given a name. Beyond that, he had no story, a common situation for the many abandoned dogs at animal impound. To skirt death, he needed a home. Eager as a birthday girl at her party, I stood on tiptoes at the counter straining to see what the veterinary technician would bring through the door.

When I first glimpsed Crosby, the image of the Bedlington Terrier from the breed identification poster flashed in my mind! My heart skipped a beat. A lump caught in my throat. There stood Crosby with a sheared coat of tightly wound white curls, bright pink skin, and a black button nose—my little lamb! My hands trembled as I took a quick picture for Anna and Mia. I knew it was time for them to step off the school bus and that they were equally anxious to see what surprise awaited. None of us could have predicted how quickly the little ten-pound package would warm our souls and turn our home upside down!

Crosby swaggered through the door securing his position as ring-master and clown with confident playfulness. He brushed by Margo and Rascal and ran for the sectional, catapulting himself onto the seat cushions. I stood by the kitchen peninsula where I could easily spy into the family room. The stillness of the three dogs forced me to step forward, to see if there was a problem. It was then I realized Crosby enticing me into a game of peekaboo. He was seated on the other side of the sectional, one black eye barely visible above the top of the back cushion. As soon as he caught my eyes look his way, he flattened himself on the seat cushion. In a short minute, he had that glossy orb peeking at me again. This time, he leaped high above the cushion then fell flat in hiding. Once more, he leapt up, yipping loudly as he ran from one corner of the sectional to another, wide grin growing as Margo and Rascal joined the chase.

We quickly discovered that if you dared to engage Crosby's mischievous eye, you would be sucked into a loud and rowdy game. With it came the possibility of waking a sleeping household or disturbing TV watchers and bearing the wrath. Crosby was so small he found nothing wrong with racing from one end of the sectional to the other while leaping over any object, cat, kid, or Joe, in his way. That game always caught the attention of Margo and Rascal, who also began to believe it was equally fine to run over people and around the sectional in a game of chase. These not-quiet moments, punctuated by laughter, were often made louder when the kids grew tired of the interruption and started yelling at the dogs to quiet down. Even if the dogs did oblige, any new catalyst entering the room, whether human or cat, would reignite the smoldering game. Crosby took no time in stealing our hearts. Soon the kids were boarding the "Can we keep him" train.

What they didn't know was I had boarded the train as soon as I saw him. I'd never told them the story of Brandy and the picture of the Bedlington Terrier. They didn't know I had searched my life for a little lamb. Crosby's adoption papers were in a tidy stack on my desk. How easy it would have been to reach over and sign them! Yet, I didn't. Instead, I retreated to my corner of the ring, waiting for time to guide me.

Time, however, remained suspended the day our little entertainer suddenly stopped entertaining. The mischievous marble eyes that started the morning with a game of peekaboo had become crusty and swollen by bedtime. Green goo sputtered from his nose as he tried desperately to clear his airway. When he stood, he wobbled. When he laid down, he whimpered. Panic filled all of us as Crosby's illness rapidly overtook him. The vet clinic for our fostering agency was closed.

Feeling helpless and scared, I took Crosby from his crate and put him beside me in Anna's bed. The girls, equally worried, huddled together under Mia's covers. I gently rested my hand near Crosby's ribs, checking frequently to ensure he was still breathing. Fitful sleep and troubled memories of another rapidly progressing disease accompanied me through a very long night.

More than a decade earlier, newborn Mia was buckled into her car seat, rolled baby blanket supporting her tiny head. Anna, proudly wearing her "I'm the Big Sister" t-shirt, was rocking her as Joe and I packed our bags to leave the hospital as a family of four. Eclipsing the happy day was Joe's foul mood and the continual onslaught of complaints he rifled under his breath out of Anna's earshot.

"Can't you move any faster?" Joe snorted like an anxious racehorse. "My head is pounding, and this hospital it too loud and hot. I need to get home." His lack of compassion after Mia's delivery tore past my heart to gather at the base of my pelvis, intensifying my pain and nausea. He huffed the strap of my small duffel bag over the handle of the wheelchair while dropping Mia's car seat heavily into my lap.

The Mona Lisa smile I fashioned for Anna faded along with the ecstasy of new motherhood after wrestling two car seats into the back seat and settling a very sore body into the front next to Joe. We drove home in a stew of angry silence, me stealing glances at this stranger whose eyes were focused on the road, hands gripping the wheel as if we'd been swallowed by a blizzard, though it was August. My hopes for a Hollywood homecoming fizzled as each mile of rigid highway unfurled. I was clueless as to why Joe had retreated to a distant corner of the ring. His behavior was so erratic, did I even want to know? The only peace surrounding Mia was the singing of one sister to another in the back seat.

Joe barely had the car in park before slamming his shoulder into the house door in a rush. Anna jumped from her car seat in pursuit of Joe. Fear replaced anger as I quickly unbuckled Mia, kissed her forehead, welcomed her home, and laid the newest member of our family in her crib. Just as her pink cap came to rest on the soft mattress, a long wail came from my bedroom. The stench of vomit met me at the door as Joe pulled the covers over his head, begging me to close the shades and block the light. Tears oozed from his tightly shut eyes. Through a barely audible whimper, he complained that his head and neck hurt.

"Waa. Waa. Waa." Short, breathy cries were coming from our newborn just learning to use her lungs. I started to turn towards Mia, but my feet refused to move. The blood had drained from my limbs to feed the boom, boom, boom of my pounding heart. *Joe? Mia? Oh my god, what do I do?* It was then that I registered the terror in Anna's eyes. I scooped her up, unleashing her flood of tears and wild screaming which drowned out the pain of Joe and Mia.

Like a scene from the movies when the clouds part and threads of gold light wash over desperate land, my parents walked in our front door after a long drive from Chicago. Their shouts of jubilee were doused quickly by our panic-stricken faces. My exhausted dad rushed back to the driver's seat as I helped Joe to the passenger side, blankets wrapped around shoulders, vomit bag ready for the ride to the emergency room.

Mom fed Anna and played tea party. I quieted Mia in the rocking chair. Our little spot in the universe had slipped into night when the shrill of the house phone pierced its peace. In a hushed voice unchar-acteristic of my dad's deep timbre, he relayed the bad news. A spinal tap indicated Joe had rapidly progressing meningitis. A culture would tell us in twenty-four hours whether it was bacterial or viral. If it was bacterial, most likely he would be dead before the culture returned. He was sedated in a dark isolation room, his pain so intense there would be no phone calls. The disease so contagious and dangerous there would be no visitors, not even me. Just when I needed him and he needed me, there was no option for either.

I communicated with Joe via a whiteboard in his cave, nurses writ-ing my greetings in large letters. He doesn't remember any messages, except for the one written during the wee hours of his second night. "Your wife is next door. Mia's in intensive care."

It was late summer. I was trying to placate Anna as she grappled with the addition of Mia, the absence of Joe, and the pulsing stress from Joe's precarious connection to life. We were having tea with Minnie Mouse and Grandma on the screen porch, an alpenglow turning the little white cups pink, when my dad stepped inside. He had just walked by Mia as she slumbered in her car seat in the adjacent room. Seeming a bit red-faced, he touched his hand to her cheek. She was hot. I checked. Yes, she was. In an instant, Anna and Grandma were left to their party as my dad whisked me and Mia to the children's hospital connected to Joe's, a team of providers at the ready per the instructions of our family physician.

We were immediately led to an isolation room in the emergency de-partment; they'd already been briefed on Joe's condition and wanted to prevent the spread of meningitis if Mia should be sick. Blood was drawn. Tests were taken. I was steered briskly from the room at 2:30

AM, sobbing, as the team began preparations for a spinal tap on a wailing, thrashing Mia. With adrenaline raging and a primal urge to steal my daughter from the torture, I dialed Loree's home phone. At the sound of her tired, confused hello, my resolve melted into hysteria. She later told me it took her five minutes before figuring out who was on the line. She'd gotten me calm enough to hear my story before an emergency room doctor tapped my shoulder. She was there to escort me through the hospital labyrinth to Mia. I hung up so quickly the worry kept Loree awake the remainder of the night.

There was no time to tend to the wave of isolation and fear as I stood before the massive doors separating me from Mia at the entrance to the neonatal intensive care unit. I needed support from Joe, but he was still isolated in the darkened cocoon where I was forbidden from giving support to him. My dad, not allowed in the NICU, was on his way to my home for some much-needed sleep. "Beep," pierced the quiet as the doctor swiped her access badge across the reader. One half of the gleaming metal door yawned, giving us entrance to the secure ward. A softly lit aquarium bubbled in the darkened, empty waiting area leading to a cramped ward of tiny babies, tucked in clear plastic boxes with tubes and wires tethering them to whirring machines. Round heads no bigger than navel oranges were attached to many shapeless bodies, only arms and legs defining them as human. A few nurses and doctors in white coats were administering care. No parent was in sight. I felt as if I was walking through a biology lab.

Mia was sleeping peacefully in her plastic cradle swaddled in a white blanket with colorful clouds. On her head a new pink hat. An IV was taped to her arm. A tiny clip monitoring her oxygen blipped from her hand. As soon as I walked in the door of the isolation room, the nurse exclaimed, "She knows her momma's here. Her breathing just increased!" I lifted a sleeping, but knowing, Mia gently from the cradle and rocked her in the padded chair. Tears of relief streamed down my checks, each one a token of our good fortunes. We had a private room. Mia was calm, no longer thrashing in pain. She was a normal-sized baby, a giant compared to the preemies. Born healthy, she'd have the resources to fight the same viral meningitis that had just been confirmed in Joe. Most importantly, the doctor's parting words informed me both Mia and Joe were expected to survive.

Loree later classified this as "perspective," a concept that engaged her mind during the long night without word from me. Raising two teens as a single parent with a distant ex-husband, she had no shortage of balls juggling and plates spinning while money disappeared in flames. She was weighing a decision the night of my frantic call. By morning's dawn, what once seemed insurmountable had become doable when placed on the scale of "perspective." Her problem, its scope, and the amount of resources to apply to it came into focus when compared to mine. Perspective helped her move forward with her decision.

Perspective was my life vest through the drowning exhaustion and busyness following Mia's admission to the hospital. Nursing, rocking, and catching a few hours of sleep before nursing and pumping so I could hurry home, dad as chauffeur, to play with Anna, sing her good night, and take a hot shower. It was then back to the hospital to navigate the maze of hallways that led to the NICU.

On day four of Joe's hospital stay, he was deemed noncontagious. I was able to visit just before his release. I brought him a gift of shaving cream at his request; he wished to tidy up before seeing Mia. Our journey from the adult hospital co-joined to the children's hospital required us to take a series of elevators. When the bell dinged in one, our heads both turned towards the lighted panel. Just as the steel doors were parting, our friends Alex and Jeff from parenting class stepped inside. Surprise hovered between our group as we quickly told them of Mia's birth and Joe and Mia's struggles. We stood in further disbelief as we learned Alex and Jeff were on their way to see their son, Carter. Six weeks older than Mia, he had meningitis, too!

A slumbering Joe missed Mia's second homecoming. He was recuperating in bed, while I received a big bear hug from Anna and my parents. Colorful welcome signs crafted by Anna hung from the railing up to the girls' room. From the kitchen came a heady aroma of tomatoes simmering in basil and garlic. My mom gently took a sleeping Mia from my arms as Anna pulled my hand, dragging me outside. She'd fashioned a "bus" out of her stroller, a wagon, and Snuka's old leash. It was time for her dolls and stuffed animals to take a ride. Together we walked the block, me as bus driver, a few early fallen leaves crunching under the wheels. As Anna sang a silly song about bananas and wheels on the bus, my weary limbs became heavier as the anxiety that'd kept them moving drained away. We returned home to steaming hot plates of pasta and a table full of family. I nursed Mia one last time before falling into my own bed for much-needed sleep.

Sleep did not come the night Crosby fell ill. My hand moved methodically from his nose to rib cage to confirm he was still breathing, while memories of Joe and Mia's ordeals had me gasping for my own breath. Anna and Mia, exhausted with worry, were splayed out on Mia's bed. I could hear muffled whispers through the wall. They'd hoped to find a simple diagnosis and home cure for his discomfort.

Instead of being assured, they felt more panic. I knew they were still hashing through their efforts as the clock ticked by.

At first light, Joe rushed Crosby to Life Care where a veterinarian determined he had an advanced bacterial infection. He was prescribed antibiotics and a prescription for plenty of rest. Quiet filled the house as we anxiously waited for improvement. Little by little, Crosby healed.

Our little comedian's personality returned as his strength improved, but a new side of him emerged, one consumed by separation anxiety. Like Odie, Crosby would pace frantically in his crate, howling and barking when we left for school or work. We tried giving him free reign of the house like Margo and Rascal. That appeared to diminish his howling. He then embarked on a new habit of wall-marking and side-of-the-couch peeing. We needed a new strategy, and fast.

Making a sandwich one day, Anna found Crosby staring intently at her while she stood at the counter spreading peanut butter on bread. His eyes never left her plate as she moved to the table. He hovered at the open dishwasher when she put the dirty dish inside. When she let him taste a lick from a spoon, his little pink tongue worked furiously at the sticky treat he once snubbed, his tail wagging in approval. He was soon running to his crate, eager to get at the smear of natural peanut butter in the center of the hollow Kong. His anxiety behaviors subsided.

Meanwhile, the pressure to keep him grew. Anna, Mia, and Joe had grown quite fond of the little joker. He'd certainly become my playful little lamb. His illness and recovery served as a reminder of the goodness gracing my life and the many reasons to be thankful. Yet a third dog in a busy household provided plenty of anxiety-inducing stress. Three peanut butter Kongs needed to be filled every time we left the house and cleaned later, so they could be filled again. Three dogs needed walking for exercise and letting into the paddock for quick relief. Three bowls of dog food and two bowls of cat food were scooped twice daily. While we fostered Crosby, we weren't responsible for his food, vet bills, or medicine. If he were to become ours, we would. We'd then have five animals in need of care. The dogs typically vacationed with us but not always. Three dogs and two cats would mean more money on house sitters and less to spend on vacations. The dollars we spent, or could be spending, on animals was adding up.

So, too, was the money we spent on kid care: counseling visits, ADHD medication, primary care visits, dermatology, orthodontics (both girls genetically predisposed to crooked teeth and overbites), and activities, mainly horses, to help them engage with life. Anna's school performance had improved to a level where college was once again a possibility. We'd finally reached a point where most of our home's problems had been fixed when I found the check- writing for kid expenses ratcheting up with no end in sight.

The money flying out the door as soon as it was brought in was also creating a rift between me and Joe. There was less to spend on our own interests, let alone our future. We'd begun to look forward to a reconnection; we'd set our relationship on the sidelines as we helped the girls get back on track to graduate high school. We even dared to discuss ideas for retirement and travel and more leisurely walks on sandy beaches. Those dreams that'd seemed so far away were quickly drawing near in relation to time, but unattainable without money to support them.

That's when I had to call on my inner strength to summon per-spective. While I had waited a lifetime for my little lamb and even written a check (the girls didn't know this), I was still unable to sign the contract.

I didn't lean on Loree this time to get her perspective. Instead, I called up the relief pitcher for my adult persona from the bullpen. I'd been grooming her long enough to gain confidence in her decisions. The kids were starting to take ownership of their mental health challenges and interventions as Joe and I continued to learn how to better captain their fleet and our marriage. But what really kept me from adopting Crosby was our fostering experience. I knew in my lifetime there would always be an ample supply of wonderful dogs in need of forever homes. There'd be other lambs.

"Growing up is stupid" was the response Anna and Mia gave to me after listening to my reasons for putting Crosby up for adoption. I know they wanted to scream "I hate you," but they had summoned a level of decorum. So, they began to bargain, much like they had done with Betty.

"If you let us keep Crosby, we promise to do more chores."

And my favorite: "We'll get up earlier to walk the dogs, so you don't have to."

I tried not to laugh, knowing that bargaining was part of the cycle of grief.

In fact, writing Crosby's profile was the most difficult one for me to craft. It was easy to put fingers to keyboard to describe the inquisitive jokester. Where I stumbled was over the tethering of lines that made our bond solid: his illness and recovery, his deep desire to engage, and his unbridled joy. Crosby looked nothing like our former loves, Snuka and Sierra, but he was their greatness rolled into one. I wrestled with logic and emotion and letting go for so long I almost missed getting him on the web before the monthly Petco Adoption event.

Thank goodness I didn't, or we might never have met Sharon and Joe, a retired couple with a fondness for Bichons who became smitten with Crosby's profile the Friday before the event. They drove across the Twin Cities, passing several Petco stores along the way, just to meet him in Roseville. Crosby and I watched from our chair in the volunteer circle as Sharon and Joe were interviewed by Lynda. We waited with Sharon and Joe as another screener conducted a veterinarian check. I then witnessed Sharon and Joe walk my little lamb out the Petco exit and into their car to begin their life together. My urge to open their car door and wrench Crosby from their arms was tempered by Lynda standing beside me. "They are the perfect couple for Crosby. I feel he'll have a good home," she said. I put on my coat and left with empty hands. No leash to hold our comedian with curly hair. No bag with Crosby's food and his favorite Lamb Chop squeaky toy. Those were already en route to his new home.

I sat in the nearly empty Petco parking to let hiccups turn to tears. Fear was not compelling my sadness the way it did when Lizzie went to her first home. My grief was loss, plain and simple.

When I got home, the usual "I hate you" was replaced by "You're rotten." The girls had learned from our pre-Odie adoption meeting with Jeff just how hurtful the three dirty words felt to me. "Rotten" was their new way to express their pain in our Crosby-less home. I leaned into that pain, letting them process their grief without forcing myself into its center. I didn't even fill the void with a new foster dog.

I would've felt immense guilt over the emptiness of a home without Crosby, except I was hiding a surprise that put his adoption in perspective. Joe and Sharon had asked me if we would be willing to dog-sit Crosby when they traveled. They knew our house was his and wanted him to be comfortable when they were gone. The first vacation date was already blocked on my calendar.

We now host "Crosby Camp" several times a year, eagerly awaiting the date of his arrival much like little kids await the unloading of ponies at a traveling petting zoo. My little lamb prances through the door, tosses his head this way and that, letting out joyous yips and yaps until he has our full attention. We spoil Crosby rotten, walk him until his snow-white fur turns to gray, then send him home happy, waiting for it to happen again.

Knowing he'll return helps soften the sorrow of loss. *If only there was an easier way to say goodbye to the other foster dogs, some way to gain more perspective.*

NINA

Chapter 13

Nina's story troubled me right from the get-go. She'd been rescued once already in her young life after a concerned neighbor called animal control to report incessant barking from the house next door. There Nina was found with feces-matted fur and no food in a cramped crate in the basement of an abandoned student rental house shortly after college graduation. She languished for a week at animal impound before being adopted into a family with an older rescued dog named Skye. Her new home had a fenced yard with plenty of room to roam. It was said Skye and Nina became an inseparable big dog-little dog duo, romping side by side and napping in a heap in the sun. All was good for the bonded pair until their family was rocked with insurmountable medical complications, and equally devastating bills. The family, forced to sell their home, moved to lower-rent housing where having pets was not allowed.

Before moving, they reached out to their longtime veterinarian at Life Care for help. In a role reversal, Life Care contacted Second

Chance for assistance. Lynda worked her foster list and telephone magic and found each dog a foster home, helping the duo to avoid the stark, impersonal kennels of an animal shelter where many animals uprooted by human complications languish.

Nina, a four-year-old, fuzzy-haired Shih Tzu-poodle mix with a kink in her left ear was waiting for me at Life Care. Another foster family had already picked up Skye, an equally furry but much larger, older dog. While keeping them together would have been ideal, no one in our fostering system, including myself, could foster the pair together. Other than a brief, bright-eyed "I'm going for a ride" moment when she got in my car, Nina's lowered head and expressionless face imparted mostly gloom. Neither Margo nor Rascal nor miles of walks with enticing smells would lift her spirits. Her hollow sadness rivaled that of April's. My heart ached for her and Skye and the family uprooted to a pet-less apartment, worrying about the dogs they left behind.

My concern for Nina was amplified by the changes looming on my own horizon. We'd come to the part in our family play where Anna would exit stage left to begin a separate life at a college in another climate zone. We'd no longer be main characters in each other's plays. Every time I felt clenching below my sternum, like a guitar string being tightened until near breaking, I tried hard to remember the sage wisdom of Jackie, the colleague from long ago who'd been the unyielding pillar that first morning I left infant Anna at daycare. She acknowledged my worry about letting go. She agreed Anna would fuss that day and many others. She assured me that with our guidance Anna would learn to lead herself and to let others guide and help her. "You'll be sad when she is on her own. As you work through the grieving process, though, you'll begin to see the gift of extra time to focus on yourself," she calmly counseled.

Jackie's were indeed wise words. I was not, however, ready to let go. I felt cheated. The roller coaster known as Anna's early high school years often had us jerking left when it appeared the track was veering right. Her ADHD, anxiety, and cystic acne often left us gasping with trepidation and plunging into outright fear. During second semester junior year, the tide turned. We began to experience loop-the-loops of breathtaking weightlessness and exhilaration, and I wanted more time with my comeback kid.

Our 'easy A' student from elementary school had clawed her way back to the graduation podium, with a village of teachers, counselors, coaches, and friends right beside her shoveling the dirt. Her sophomore science teacher had dangled the first carrot: if Anna got a C or better second semester, she'd reverse the first semester record from fail to pass. With the help of Anna's school counselor, who met with her to review assignments and set priorities, and Dr. Jeff, to ride shotgun on her anxiety, Anna took the academic challenge and erased her failed science grade. Her GPA, however, barely budged from the dead weight of the F in math.

She remained undeterred junior year, taking her medication to help with focus. After two semesters of straight A's, it was safe to say our "E for exceptional" student had returned. All that hard work, however, barely budged the GPA needle. The failed math class kept coming back as a slap in the face. Joe and I sat on wooden bleachers in the stuffy school gymnasium on a warm May evening to watch Mia shake hands with the principal during an academic awards ceremony. We were thrilled with Mia's successful fight to manage ADHD, but her name was the only Ojczyk listed in the evening's program. Straight A's for two semesters earned Anna nothing more than a seat next to her parents.

Anna and I also spent a good portion of her junior year touring colleges on the advice of Dr. Steve. He was the one who told us to stop worrying about Anna's grades. "There'll be plenty of schools trying to get Anna to fill a seat as long as she's on a path to graduate." His words rang true after Anna took her first ACT test. Postcard after postcard came from colleges inviting her to campus tours. Anna's ego soared, as did her confidence.

No matter how many postcards came, Anna's school choices were limited to those with an equestrian riding team. She wasn't willing to let go of her goal to compete at the collegiate level. In the end, she picked a small university in the middle of farm country.

The school wasn't what I'd envisioned for Anna, and neither had Joe. At the advice of Dr. Jeff, we'd stepped out of Anna's decision-making process, and—by default—the blame for her decision. Dr. Jeff had become Anna's guide instead. By night he was a psychologist. By day he was a high school guidance counselor. *Who better to inform her college selection process?* Anna told me they spent several sessions on that very topic. True or not, it was her decision to own, no matter the means for arriving at it. The consequences, whether good or bad, would be hers, too.

I felt like we'd given Anna a gift, our trusting her enough to step out of the way. When I did my own nest-leaving at age eighteen, it was more like a slow drive down a carefully charted path of my parents' design rather than a flight of my own planning. I wanted more for Anna, for her to experience the elation of a good decision and to develop self-confidence from righting an off-kilter course. She needed to believe she could be her own leader and that we'd have her back.

As good as it felt to trust Anna, doubt was creeping in like soldiers scaling the block walls of the castle, battering the door to my adrenaline and my resolve to keep my mouth shut. Anna's school of choice happened to be the same as her longtime boyfriend's. Joe and I agreed: clinging to her boyfriend did not seem healthy. *Or was it? Didn't Dr. Bonnie tell us it was important for Anna's mental health to have one good friend?* I couldn't help but hope the boyfriend would encourage her to stretch her wings in unfamiliar territory. To kick her in the proverbial butt when she needed it.

Joe and I also noticed how the college she chose was no bigger than her large suburban high school, the one she complained had so few options for friends. Yet I could rationalize that choice, too. The college had a freshman student-to-teacher ratio of 17:1. By junior year, class sizes in her major would be 7:1. The college had only one teaching auditorium holding fifty students max. Anna's K-12 public education had been in classrooms averaging 31:1. Anna also justified her decision by confidently stating, "Smaller classes will keep me accountable. I won't be able to skip once the teachers know me." A valid point coming from a kid who'd become a truancy expert her sophomore year.

What *did* attract me, and Anna, to the agriculture school in sugar beet country was the equestrian center she'd call home. I'd traveled with Anna and Mia across the Midwest for horse-related events held at sagging, musty barns adorned with dusty cobwebs, creaky doors, and fencing in need of paint and repair. Anna's new school rivaled the riding facilities Mia and I'd seen at the Kentucky Horse Park. Varnished wood, high ceilings, swept floors, roomy stalls, stadium seating. It was the shiny bling I dreamed about as a kid when I took riding lessons on my rental horse, Gravel.

Anna accepted the school's admission offer in late February of her senior year. Two carrots were dangled. Her new coach offered a partial riding scholarship dependent upon Anna's submission of a video demonstrating her equestrian skills. The school offered the second carrot. If Anna met their GPA threshold by the end of second semester, she'd receive a partial academic scholarship. That alone was the value of attending a small school looking to fill seats.

Anna continued her straight-A streak through senior year, budging her stubborn GPA into a high school academic award category, earning her first academic recognition. She picked out a new dress. Joe and I arranged our work schedules to ensure we could attend. Just as I was leaving work to meet Joe and Anna at school, I received a panicked call from Anna. A landscape truck backing onto a neighbor's yard had gotten stuck in the mud, cutting off the road and all access in and out of our small neighborhood.

Joe and Anna sat impatiently at the roadblock waiting for the truck to move. Time marched on as the lines of cars trying to get in and out grew longer. A new parent with a crying infant left her car alongside the main road and hitched a ride from a neighbor on the inside who took them home. Two neighbors on opposite sides of the bottleneck swapped cars so they could get where they needed to go. Our neighbor, Jan, stuck on the outside, walked through the woods to talk to Joe and Anna. As soon as she learned where Anna was supposed to be, she offered to drive them ten miles to school. They locked our car, walked through the woods to Jan's, and arrived in time for Anna to line up with the kids in her class. We settled ourselves on the wooden bleachers to watch Anna, shoulders back and smiling, walk in with her peers.

It was late May. People began to fan themselves in the growing heat. A flutter caught my eye. A slight breeze from an open door rustled one of the hanging banners awarded to the varsity hockey team. My mind wandered. I wasn't raised in Minnesota, the "state of hockey," yet, I was a keenly aware of skating icon Wayne Gretzky. While his shooting average in the National Hockey League was less than twenty percent, as a motivational speaker, he was legendary. His most famous off-ice quote, "You miss 100% of the shots you never take," became the mantra for my life and the belief I hoped to pass along to my kids. As I watched Anna shake hands with the principal while receiving her award, I knew she'd taken many shots to truly earn this one goal!

The next day, I bought Jan a bouquet of flowers to thank her for her act of selflessness. She'll never know how important that awards night was to us. Nor will she know the boost it gave me as a parent ready to let her child take wing. Knowing Anna was on a good path with others there to help made letting go more tolerable.

As I pondered Nina's plight, I thought of Anna and Jan, and situations that look hopeless made possible by others who care. It was the motivation I needed to try and reunite Nina and Skye. I began in earnest to tell their story. I printed posters for coffee shops and vet clinics. I did a digital blitz using social media, email blasts, and a profile on Petfinder.com. I didn't write a "Nina story" but a "Nina and Skye story." I wove together their pictures and personalities intending for readers to see them as an inseparable package. I knew full well that waiting to find the right adopter could take longer with a bonded pair.

Lynda was at Life Care updating the concerned staff on Nina and Skye when a retired couple shuffled slowly out of a clinic room, weighed down by grief. Waiting in line to pay a bill no one ever wants to pay, they listened passively to Lynda's story. Suddenly, Gerry, the husband, stepped out of the line. Grief grew to grin. Brightness filled his eyes. He said that with the consent of his wife he would like to adopt the pair, because "It was the right thing to do." Lynda, surprised by the kindness and the suddenness, suggested they take a few days to grieve. She wanted them to think about filling the void of their beloved dog with two strangers.

At the start of the new week, Gerry called me to talk about Nina. He and his wife, Corrine, had just returned from Wisconsin to meet Skye at her foster home. Their love for her was instant. Convinced it would be the same with Nina, they were anxious to meet her and reunite the duo. While I waited for Gerry and Corrine to drive to my home, I began in earnest to prep Nina for the meeting. I was hoping my excitement would change the sadness in her eyes. When that didn't work, I grabbed a brush and ran it through her curls.

Nina clung to me like a shy toddler meeting a stranger when Gerry and Corrine walked in. We stood in the entryway for a few minutes and exchanged pleasantries. Nina, overcome with curiosity, peeked out from behind my ankles. She lifted her chin from the floor for the first time in two weeks to get a better look at Gerry and Corrine. Gerry, wanting to make a good first impression, laid on the floor in the entry to be eye to eye with Nina. She began a slow and methodical process of sniffing him from head to toe. He talked calmly to her about a variety of topics including their home, their dog that died, and the good life he and Corrine could offer the duo. Gerry eventually sat up, crossed his legs, and encouraged Nina to sit in his lap. She soon relaxed into his embrace and the goodness of letting him pet her head.

Corrine took that as a cue and sat next to Gerry, her hand stroking Nina's fur. Nina melted. Gerry and Corrine soon began asking about adoption; they were sold on caring for the pair. My intuition was flying green flags as the two adults sitting on my floor by the front door continued to lavish attention on Nina. We began imagining what the reunion would be like for Nina and Skye. I saw rainbows and wagging tails as they frolicked shoulder to shoulder towards a golden horizon.

My fairytale reunion was not to be. When I called Gerry to follow up on their first day with their newly adopted dog family, he told me Skye and Nina looked like a nervous couple on an awkward first date. They wandered about aimlessly in Gerry and Corrine's unfamiliar backyard, Nina with her chin to the ground. Any glimmer of familiarity communicated between the two dogs was lost on the disappointed adults. It was not a day for magic.

Day two, however, was fabled. Nina and Skye awoke as if they'd never been separated, romping in the dewy backyard like it had always been theirs. Late in the day, they found a patch of sun and curled into one furry heap. I closed the chapter in our Nina story, satisfied our foster team continued to take shots until we scored. I hoped the good news would reach the family who had surrendered the pair. I wanted them to have closure, to know many people stepped in when they were forced to exit stage left. It served as a good reminder for me, too, as the curtain on our family play began to close.

SIDNEY

Chapter 14

Sidney was waiting for me at Life Care. Complications at work, however, were standing in my way of springing him from his kennel by closing. Mia, eager for her first taste of foster pickup offered to go in my place, so she could be the first to see Sidney emerge from the back room. Judging from the multitude of pictures Mia sent from her phone and pasted on social media, I knew she was squealing with delight over the nine-pound dog with waves of strawberry blond fur and a fluffy tail that gave him the look of a miniature golden retriever. I also knew it wouldn't be long before I heard, "Can we keep him?"

Thankfully, she didn't ask right away. Instead, she drove Sidney home, walked him in the back yard, introduced him to Margo and Rascal and lavished him with attention. She crated him with a peanut butter-filled Kong in the family room under the big ceiling fan rather than the normal foster spot in my office where the summer air was still and warm. Mia then left to carry on with her busy teenage day.

Later, when I entered the room to see the beautiful dog from Mia's numerous texts, I immediately noticed the cover of the armrest dangling precariously from the sectional. It struck me it was out of position; it hadn't moved once during its many years of service. Then I noticed the large holes chewed through the fabric, and one torn end protruding from Sidney's crate. Instantly, an image of Charlie Brown trick-or-treating as a ghost in a white bedsheet with too many eyeholes popped into my head. I wasn't sure whether to laugh or scream until I saw wide eyes of desperation on Sidney's face. I flung open the crate door. Sid sprang into my arms.

The destruction of the armrest protector was just one indication of Sid's unease resulting from his abandonment. We learned quickly to be careful around open doors. He was smart enough to know people leave through doors; he didn't want to be left behind. On the occasions he snuck past our feet, he ran to a car, waiting patiently to be invited inside. When crated, even with a tasty snack and plenty of toys, he howled his disapproval and shredded blankets and crate pads. Eyes, noses, and squeakers would be ripped from toys. Spilling through the grates would be clouds of stuffing. Sidney didn't challenge Rascal's dominance; instead, both worrywarts followed me everywhere, stuck like June bugs on a screen door.

Oftentimes the worry reminded me of toddler Anna, who sat me down one day to tell me a story about her baby sister. She was tired of Mia taking my attention. She wanted Mia to go back from wherever she came. She was done wanting a sister much the same way Rascal's worried eyes told me he was done with Sidney.

I suspect many parents hear similar stories from siblings throughout their years. Since Anna's request was not practical, we had to devise scenarios where she associated Mia with fun. Walks to the neighboring barn, trips to the library, visits to Como Zoo, and lazy afternoons on the shore of a local lake filled our days.

Family vacations most often centered around water. Joe was happiest in a boat or walking a sandy shore. During one of our first trips to Florida, Joe took a predawn stroll following a particularly stormy evening. He placed his collection of shells on the dresser and climbed back into bed. We both awoke to the clicking of shell against shell as the treasures he had collected in the dim light scuttled about looking for the sea. Joe gathered the shells he once thought were abandoned and took them back to the beach.

From that day forward, we became beach glass collectors. When one of us took a solo walk, our return would be peppered with, "What did you find?" When we walked side by side, we would stop to admire the pieces each had plucked from the sand. We would often compete to see who could find the most. Years have gone by, and the piles have grown as we visited the shores of great lakes and oceans where relentless waves and sand transformed other people's trash into our frosted treasures.

The glass is stored in clear bags. On occasion, we sit around the kitchen table, idly fingering the pieces, faint jingle of glass on glass, sharing stories and searching for one fragment that stirs a particular memory. We then begin to scheme and plot about our "someday" project, the perfect art installation to memorialize a lifetime of shared interest.

To help Sidney heal and to build Rascal's trust, we spent as much time doing the things both dogs loved most—being outdoors. They could spend hours nosing between the fieldstones that bordered the gardens and harbored a scurry of chipmunks. As Sid recovered from neutering surgery, we began increasing the distance he could travel. He loved to walk miles with me and Anna through the woods and around the lake. He wasn't interested in challenging Rascal, so three dogs on three leashes almost always pointed down the road.

This love of walking made him the perfect dog for our first-time participation in the White Bear Lake Manitou Days Parade. We'd been spectators sitting in lawn chairs on the parade route for many years. Streams of marching bands, firetrucks, and floats from community organizations would pass by while Anna and Mia ran to catch candy thrown from smiling float riders and clowns. Even as the girls got older, they enjoyed watching the parade, if only to catch up with friends and to sneak a piece of candy.

During the summer of Sid, a local group supporting the American Cancer Society's Bark for Life division decided to walk the parade with their dogs to raise awareness for the healing role of animals. For a small donation, we could walk behind their banner with Sid and carry our Second Chance Animal Rescue signs. The timing was perfect; Sid was ready for adoption. What better way to let several thousand people know he needed a home?!

On the day of the annual event, I carried our Second Chance signs to the parade staging area. Anna, Mia, and Mia's friend Shelby, took turns carrying Sidney so he wouldn't tire before the parade. When we met up with the Bark for Life group on Clark Street, everyone was vying for a cooler position under the shade of a tree. Many dogs, large and small, were sporting their purple Bark for Life bandannas. An old gray poodle was curled on a blanket in a bright red wooden box set on wheels like a stroller. A few small dogs were riding in makeshift backpacks and wagons, one in a baby front-pack. Oblivious to the crowd of people, a giant black lab with a face covered in drool frantically ran from ball to owner and back.

Sidney, a recently neutered male still motivated by hormones to mark, walked over to a woman with her back against a tree. He sniffed her shoes, then her knees, then her shorts. The woman was nearly finished asking me if she could pet him when Sidney lifted his leg and "rained on her parade." Her tiny dog popped up from her side by the trunk, barking furiously amidst the woman's laughter. Thank goodness she had a sense of humor and calm sensibilities! Otherwise, our parade would have ended before the grand marshal lifted her baton.

Sidney didn't win the hearts of any one family that day, but the Bark for Life section of the parade stole the hearts of the parade-goers. Crowds of kids rushed from their seats for a chance to touch the dogs. Anna, Mia, and Shelby would show the kids how to approach Sidney with care while patiently talking with parents interested in other Second Chance dogs available for adoption. Often, I would I look up to see the float in front of us at least a block away. Parents would then hoist thrashing kids back to their seats while the boom, boom of the drum section behind us drowned out their cries. It took two hours to walk the one-mile route and secure the parade as the most memorable of my lifetime, complete with one spinning helix and two sisters aligned.

Following the parade came two weeks of stifling weather, much like during the year of Sierra's death. Margo, Rascal, and Sidney spent a good amount of time lounging in the breeze of the shady paddock while summer heat accumulated in our air conditioned-less house. The spinning helix of two sisters, like the Wheel of Fortune, slowed, tick, tick, tick, until the flipper took its final flap and landed in "bank-rupt."

"Mommmmmmmm," screamed Mia, running down the hallway, hairbrush in hand, tears spilling over red cheeks. "Anna's bullying me. She pulled my hair and called me fat."

"Mommmmmmmm. Mia's picking on me," howled Anna through clenched teeth, the whites of her eyes pronounced.

I ran from my bedroom to the hallway to find two young women embroiled in a rage of fisted hands pushing at shoulders, while strong sun from the clerestory windows illuminated them like a police spot-light.

"Mia started it. She hit me with the hairbrush."

"I didn't hit you. You hit me. Mom, she's a liar!"

"You're the liar, you little baby. You even have the hairbrush in your hand. So there!" snorted Anna while she stomped her foot for emphasis.

"Enough," I bellowed, thrusting myself between them as if I was an umpire and the two were batter and catcher fighting over an erratic pitch. "Start over and tell me what happened," I demanded, holding my arms out stiff to block them from each other.

"Why should I explain anything. You'll just take baby Mia's side," shrieked Anna. "All she has to do is cry and you believe her."

"Oh, yeah. All my life it's been about you! Anna's hungry. Anna's tired. Anna wants to hit something. Everything stops and ALL atten-tion turns to you," roared Mia, poking a threatening finger at Anna's agitated face.

That same agitation, with Anna spitting like a volcano before it blows, was what had led us to a different Dr. Steve and a dusty paddock on a crisp autumn afternoon several years before Anna's ADHD diagnosis. Unusual outbursts and self-isolation were ushering in her puberty, and our family boat was beginning to thrash about in her gale. The girls loved horses. I figured why not use what they enjoyed to right our boat. Wrong! Anna and Mia wanted to ride horses, not stand in a "stupid" paddock and talk to a "stupid" therapist. Joe immediately took their side. He was not a horse person, finding them smelly and intimidating. I made them go anyway.

"The human-horse relationship is the foundation of my equine-assisted therapy practice," said the imposing man in a quiet, yet powerful voice. "Horses may have been domesticated by people, but people have not been able to get horses to stop reacting as prey animals. Horses are still very sensitive to human emotions and behaviors." As he talked, Honeybun, a short-legged, roly-poly chestnut pony with a blond forelock tangled in her long eyelashes, walked up to Dr. Steve and nuzzled his shoulder. Snickering, she put her nose in his palm, looking for a treat.

"When horses feel comfortable with you, they'll stay. Make them worried, they'll flee. Honeybun will be my yardstick, my way of measuring how you really feel when we talk. If you respond in a controlled and honest manner, Honeybun will reward you by eating from your hand. She'll even follow you without a lead rope."

As if she were a show dog on cue, Honeybun began to trail Steve around the paddock as he walked to the gate to let Anna in.

"Here. Give Honeybun this treat," said Steve, gently laying a crunchy biscuit in Anna's open palm. Honeybun snorted as she sniffed Anna, grabbing the treat with her tickly lips. Anna giggled. Steve gave her another treat. He then instructed Anna to turn away from

Honeybun and walk around the paddock. As she did, he began to engage with Anna.

"Anna, what is the name of the horse you ride?" "What is your favorite riding memory?" "If you could have a horse of your own, what kind would you want and what would you name it?"

Her answers were peppered with laughter and excitement. Honeybun followed close behind, her eye on the treat in Anna's hand.

Steve changed his tone.

"Anna, tell me what was bothering you when you yelled at your dad in the restaurant in South Dakota?" "Can you remember why you didn't want to invite classmates to your birthday party?" "What did Mia do for you to call her stupid?"

Anna's brow furrowed and eyes darkened as Steve peppered her with questions she didn't want to answer. Honeybun turned quickly from Anna and retreated to the other side of the paddock. Anna kicked at the dirt with head hung low, shoulders slumped.

Steve returned to asking happy questions. Anna relaxed. Honeybun ambled to Anna and nuzzled her palm. Anna uncurled her fingers as Honeybun slurped the treat from her hand.

"See. As easy as that. Talk to me calmly, and Honeybun will follow. Let your anger drive your behavior, and you'll drive Honeybun away. No different than with people." Laying a peppermint in Anna's hand, Steve turned to all of us as Honeybun crunched, a soft murmur of pleasure vibrating in her throat. "Our goal through therapy, is to let Honeybun be the therapist. I'll ask questions, but she'll tell you if you've responded in a way that will make her want to listen."

"I wanna try," yelled Mia. The two girls switched positions. Honeybun trailed Mia or trotted to the far corner, depending on the question and response.

Joe wasn't sold on the value of the therapy, but Anna and Mia quickly bonded with Steve and Honeybun. For the next few weeks, we made the trek to the little farm nestled in the big woods. We alternated turns in the dusty paddock, horse and patient, while Steve talked to us about school and work and home. Anger boiled. Tears fell. Feelings were discovered. But Steve always guided us to a place of peace and calm where success was measured by the quantity of treats consumed by the willing pony.

A brisk wind whipped at our back, snapping the nylon fabric of my jacket like a sail, on the day Dr. Steve led us to an expansive, rolling pasture where four mares came to greet us. There was no happy Honeybun in the sizable pasture. We'd never seen these horses that were towering above us, nostrils flaring in and out, using their breathing to size us up. Dr. Steve stroked the forehead of the leader as he described our challenge for the day. "I have one simple task for you to do as a family. When I tell you it's time, you'll climb over the fence to get into the pasture with the horses. You'll then work together to herd the horses to one corner."

"Remember how Honeybun followed each of you in the paddock when you were calm? You didn't need anything but your confident manner and her curiosity and motivation for food to get her to do what you wanted. These four mares will do the same. They will gladly follow a strong, calm leader. The difference in this exercise is you'll have to be that leader together."

Dr. Steve took a moment to push aside the hair blown across his face by the wind. He turned his side towards us, yelling louder than the gusts. "To get these four horses to do what you want, you have to appear as one." Looking specifically at me and Joe, he continued, "You'll have to let each other talk. You'll need to listen to each other to find agreement. You'll have to be equally confident in your approach. If one of you feels angry, frustrated, and unheard, the horses will know. They won't come near any of you."

Casually taking treats from his pocket, he moved from horse to horse as he continued, "You've practiced with Honeybun for six weeks. I know you have the skills to complete the job. It's a matter of whether you'll let yourself use them to succeed. When you've managed to get the mares to gather in the corner with you, we'll know you stayed calm enough to communicate."

Steve hiked his large frame over the sturdy wooden fence, landing with a loud humph. All four mares began to nuzzle his shoulders and hands. "Good girls," he said quietly to the horses.

I saw Joe's face turn ashen. The equine-assisted therapy sessions had pushed him to the far edges of his comfort zone. Asking him to get in the pasture with his family and four unpredictable animals was like asking Loree to feed a live rat to a snake by hand.

As I lifted my right leg over the fence, I shuffled through memories of Temple Grandin's books and Mia's milk carton town, tripped up by the word "communicate." *Remember, don't tell but talk and listen.* Our feet had barely hit the ground when the mares sensed our disorganization, and some discontent. Sixteen hooves kicked up a cloud of dust as they bolted with fear. We watched with mouths agape as the mares galloped over a ridge and out of sight.

"Mom! Dad! Come on," Anna and Mia yelled in unison as they pursued the horses.

Joe and I staggered, breathless, over the ridge to see Anna and Mia standing surprisingly close to the resting herd, nibbling grass not far from the corner. The girls were holding hands, their free arms stretched outward, parallel from the ground.

Mia yelled through a whisper, "Anna and I came up with a plan. Come grab our hands. We'll make a human fence."

"Yeah, together we'll slowly drive the horses to the corner. It won't take long. Look how close we already are," insisted Anna.

Joe and I, propelled by adrenaline, were in no mood for discourse.

"Get out of the pasture now before you get hurt!" Joe ordered through clenched teeth, thrusting his pointed finger towards a gate on the other side of the pasture.

The girls stood united in their plan. Eyes fixed with confidence. The horses picked up their heads in unison, eyes wide, ears twitching forward and back, chest muscles quivering.

"Come on, Mom. Tell Dad we know what we're doing," pleaded Anna and Mia, hoping I'd convince Joe to listen. In a louder tone, they both cried, "This will work! We know it will!"

The four horses, sensing the growing friction between us, galloped past us to another part of the pasture.

"You didn't even try our idea. Now they're gone," sobbed Mia, hands covering her face.

A frustrated Anna continued, "The horses were calm when you got here. They knew we weren't going to hurt them. YOU didn't even give US a chance." She turned abruptly and bolted down the hill. "Come on, Mia. Let's go follow 'em."

In no time, Joe and I were alone on the hill, the realization growing that they were right. We hadn't listened to their idea. We tried to take charge, doing the very thing Steve warned us not to do.

Humbled, we ran after the girls. Gathering them in a big hug, we offered a sincere apology and stood as calm as we could under the threatening sky, listening to their plan. Once briefed on our roles, we ran to find the horses. Joe and I steeled our anxieties while locking hands with Anna and Mia, arms outstretched to form a human fence.

Our two young leaders began to talk soothingly to the horses, and to us.

"It's okay."

"Breathe deeply."

"Move slowly."

"Good job."

In a matter of minutes, the horses walked calmly to the corner and ate from our hands. Audible relief came from Joe as he strode quickly though the now-open gate and continued until he was seated in the car. Mia and Anna whooped and hollered, jumping up to give each other high-fives once they were out of the pasture. I was overjoyed to see their exuberance, but a bit deflated that I hadn't listened to them sooner. I walked quietly to Honeybun's pasture to say goodbye. The four mares had been our final test. Honeybun had prepared us well. Steve stood beside me, and said, "Your family did well here. You'll do well at home if you remember what it means to be a confident leader, one that attracts rather than repels. Breathe calmly, listen, discuss. The minute you try to force your will, the faster they'll turn and run."

"Thanks," I murmured.

"Oh yeah, one more thing," he added as I turned to join my family in the car, a gentle rain turning dust on the windshield into muddy rivers. "Go easy on yourself. You can never achieve perfection in parenting, but practice goes a long way."

I was trying to recall our sessions with Dr. Steve and Honeybun as the hairbrush fight in the hallway intensified. What came to mind instead was the code Loree and I used to use with each other when our parenting frustration escalated. If one of us uttered the words, "I want to eat my kids," the other would know instantly something was amiss. I knew I should walk away from the fight to dial her phone, to vent to a good friend. Steam was building, pushing against the hinged lid of the spout, but the intense energy created by two teenagers fighting like giant toddlers sucked me into their fury like a magnet.

"STOP! IT! NOW!" I roared like a stoked fire in a steam engine.

"WOOF!" responded a fretful Margo from the paddock. Her "Woof, woof, woof!" was joined by a stream of high-pitched yip, yip, yips from Rascal and Sid. My head immediately turned in the direction of their distress.

"Go ahead, Mom," Anna retorted. "Go check on the dogs and leave me here with Mia. You love them more anyway," she sneered, looking down at me from her much greater height.

"Really? That's your response? Does that mean you really did hit Mia?" I asked, hoping my backhanded accusation would stymie her posturing.

"I knew you'd do it. I knew you'd find a way to blame me. You always think I'm the bad one!" Anna turned abruptly, the loose bun of her ample hair bouncing with each heavy step, until bam! The door to her room slammed shut.

"Mia," I raged to the only body left, "Why did you hit your sister?"

"God, Mom. You're such a sucker. She challenges you, and you cave," she countered. "Think about it. Why would I hit her? So, she can hit me back? Do you think I want to tangle with her strength?" I thought about that very point as Mia, almost my height, tore her eyes away from mine and retreated to her room with an equally forceful slam of her door.

Anna's ADHD was considered "hyperactive." On one hand, she produced too much adrenaline at the wrong time and place—class lectures, restaurants, fights with her sister—and not enough when focus was needed, like during class lectures, homework, and resolution. It was easy to blame Anna as she was often the one caught poking and prodding her kid sister, who suffered from "inattentive" ADHD. It bugged Anna that Mia didn't have the same energy level she had, complaining often that Mia was lazy and spoiled. Mia would counter that Anna was a bully and disruptive. Both were right and wrong. Yet neither girl was standing before me to engage in discussion.

That's when I remembered psychotherapy never works when the horses are running away. I should have entered their turbulent situation in a calm manner as the confident leader. But I didn't. I'd thrust myself into their mayhem. "Duh," I exclaimed to no one as the palm of my hand thunked my forehead and dislodged the wise lessons of Dr. Steve.

"I'll have to give them time to vent, then have a calm conversation," I said to no one in the empty hall.

I retreated to the paddock to check on the dogs. Three barking canines greeted me with toothy smiles and dangling tongues. Rascal and Sidney hopped on their back legs, front legs pawing at the air, begging me to pet them. Margo laid a gentle paw on my leg. *Yes, sometimes, it was easier to love the dogs. That didn't mean I loved them more.*

Three days later we had a call from a potential adopter drawn to Sid's profile on Petfinder. Dione, a schoolteacher, and her eight-year-old daughter, Grace, came to our house to meet him. Anna and Mia were holed up in their stifling rooms, still hating the letting go part of fostering and still angry at me for not picking a side in their fight. Sidney relaxed in Grace's arms as she told me how she longed for a pocket dog she could dress up at play time and snuggle with at night. Rascal and Margo let out little whimpers, toenails clinking, as they chased rabbits in their dreams under the cool breeze of the ceiling fan.

A gentle rain began to pitter-patter on the roof as Dione backed out of the driveway with Sidney. Unable to unleash my sorrow on the garden weeds or the winding road, I grabbed our bags of water-worn beach glass and emptied them on the table in the screened porch. No artistic inspiration came, so I sorted the misshapen pieces by color. It always seemed we collected more green than white, but the pile of white was growing bigger than the green. Off to the side was a smaller pile of beer-bottle brown and a tiny pile with four red pieces. In the center of the table I placed one pale pink-frosted gem.

Anna and Mia, unable to stand the summer heat of their rooms and the stillness of the house, subtly sat themselves at chairs around the table, fingering pieces of glass, putting a few together, gently tossing them back, taking more. Nothing was said as distant thunder rolled gently through one screen and out the other. Rascal, while not as scared of storms as Sierra had been, curled his body on my feet. Margo laid down between Anna and Mia. She looked up from slumber when Joe slid himself into the last seat to let the etched glass pieces sift through his fingers.

Retreating to the corners of the ring hadn't solved the discord between us, but it did provide a much-needed cooling off that would yield a platform to talk calmly and to listen. Someday. Hopefully soon.

WRIGLEY

Chapter 15

My neighbor Gracie, with bouncing blond curls and cherub cheeks, peered longingly at Wrigley, an all-golden Puggle that looked neither pug nor beagle with enormous puppy dog eyes. "Cindy, can I pet your dog?" she uttered with an almost inaudible peep. When I gave her the go-ahead, she gingerly walked forward and stretched her tiny, kindergarten hand towards Wrigley. She was no closer than ten feet when he decided it was his decision, not mine, to meet her. In the blink of an eye, Wrigley backed away from the taut leash, rolled his shoulders forward with head down, and slid free of his harness, sprinting away from Gracie as if she were a stalking wolf.

I rushed after him, fear choking me as the distance between us lengthened. Wrigley had been with us just three days. We had no bond. He was hundreds of miles from the South Dakota Indian Reservation where he'd been rescued before the round-up.

I finally reached the crest of the hill in time to see Wrigley descending the other side. As he neared the spot where I'd scooped a trembling

Poet from the pavement before rushing him to the emergency clinic several years before, a mallet began banging a steady beat in my head, the internal pounding a stark contrast to the tranquility of a neighborhood drenched in autumn sun.

I saw my neighbor, Jan, round the bend below my house. I would've screamed, "Freeze," to keep her from spooking Wrigley, but the heaving in my chest prevented any sound from leaving my throat. It didn't matter. As soon as Wrigley spied Jan, his eyes grew wider. Pivoting like a quarter horse around a barrel, he ran up the hill and into me!

Wrigley's reactive fear provided plenty of opportunities to reflect on parenting teenagers with anxiety and ADHD. Too much push in a direction for which they weren't ready, and they'd roll their shoulders like Wrigley and run. Too much pull on the reins of control, they might thrash their heads and buck authority.

Prior to Mia's ADHD diagnosis, she ran with a pack of kids we knew and liked. They treated each other respectfully and enhanced each other's goodness. Mia's twelfth birthday, however, ushered in kids also struggling with puberty, self-image, and a host of mental health issues. One of the new friends that emerged after the cell phone bullying incident was a quiet girl named Abby whose parents went through a tumultuous divorce during her freshman year. The mom often answered the door with a hard drink in hand, clear liquids sloshing over the rim. Adults without jobs, sometimes accompanied by kids, were transient boarders in Abby's home.

A few years passed without much drama until the summer Anna prepared to leave home. One morning when the bulb of the thermometer threw a tantrum and nearly boiled over the top, I drove to Abby's to drag a surprised Mia home from a sleepover. Anna had willfully remarked that Abby's unemployed, often-drunk aunt, now living with Abby and her mom, planned to take the girls and a few other friends to a secluded beach along the river. Anna worried out loud, "Do you think she'll try to be the cool aunt and provide beer to the girls?"

"Screw you, Anna. I'm never going to tell you anything again," shouted a pissed Mia, hands clenched, arms stiff at her side.

Anna, smirk on her face, retorted, "Not my fault. You shouldn't hang out with such loser friends."

"Talk about a loser, tattletale Anna." Mia's face contorted. With her naturally arched eyebrows deeply furrowed, she blasted back, "Did you think Mom would love you more for telling on me?"

A knot pulled tight in my stomach. I'd eagerly taken Anna's bait, knowing Anna tattled out of spite, amplified by a healthy dose of fear for Mia.

Two weeks later, I sat at my desk as Mia rushed out the front door with a quick "Bye, Mom. See ya tomorrow." The deafening, chug-chug-chug of a muffler-less car drew my attention to the front of the house as Anna burst in to my office.

"Mom," she started. "Did you know Mia's not going alone with Abby but sneaking out with boys?"

I willed myself not to look out the window as an argument brewed in my head: prove Anna wrong or prove Mia wrong. I wasn't sure which outcome was better. Desire for resolution forced my eyes in the direction of the deafening noise. As I did, I saw Mia slide quickly into the back seat, not the front seat with Abby, to sit next to a male I didn't know. This wasn't a girls' trip to the mall as I'd been told. Tattling Anna had been right. I grabbed my keys and jumped in my car. Revved up, I was prepared for a high-stakes chase to the mall. Instead, Abby drove home. Two mid-teen girls emerged from the car with two young men.

I slowed my car to let them enter the house, oblivious to my rotating tornado picking up speed. I rang the doorbell, predicting Abby's mother would answer with drink in hand. She didn't disappoint.

"Where's Mia? Who the hell are the young men with the girls?" My voice was high-pitched and quavering.

"Phun iss Abby's long lost cushin," she slurred. Flicking her hand in a casual manner and giggling, "Heeee's stayin hur wif mee." The "distant cousin," twenty, and his nineteen-year-old friend, were the newest guests in her transient hotel. Registering the horror in my eyes, she straightened a bit and added, "Thon't worry. Nofing badddd can happin. I put Abby on the pill yurrrs ago."

"Don't worry? The pill?" I shrieked, no quivering voice now. "Mia is fifteen years old. She's not old enough to be hanging out with a twenty-year-old man!"

Abby and Mia (the two guys long gone) peered through the wooden spindles behind their perch on the stairway, looking like guilty puppies in a crate.

Mia squared her shoulders. "Mom. You're overreacting. They told Abby and me they like being with us because WE aren't like girls their age."

"Oh God, Mia. You fell for that shit?" Using air quotes, I continued, "They 'like' you because YOU aren't experienced enough to know when you've being played! Forget pregnancy and the pill. Think about manipulation, the potential for sexual assault!"

I turned to Mia and told her I would walk out the door without her if she could look me in the eye and tell me she felt 100% safe with two guys she didn't know, being defended by an inebriated adult. In what I can only describe as a small miracle, Mia's ability to self-advocate, once held captive by ADHD and low self-esteem, broke free. She grabbed her bag and left with me. It was a giant step upward from the downward spiral.

The spiral, however, didn't spin quickly enough to align two sisters. Anna felt smug about the incident. Mia expressed relief she was safe but outrage at Anna for tattling. Mia and I skated on separate sides of conversation while glass on the highway to Anna's departure continued to shatter, releasing shards of bickering, and jabbing that continued to D-day.

Anna was packed days before leaving, all the boxes on her checklist checked. The kid who seemed so worked up over change was ready to roll at sunup on freshman move-in day. Fields flush with spinach-green sugar beet leaves, stalks of golden wheat, and unending rows of cheerful sunflowers stretched across the table-flat river valley towards an azure horizon. Little was said on the five-hour drive. I could feel Anna's emotional roller coaster colliding with mine. Excitement. Dread. The flapping of wings before soaring. A tightening in the gut just before feet let go of the edge.

We channeled our energy into shuttling stuff from car to dorm room. Joe busied himself with trips to the local store for items forgotten or things we didn't know we'd need: a few extra hangers, magnets for a white board, a surge protector. Anna arranged as I unpacked. Pleasantries were exchanged with the strangers moving their daughter into the room. As the small space became more chaotic with people and stuff spilling out of boxes and bags, overstimulation engulfed Anna. I noticed her casting dark glances at her roommate, a stranger with whom she had so little in common except they both checked a box for "early to bed and early to rise" on the college questionnaire. Soon her agitation turned to me since Mia wasn't there to poke and prod. "I can do this, Mommmmm. You don't need to help." By evening's end, she complained her stomach felt like someone was pulling on both ends of coarse and knotted rope.

Joe and I, tucked into a small motel surrounded by the stubble of harvested wheat fields, quarreled over what to do about her pain, welcoming the argument as a distraction from the loneliness on our first night without Anna.

Nothing was unusual about the onset of Anna's pain. It arrived the same way many other anxiety-induced ailments had come. Discomfort would sneak into Anna's pores, congregating as an angry crowd in her gut, then erupt as fury when the pressure exceeded her limit. Joe thought maybe the pain in my heart was blurring the current situation and amplifying my fear. *Maybe.* We tossed and turned and hoped Anna would prove us wrong.

A complaining Anna greeted us at the cafeteria for breakfast. "Mom, I really feel sick. I tried to vomit, but I can't. My head and neck are killing me," she grumbled as she lowered her head to her outstretched arm resting on the table. I touched the back of my hand to her reddening forehead. I gobbled some toast. Joe poured his coffee into a to-go cup. We drove to the only health clinic in the small town as my mind raced to meningitis and the awful days when Mia and Joe were tethered to hospital equipment in dark isolation wards many years before.

A brief check-up and suite of x-rays yielded nothing conclusive but the potential for early-onset strep throat. We rushed out of the clinic, made a mad dash through a pharmacy, and pulled into the dorm parking lot in time for the parent forum and freshman orientation.

Two hours later, it was time for our inevitable departure. Anxiety was the driver with words spilling out of our mouths to fill miles of highway that would soon be between us. I couldn't help but remind Anna about the prescribed medication.

"God, Mom. I'm eighteen, not two. Leave me alone," she protested as she reeled away from me. My head nodded in agreement while a leash tangled around my throat.

"Sorry, Anna. You're right. I've been parenting so long it's hard to give it up."

She pulled my leash tighter. "I'm sorry, Mom. I'm sorry for being such a jerk over the summer and for snapping at you now."

I could feel her toes gripping the edge of the nest, preparing for that final push. The quick amends to enable a clean break. We hugged, tears spilling onto shoulders locked in a tight embrace. Joe, growing impatient with our unending Minnesota goodbye, honked the horn, flashed the lights. I stepped back to watch Anna's wings flap—one more test of strength and resolve. She flew, or I pushed, or some combination of both finally steeled her from the nest. My last memories are my tears contorting her face and her waving arm growing smaller in the rearview mirror.

A few hours later, when the last of the tissues were gone and acres of golden sunflowers ended, I thought of Jackie from many years prior. She had warned me about this day, of the uncertainty and fear of letting go. She said I would be consumed with a sadness that would heal with each tick of the clock. Into its space, would be a new focus on me. A deep sigh escaped like a large bubble bursting at the surface of a lake. I couldn't imagine that day would come.

Mia, with Margo and Rascal in tow, greeted us in the driveway, anxious for an update on the weekend we'd all been wondering about for so long. Into the hurried space of a kid ready to get on with her day, we exchanged a few sentences. She gave us each a hug, then rushed to her friend Michelle's for the night.

I immediately busied myself to keep from being swallowed by the quiet. The animals were hungry. The dogs needed brushing to remove burrs from their fur. Laundry was waiting to be sorted and washed. I walked to my closet to empty the suitcase carried upstairs by Joe. An envelope propped on the window ledge over the sink caught my eye. There was no external salutation, so I turned it over to lift the flap. Inside was a handmade card, itself a collage of handmade papers created a decade before on one of our craft days with Loree. Written across both pages was a thank you letter from Anna to Joe and me.

My mind flashed back to the morning we left for college, of Anna unbuckling her seat while we were still in the driveway. "Wait," she implored. "I need to say goodbye to the pets one more time." It must have been her ruse to plant the letter in our room. Or perhaps she did say goodbye to the pets, knowing she'd asked Mia to put the letter in the window for her.

Anna's words painted a picture of a daughter grateful for the gifts of tenacity, independence, and compassion that prepared her for leaving. She wrote how Joe and I exhibited friendship, teamwork, and love. She spoke of being hopeful about her future. I was careful not to let my tears blur her carefully penned words. I tucked the letter into the envelope and placed it back on the ledge. A smile spread upwards from my heart as I remembered my letter I'd written to Anna and paperclipped to the first day of school in her college planner.

Mia and I spent the following afternoon at the Minnesota State Fair, one of the largest fairs in the country. We'd picked a weekday in hopes the crowds would be smaller and lines shorter, making the late-summer day feel less hot. Our first stop, as usual, was the pig barn. Mia enjoyed taking close-ups of wet pig noses as they squealed for food. Her intent: to send as many videos and photos to Anna who was unable to attend the fair for the first time in years. We walked the horse barns and said hello to a friend of Mia's standing with her horse in the Parade of Breeds exhibit.

In the Coliseum, Mia and I watched the draft horse teams compete in a show of beauty, might, and technical expertise. I swallowed deep sorrow as memory after memory of a week several years before when Anna and her rental horse, Theo, competed in a show jumping competition in the same arena. Then a quick smile spread across my face as I remembered the final picture of the day, one of goofy Max wearing Anna's show coat over his man-capris, with sleeves much too short for his long, thin arms. Next to him stood Anna's grooms for the day, Mia and vaulting friend Lexi.

Mia and I were stuffed with fair food and exhausted from walking as we slumped in a suspended state of fair bliss on the shuttle bus to the park-and-ride. I was unprepared for Anna's hysteria when I pressed answer on my phone. "Stupid coach! She just told us we need a physical on file in order to ride in an NCAA facility, a little detail she failed to tell us freshman over the summer. If I don't have the physical by end of today, I can't ride at tryouts," she sobbed.

"I don't understand?" I spit out in a whisper, trying not to attract attention on the bus. "Tryouts? I thought you were already on the team?"

"I am on the team, but I can't ride until I have a physical," she wailed. "That won't be until Thursday. I'll miss much of the week. What will my teammates think now?" My heart rate increased to keep time with Anna's. I'd been beside her the many days she battled judgment, real or perceived, from her peers. She spent high school clawing her way back to normalcy, working to prevent the stares caused by disfiguring acne and impulsive behavior from ADHD. The opportunity to ride the first day would have put her on the inside of the ring. No physical on file meant she had to stand outside on the throne of judgment—again.

My mind twitched at the second realization afforded by distance: I was truly no longer in charge. At eighteen, it would be up to Anna to navigate doctors and coaches and teachers and therapists all on her own. I felt dark water swirling and rising.

Two days later, I was still fretting over the immense changes brought on by Anna's departure when I pressed "answer" in response to another call from campus.

"Mommmmmmmm," she railed. "Stupid small-town doctor. He won't sign the physical. Now I can't ride at all." She wept as I dug my fingernails into my palms, forcing myself to focus on my physical pain rather than react to hers. Instead of calm after the train leaves the station, an engine barreled around the bend in my head and shot off the rails, slamming into the wall of my skull as Anna wailed, "I have mono!"

"What? Mono? I don't understand."

Weeks of reoccurring stomach pain before she left for school. Fever, but no strep throat. Anna's gasp of pain when the doctor palpated her abdomen. Mononucleosis, a viral infection that simmers four to six weeks before percolating into a full-blown fever and enlarged spleen. It all made sense with the lens of hindsight.

Our kitchen took the brunt of my energy. The large stockpot banged against the metal grate of the cooktop and metal spoon clinked against metal pot as each ingredient for homemade chicken soup went into the mix. Heat multiplied in the August afternoon as bread baked in the oven. Joe packed the cooler and the car for another trip through farm country. He and Anna spent the next four days holed up in a suite at the motel surrounded by wheat stubble, Anna sleeping, doing homework, eating homemade meals, sleeping more. When Joe finally pointed the headlights home, he watched a much healthier, happier Anna return to a more stable college life.

I wanted to go with Joe but couldn't. Mia and her vaulting team were part of the State Fair entertainment in the Coliseum. Much like their event at the Midwest Horse Expo a few years before, the story of vaulting would be told through three horses and a team of girls in ballet slippers and glittery costumes.

The thermometer climbed into the upper 90s while holding hands with the humidity. Large ceiling fans in the old horse barn whirred as box fans attached to stalls kept the horses cooled. Parents and vaulters would take turns standing in empty stalls for a bit of dusty breeze.

Tensions were high in the practice arena as girls fell off horses when they'd normally stand. Teammates shouted rather than encouraged. The lungers tried to control horses attempting to flee the discord. It was one thing to vault two hundred miles from home to an audience no one knew. It was another to entertain the home crowd. Sensing the rising disarray, the coach gathered all the girls into a circle, arms cinching waists, to chant away the nervous energy. She soon had the circle unfurling like a fiddlehead fern into a line arranged shortest to tallest. Step, step, step, they marched in unison into the Coliseum to the encouragement of a scattered crowd.

The lights dimmed. The music began. Into the circles created by lunger and horse, vaulter after vaulter, sometimes solo, sometimes as a team of three, mounted the horses to dance and leap and twirl. Ten minutes later, the music stopped, the audience cheered, and the vaulters marched out, releasing an audible bubble of relief that floated to the ceiling and popped. Horses were groomed and fed. Shorts and t-shirts replaced hot tights and costumes. No longer the entertainment, the kids dispersed into the crowds of fairgoers to be entertained.

The next morning, with one day shouldering the end of summer and the start of school, Mia woke me, tears spilling down her beet-red face. She complained of intense itching and pain. My blurry eyes shot open at the sight of my youngest child, swollen from head to toe. We spent Labor Day in hard waiting-room chairs at the emergency clinic. When we finally met with a doctor, Mia received more of a grilling than a checkup. Did Mia use new makeup for the State Fair event? Did she eat anything unusual at the Fair—shellfish, mushrooms, nuts? Had we switched laundry detergent, shampoo, or lotion? Had she slept at a friend's house where she would have used new laundry detergent, shampoo, or lotion? To every question Mia answered no. Until the last when the doctor asked, "Have there been any changes at home?"

I was so affected by Anna's departure I hadn't considered how change was impacting Mia. Well, that wasn't true. I'd assumed Mia was fine, and probably relieved that Anna's leaving-for-college bluster was hundreds of miles from home. As silence settled over our house, Mia's anxiety amassed. Unlike Anna, whose agitation usually exploded in fireworks with shrapnel, Mia's turbulence turned inward. Night terrors and sleepwalking were her way of "working things out," as our family doctor used to say, when she was younger. The onset of puberty delivered lethargy, headaches, and body aches. She stood before me and the doctor in the clinic exam room as a head-to-toe hive. She missed the first day of junior year, lying in bed waiting for prescribed steroids to relieve the physical manifestation of change. I called Dr. Jeff. Mia and I needed help charting a better course through this life-altering event.

I knew it would take a similarly enormous amount of attention and intervention to help fearful Wrigley navigate the upheaval of being in a new home after years of suspected abuse in his old. Safety was priority one. He became the first foster dog to don my two-leash system—one leash attached to his harness and the other to his collar. Should our little Houdini try to sneak out of his harness, he'd still be clipped to a collar. I also put Mia and Joe on high alert around doors, urging them to check for the golden ghost likely to streak past their feet.

Mental wellness and trust were combined into priority two. Wrigley reminded me of our visits with the roly-poly pony Honeybun. Both dogs and horses need to know they are in the capable hands of a human before they unleash their personality and shed their trauma. There is no defined timetable for the process. It can be quick, like the confident Schipperke Betty's brief stay in our home. It can take months, like

Shelby's transition from puppy-mill-discard to family pet. Lynda once told me it could take a year for some dogs to believe they are home.

For Wrigley, trust began with the walk. Walks were short at first, out and back along the same route to assure him he wasn't being dumped. He became a happier dog with an empty bladder and seemed to enjoy his time with Margo and Rascal, unearthing smells and disrupting rodents along the route.

Wrigley, like Rascal, rarely tired. Walking merely primed him for boisterous play. We'd often attach the long lunge line to Wrigley's harness, like we did with Poet, and let him run circles under our watchful eyes. Once inside, he would toss toys from baskets and wrestle Margo.

Wrigley opened his circle of trust one person at a time. I was first. Mia, a reluctant second. He often rebelled like a stiff-legged toddler when she'd try to get him into his crate. The needle on his trust meter, however, moved far right the night she gave in to his fight and let him snuggle under the covers. From then on, they were best friends. That trust was quickly transferred to Mia's longtime friend, Michelle, whose relationship with Mia had ebbed during the Abby years, but was now flowing as it did when they were toddlers. There was no happier dog than Wrigley when he was wedged between two good friends during a sleepover.

Michelle's growing love of Wrigley turned into a full adoption campaign she unleashed on her parents, Robyn and Charlie. Their family dog, Jake, had died, leaving their Chesapeake Bay Retriever, Gunnar, without a playmate. Michelle thought playful Wrigley would easily become Gunnar's best friend. The two girls were in Mia's room when I heard a knock at the back door. There stood Robyn and Charlie who'd rushed to our house after Michelle's panicked phone call, insisting they had to meet Wrigley now or never.

As I expected he would do, Wrigley shied away from these strangers, clinging tightly to my legs. Robyn, however, was smitten with the little dog that looked like a mini golden lab with an underbite. She sat beside me on the sectional and rubbed his ears until his stiffness melted. He soon leaned into her.

Charlie, like Joe, couldn't get close. Wrigley appeared to have a fear of men, along with his fear of kindergartners. As soon as Charlie tried to approach, Wrigley became stiff-backed and wild-eyed. Rascal and Margo took it as a cue to sneak onto the sectional for attention from Charlie. Soon, three adults and two teenagers were wedged with three dogs on the cushioned L in the family room. Talk centered on Wrigley, house training, and his complex character. It shifted to Robyn and Charlie's Wisconsin cabin and our trips north with them. We laughed and joked. Midday turned to late afternoon. Into the ease of friends, Wrigley rolled over to let Robyn pet his belly.

It was fun to reminisce with Robyn and Charlie, but I didn't have a strong sense they were interested in Wrigley. Several days later, Robyn proved me wrong. She was so committed to his healing she'd already formulated a multistep, multi-month plan to transition him to their home. It was so like Robyn to analyze a problem then craft a solution to conquer it. What bewildered me was their choice of a reluctant dog like Wrigley. Charlie was used to puttering about his multi-acre yard with two loyal, obedient dogs at his side. Wrigley was neither.

A month after Wrigley's adoption, I rang Robyn and Charlie's doorbell. Under Robyn's watchful eye, Wrigs was making significant progress. He was hiding behind a chair in the family room when I entered but bounded quickly to greet me when he heard my voice. He alternated between catapulting his body into my legs and jumping like a pogo stick to try and lick my face. Soon he and big Gunnar were running circles around the furniture and playing tug-of-war with an old toy.

At some point, Robyn sensed Wrigley's need to relieve himself. She rigged up his double-harness system and led him out the door. There she hooked him to a long tether Charlie had fabricated to let him easily expend energy without worry he would bolt. Wrigley and Gunnar resumed their dog game outside.

Over the months that followed, and after the parade of kids and extended family who visited, Wrigley stopped hiding behind the chair when the doorbell rang. He began to anticipate good things: ample petting by guests, hidden treats, extra time outside with Gunnar. People no longer frightened him—not men nor kindergartners! Joe could stop by for a beer with Charlie and get a warm greeting from Wrigley. Under the watchful, caring eye of his new village, and the right blend of push and pull, he was becoming a less fearful character. The trauma of his past receded. That fostering victory served as my reminder that time can be a great healer if I stand out of its way.

SKIP

Chapter 16

Skip's ears could end wars, prevent heart attacks, and pacify teething toddlers. Black like an elegant party dress, they were soft as a puppy's belly. Many tried to pet him without touching his ears. Everyone failed, falling victim to the magically soothing fur radiating from the top of his magnificent black head. It still upsets me when I think about that beautiful puggle tied to a tree while the winter temperature dipped below freezing.

Skip was discovered on a South Dakota Indian reservation during "round-up," a barbaric method of shooting untagged and roaming dogs when no other resources exist to reduce the population of canines. Skip must have hated each moment tied up. His lack of leash skills indicated that a collar around his neck and a tether to a human were not part of his daily routine. Our first walks were chaotic and comical. Skip would shy away from the lead. Rascal would zigzag to get away from Skip. Big Margo would prance around the two in anticipation of some new game. Entangled in three dog leashes, I felt like a lassoed jackrabbit in a cartoon Western.

After one such episode, I let down my guard to untangle my wits. All three dogs were busy, noses to the ground, snorting and snuffling over some unseen goodie. At once, all eyes were drawn upwards to a chattering squirrel on a low branch. We stared in amazement as the squirrel fell with a thump to the ground at the feet of the dogs. This odd turn of events startled us all but only for a moment. While my brain played catch-up to those of the dogs, Skip lunged like a jaguar. As the leash snapped to attention, my elbow wrenched wickedly from its relaxed position. The short leash saved the squirrel, but I nursed my injured elbow for a whole year afterward.

Skip's initial disdain for a leash contrasted with his love of people. Any attention paid to him elicited exuberance and unbridled wiggling, his curly pug tail flip-flopping. He knew no personal boundaries, attempting over and over to weasel his thirty-pound body onto laps whether they were seated at the dinner table or on the sectional. Yet, he never challenged Rascal for the alpha position.

His strong desire to be in motion was the very thing that led to his love of the leash. He was soon sitting, butt squirming, in patient anticipation of the leash being clipped to his collar. I often brought the lunge line with us to the marsh at the bottom of our hill. I would hook Skip to the line and watch him and Margo crash through matted reeds and jump like ponies over fallen trees. Skip's smile would stretch ear to ear below his wrinkled nose.

Anna, several months under her saddle on the college riding team, was wearing her own smile. She'd been jumping rails and following hunter patterns in outdoor and indoor rings at colleges across Minnesota. She was glowing in success. Joe and I would pack a picnic lunch and drive hours to sit on dusty bleachers with other parents grasping glimpses of our kids paving a new way for themselves.

Jeff and Joanne were an easy-going couple whose daughter, Rhiannon, rode with Anna. I was thrilled Anna had forged a friendship with her; Rhiannon was that one good friend Dr. Bonnie said everyone needed to enjoy good mental health.

I was deep into a writing project after the last horse show of the semester when the sing-song ring of my phone distracted me from shuttling words from my brain to computer. Anna's name flashed on the screen, tripping my annoyance button. I'd quickly settled into the new rhythm Jackie said would come, the one where my days would become more about me than my kids. I could write or design during the day when the house was quiet instead of waiting till the wee hours of the night when kids and pets were tucked into bed. I was considering the idea of pressing the "In a meeting now. I'll call you later" button when I remembered a similar moment years before. And was I immediately sorry.

I'd finally secured a meeting with the head designer from a firm seeking partnerships with independent contractors. Negotiating a deal would've enabled me to meet a quarter of my sales goals with one client. We settled ourselves into wood chairs at a hip coffee joint. Two lattes with hearts swirled into foam were gently pushed aside as I opened my digital portfolio. I'd already swiped through several images when the phone in my purse vibrated. I ignored it, letting its sound blend into the whir of the espresso machine. One minute later it vibrated again, just as the table next to us erupted in laughter. I ignored that series, and a third, even though our family uses the three-call system to signal an emergency. I let the ringer vibrate till the end and continued with my sales pitch; dollar signs had buried any thought of family need. The last swallow of bitter coffee tempered by steamed milk brought a handshake and a deal. I did a happy dance in my car as I dialed Joe. The burnt aroma of roasted coffee beans wafted from my clothes as I waited for him to answer.

No answer. I dialed again. And, then a third time. Still no answer. I called daycare. I learned Anna had stepped off the bus with Mia to a chorus of the little kids singing them a silly song. Anna and Mia looped arms to dance with them in a circle. A mingling of feet resulted in Anna tripping face first into the pavement. She tried my phone. Then Joe's. He rushed her to the dentist, chip from her tooth in hand.

Mother guilt washed over me. *I should've excused myself to answer the phone. I should've been there for Anna.* Reason pushed against remorse. *But Joe was there. He took care of it. It doesn't always have to be me.* Guilt and logic continued to duke it out as I drove home. I rushed to wrap Anna in my embrace. She turned her road-rash face towards her pillow, snubbing me. Joe had been her hero that day.

Anna is in college now. I don't need to react to every call. Logical thinking? Yes, but fear of letting her down made my finger swipe the green button.

"Mommmmmmm, there are cats and kittens everywhere. Some dead. Some alive. The farmer said he doesn't care." Words were spilling from her mouth like a coffee cup tipped on a counter. "The few kittens still alive have crusty eyes and green goo sputtering from their noses like Crosby. Please," she deplored, "Can I rescue two kittens?"

"Farmer? Kittens? Where are you?"

"Rhiannon and I are on a field trip for our animal science class. We're visiting a dairy farm. The farmer said he only keeps cats on the farm to eat the mice. He doesn't provide vet care. When there are too many, he drowns them in the pond!" More gasping as she tried to reconcile the reality of farm culture with our effort to save each of our foster dogs. "I can't leave here and leave the kittens behind. I can't shut my eyes without seeing those kittens dying in the cold. I can't unsee what I saw." I heard Anna's plea, but my mind raced to Loree. She'd said that same expression to me on numerous occasions. She must have said it to Anna as well!

Loree was also the one who often reminded me, "Once you teach your kids to care, you have to be prepared for them caring." I knew her periwinkle eyes would sparkle when I'd tell her the story of Anna's kittens.

"All right. Take the two kittens with you. Bring them to the Humane Society. I'll pay for the donation with the surrender." I hung up the phone feeling pleased. Anna had seen a need. She called for advice before acting. We had a plan.

"Mom. Where did Anna get all these kittens?" Mia nearly bumped into me as she walked into the kitchen, head down, shuffling through Anna's text.

"What do you mean 'all these kittens'?" I hurried to look over her shoulder. In one video, seven—not two—dehydrated and disheveled kittens were hungrily eating at small bowls on the bathroom floor of Anna's dorm room. In another photo, a triumphant Anna and Rhiannon were framed by mangy kittens with matted fur and gooey eyes. I quickly dialed Anna.

"Anna," I shouted over the cacophony of mews. "We discussed two kittens. Why are there seven?"

"Mom, when Rhiannon and I went back to the farm more kittens had crawled onto the hay bales than had been there before. We couldn't just leave with the two we'd originally found. The new ones looked as near death as the others."

"Will the Humane Society take them all tomorrow?" I asked.

"Well, nooooo." A long pause was followed by a sobered Anna. I could hear her back slowly slide down the bathroom wall. Then a thunk as her butt hit the floor. "They won't take any of them. They have no space. They're overrun as it is." Voice rising in panic, she continued, "Mom, we don't know what to do. I can't keep seven kittens in my bathroom. Rhiannon's roommate is allergic to cats." She pleaded again. "Mom, tell us what to do!"

Silence surrounded me as I retreated to my corner of the ring.

"Mom! We need to know what to do," repeated Anna.

"I don't have an answer, Anna. Seven kittens are much harder to place than two. I'll have to make some calls tomorrow. Let's find out what our options are, then we'll make a plan."

I spent a full day making phone calls, trying to place seven kittens, with no luck. In the end, it wasn't my hours of effort that landed the plan. The kids rose to the occasion. Rhiannon would drive the kittens to her home halfway between the university and our home. Her mom, Joanne, would take them to their local vet for a quick checkup, and then host them through the night. Joanne and Jeff would choose one as a family pet, then drive the remaining six to a meeting spot between our homes. I'd rush three to a local vet clinic, where one of the partners would care for the kittens and find them homes. Anna was friends with the partner through the horse world who'd learned of Anna's plea for help via social media. Mia called our vet clinic and her place of employment. They offered to house the remaining three until we tested them for feline leukemia. Once cleared, the kittens would come home to the refuge waiting in Anna's bedroom here at home.

Rhiannon and her dad, Jeff, drove to a strip mall where Mia and I met them in a parking lot. As shoppers around us were loading their trunks with holiday gifts, we were stuffing six protesting kittens into the cat carrier in the back seat of my car. They'd been stuck in a cardboard box for the hour's drive from Rhiannon's farm. Hungry, they tried to suckle on our fingers as hands pushed each one into the opening. Mia buckled herself into the back seat while I ran to the driver seat eager to get the rowdy bunch on the road. I was just about to turn the key in the ignition when I heard Mia giggling with delight. I whipped my head around to see Mia, with a pie-eating grin, proudly displaying a bouquet of disheveled kittens in her hands, empty cat carrier by her side.

I'm always amazed how my adoration and frustration with my children can flip flop at a moment's notice. The genuine smile stretching across Mia's face was joy personified. Her deliberate disobedience was frustrating. I thought again of Loree. If I called her, she'd joke, "I bet you want to eat your kids!" Before I could unfurl a litany of anger, Joe's words from the girls' toddler years popped into my brain. "Stop fighting with them. Let them go outside without a coat. Let them get cold enough to remember to wear one the next time. Consequences. They've got to learn consequences."

I turned back to the steering wheel and put the car in motion.

"Mom! The kittens are crawling everywhere. I can't get them back in the carrier. What should I do? *Mommmmm.* Pull over! Help me!"

I glanced in the rearview mirror and caught the distress in Mia's eyes. I quickly turned my attention forward. She did not see my smile as I thought of consequences! Teaching Mia a lesson about consequences meant I, too, had to endure the mewing and the stink of kittens long in need of a litter box. I drove quickly to the two vet clinics waiting to receive our kittens. Our quiet car was barely in park in the garage when Mia jumped out of the back seat, making a beeline for the house. But I ran faster.

"Not so fast," I exclaimed, wedging myself between Mia and the door. "No one goes anywhere until the dogs are walked and the car and cat carrier are cleaned. You pick." Soon I was leashing up three dogs, happy to breathe fresh air as she donned cleaning gloves.

Two days later, Mia brought home our three kittens. She slipped them into Anna's room while I walked the dogs. It didn't take long for our two resident cats to know something was amiss. After wiping down the dogs' paws, I rushed upstairs to find Sunny and Brantley keeping vigil at the base of the bedroom door, letting out low grrrs of warning to its new occupants.

Mia distracted the cats with treats while I snuck into the room. Three exhausted kittens were curled in a heap in a dog crate. I spread eye salve on their crusty eyes, wiped their fur with a damp cloth like a mother cat, then filled their food dish. Closing the door behind me, I remarked how much easier it was to bring home kittens than a foster dog. Clean them up. Shut the door. Get on with the day.

Day two served to humble me. I staggered backwards from the stench of kitten poop greeting me at the door. Three feisty kittens wailed, pawing at the wire enclosure. They discovered the litter box, used it as intended, then played like toddlers in a sandbox. Clean litter, litter waste, and cat poop were scattered over the carpet. The bedding in the dog crate, soiled. The matted kittens—mattier. As I opened the little door to the crate, all three kittens sprang loose like Sidney the day I met him. They ran up my jeans, digging their sharp claws into my skin. I wrenched them from my pant legs, catching loops of fabric, and settled them in front of a fresh bowl of food. Quiet.

"MIAAAA," I wailed. "Bring the floor cleaner, lots of towels, a bunch of sheets, a garbage bag, and another crate."

"In a minute, Mom. I'm eating my breakfast," replied Mia.

"NOW!" I emphasized with the threat of a mother who means business.

She rushed upstairs with the goods, handing them to me carefully through a crack in the door.

"Hurry, Mia," I implored.

"MOM. I can't go any faster. I only have two hands to keep five pets from rushing past this door," she replied in exasperation.

"Get the baby gate," I yelled. "Put it in the middle of the hallway. Get the animals on the other side, then run in here with me."

Mia had just enough time to open the door and step inside before our two cats jumped the gate, leaving three barking dogs on the other side.

We cleaned quickly, spread sheets over the carpet, connected a second crate to expand the kitten condo, and restocked the litter box. I was just about to leave when Mia asked me to stay.

"Look, they feel better already," she said as three playful kittens batted at the string she was whirling over their heads. One spotted a little ball and wobbled over to pat it with its paw. The room filled with happy little mews as they jumped on our legs and suckled our fingers. I took the phone out of my pocket to take a picture.

"Oh my god, Mia," I exclaimed, "We've been here for three hours! I have a ton of work to do." I departed quickly, barely catching our adult cats before they sprang into the room.

That night, I dreamed of the White Ghost of Death, which was less of a dream than a remembrance of the risks of creating a prey-predator relationship inside one's home. A client of mine had asked us to watch her son's pet hamster while on vacation. The abundantly furry teddy bear hamster sat on a table near my desk. Bricks and thick books surrounded the outside and top of her cage to deter our predators from nighttime hunting.

Week one with Sophie was so successful she came back to our house late summer. We arranged bricks and books on her cage as we'd done before. One night, the slightest of peeps woke me from a deep sleep. Rascal was dreaming quietly at my feet. Margo, sitting up and staring intently at my eyes, had her ears cocked towards the kitchen. We both held our breath and listened. Nothing. Margo laid back down on the floor. I fell back asleep.

"Good morning, Sophie," I exclaimed, like I did every morning as I walked by her cage. *Hmmmm. Weird. She usually squeaks at me when she hears my feet on the stairs.* I detoured to my office, quickly removing the top bricks. My hand began lifting toys and digging through bedding. *Oh my god. Where's Sophie?* I sank to my hands and knees, looking under and around my desk, the filing cabinet, plants, dog beds. Nothing. I ran to the kitchen, grabbing a flashlight from the junk drawer, aiming it at the toe kick under the cabinets. Nothing. Just as the last beam of light left the underside of the refrigerator, I caught a flash. I flattened myself to the floor to get a better look. Instead of Sophie, I found an array of cat toys just out of reach. I was about to grab the broom to retrieve them when an odd shape on the floor in the dark pantry brought me back to the task at hand. *Oh god!* It was the tiny body of a skinned Sophie.

I was sitting on the floor of the pantry, hands cupping my face, catching the tears of shock when Anna walked in.

"Mia!" she wailed before remembering her sister was at her friend's. Anna ran upstairs for a shoebox and towel, then bounded down the stairs for art supplies from the basement. She was decorating the little casket when Mia walked in with Joe. Upon completion, we carried Sophie and the box to the backyard so Joe could dig a hole. We took turns saying a few words of remembrance before the last shovel-full of dirt covered her resting spot under the boughs of the wild cherry trees.

Sophie's death remained a mystery for about a week. We couldn't figure out how she escaped a cage she'd lived in for two years. The door had been locked. The bricks and books had been undisturbed.

One day as Mia walked by the empty cage, she noticed Sunny sitting next to it. "Mom! I know how Sophie got out of the cage," she proclaimed through raspy breath from running outside to the garden where I was cutting flowers for a vase. "I bet Sophie was sniffing Sunny near the wires of the cage when Sunny grabbed her by the face and pulled her through."

Mia was probably right. We were so worried about our pets knocking over the cage we hadn't thought about Sophie being able to fit through the gaps between the wires.

Later that day, I stepped into Anna's room to gather a few items for the washing machine. My eyes immediately focused on a hand-drawn picture of a white cat with evil eyes in the spiral notebook on her bed. Beside it was a poem titled "The White Ghost of Death." Awe tugged at my heart as I admired Anna's masterful use of words and rhythm to convey her anger at Sunny, her all-white nighttime companion turned hamster-killer.

I reminded the girls of the White Ghost of Death the night we discussed options for rescuing seven kittens. Any small creature we'd bring home would be at risk from the natural instincts of five predators in our home, especially Sunny and Rascal, proven hunters. I assumed Skip, from the grasslands of South Dakota, was a hunter, too. To reinforce the hallway, we added a second baby gate above the first one. The cats couldn't jump or climb over it, giving us enough time to get into the bedroom without worry of predators at our heels. A week went by as Mia and I juggled feeding and cleaning and playing without incident. But hungry kittens don't stay little. Our three soon outgrew their two-crate home. We had no choice but to give them full reign of the bedroom.

Oddly enough, giving them more space made them less destructive as they expended energy running from wall to wall, batting toys, and wrestling. The litter box, situated in a bigger box to contain the mess, became a place for business, not play. Our confidence was rising as each kitten was able to meow loudly with clear eyes and fluffy fur.

We were three weeks into kitten wrangling when I took a long break from their care to dedicate the late November afternoon to the dogs. Inordinate amounts of my time had been spent with the kittens, cleaning and playing and playing while cleaning. My computer called me to work as I hurried passed it to attend to the forgotten dogs.

I sat on the gentle slope leading to the marsh, watching Margo and Skip chase each other through the frosty reeds. Rascal, nose to the ground and ears pricked forward, scurried about the edge of the marsh, trying desperately to catch whatever creatures were scampering from him.

Guilt and annoyance that'd surfaced with the kittens' arrival eased with each ray of sun warming my face. Memories of the brief "me time" I'd enjoyed once Anna was settled at college rose to my attention. I sighed. Anna's phone call from the farm had erased the inroads I'd made. The eight animals in our care meowed and woofed louder than my personal and business needs, again.

An hour of idleness slipped by when a nudge at my elbow from Margo drew my attention. She was prancing foot to foot, signaling dinnertime. I clipped leashes to Rascal and Skip and walked home. Speckles of color danced across the frozen earth from holiday lights wrapped around our river birch trees. Two garage lights were casting green shadows up and down the west wall of the house.

"Looks like you got a jump on your holiday decorating," I called to Joe who was half-way up the ladder against the house. "Makes it feel like Christmas is coming. Now, all we need is snow."

"Don't wish for that, just yet. I have more lights to go," Joe yelled to me, as green light washed across his wide smile.

I fed the hungry pets and then left the dogs to slumber on beds in my office. Sunny and Brantley retreated to the basement. *That's odd. They usually follow me upstairs.*

With a fresh bag of kitten food and a few spoonfuls of tuna in hand, I removed the top baby gate, stepped over the bottom gate, replaced the top gate, and walked the length of the hallway to the closed door. I wrapped my right hand around the knob and wedged my right foot into the small opening, like a linebacker at the scrimmage line preparing to block the kittens from escape. As I peered into the kitten sanctuary, I was engulfed by quiet then panic. *Oh my god! Oh my god! Oh my god!* The kittens were normally like zoo animals at closing time, squealing by the door, demanding their food.

I hurriedly placed the bag and bowl on the floor, falling to my knees to check under the bed and chair for sleeping kittens. Nothing. I opened the closed closet door. Nothing. I looked on the dresser, behind the dresser, under the protective sheet on the bed. Not a trace of kitten anywhere.

"Mia! I need help! Come now! Pleazzzzze!" I pleaded through the open door. She barreled through the baby gates in reply to my panic.

"Where are the kittens?" she exclaimed as she ran in the room.

"I don't know! The gates were up. The door was closed when I came with their food."

Mia began to retrace my steps, looking under the bed, in the closet, behind the dresser. She was close to the old, crackled leather captain's chair when we heard a faint mew. We flattened ourselves on the carpet but saw nothing. Another mew joined the first. We looked around but no kittens. Mia grabbed the bag of food, shaking kibble against kibble. A hungry chorus of mews responded. I tipped the chair backwards until it leaned against the wall, and we could see the bottom. Little kitten bodies were stretching the canvas covering as if they'd been sleeping on a trampoline. Mia and I quickly grabbed the edges of the fabric, pulling it loose from the staples attaching it to the wood base. As we did, a pile of kittens fell to the floor, making a beeline for their food dishes. When my heart finally resumed a normal beating pattern, I looked squarely at Mia and exclaimed, "It's time to find them homes!"

Mia, Anna, and I reached out to our network on social media. The sweet, fragile kitten faces of Stormy, Squirrel, and Crookston pleaded to our friends. Within days, all three left the kitten sanctuary in Anna's bedroom to live forever with their new families. Timing couldn't have been better, as their leaving created space in Anna's bedroom for her first Thanksgiving break.

That same week, I called Reece and Joe. The two had been to our house the month before to meet Wrigley. Neither got that "love at first sight" feeling they hoped for. They left our home without adopting him.

The day they came to meet Skip, Joe and Reece brought their brindled puggle, Frank. They had a good feeling about Skip and hoped Frank would feel the same. Joe and Reece lived in a pet-friendly condo in downtown Minneapolis. A second dog would have to fit their urban lifestyle, enjoy long hours alone with Frank, and find joy in daily romps at the corner dog park. I'm not sure the meeting convinced Frank to embrace Skip, but their disinterest in each other was a better sign than aggression. Joe and Reece, however, were in love.

I entertained Skip and Frank with toys and treats while Joe and Reece read through the adoption contract. This was their last opportunity to opt out of the deal. I wanted them to be sure they understood their commitment as adopters. Thankfully, it only made their resolve to care for Skip more complete. They signed the contract and completed the application form. The family of three grew to a family of four with two puggles that looked neither beagle nor pug. Skip joined Frank in the back seat of the car. His beautiful black head wearing a wide grin was the last thing I saw as they rounded the corner at the bottom of the hill.

It wasn't, however, the last of Skip. Anytime I wanted a refresh, I'd stop by the store Joe managed at the mall to see photos and videos of Skip. During my first visit, I was surprised to learn Skip's name had been changed to "George Michael" after Joe and Reece's favorite TV character. Joe also sent occasional emails and texts with pictures of George and Frank, big smiles and white teeth, a bonded pair.

Those few weeks with eight animals in a prey-predator competition ranked as some of the most chaotic of our fostering years. I might not have noticed the pandemonium had Anna not left for college nor had I filled the void left behind with a focus on myself. The difference between bedlam and calm might not have been so great if only one animal had gone to a forever home instead of four. The extreme quiet, however, ushered in a new sort of nagging at the edges, something champing at the bit, waiting to thrust itself into the vacuum. On those occasions I'd pine for the soothing nap of George's velvety ears.

ODIE THE PUGGLE

Chapter 17

O die was the third puggle in a row to find a temporary home in ours. Like Skip, he had the characteristic wrinkly black muzzle of a pug. Like Skip and Wrigley, Odie had the square shoulders of a pug and a curly tail that flipped and flopped like an electric meter with a short circuit. Odie was the only one of the three puggles, however, to sport the handsome tricoloration of a beagle.

His delightful nature was surprising given he'd been seized from a property where he was found tied to an outdoor post in the deep freeze of a Minnesota February with no shelter, no food, and a bed of ice where his body tried to nest in the snow. He'd shed any trauma he might have harbored by the time he became an interim member of our household.

Odie was a toddler trapped in a dog body. When I tried to relax on the sectional, he'd tussle with Rascal, both pups pawing at my arms until I petted their heads. When Rascal would succumb to slumber, Odie would crawl onto my lap. If I wasn't sitting next to him, Odie would settle himself by sucking on toys like a pacifier. On a particularly sleepy day with no toys by his side, he tugged on the protective sheet covering the sectional until he got enough fabric in his mouth to form a nipple. As he drifted off to sleep, a puddle of drool formed a halo of damp fabric to frame his peaceful head.

Odie ate his meals with exuberance and sat eagerly for treats. His attention to food made it easy to use rewards as the incentive in house training. In less than two weeks, he'd earned our trust. With it came the opportunity to have run of the house with the other dogs. He'd dart from window to window to watch the chipmunks scurry among the garden rocks. He'd race Margo and Rascal to the front door at the crunch of encroaching feet or the dingdong of the doorbell. Odie especially enjoyed the freedom to tackle Mia when she came home from school, lavishing her with giant, sloppy kisses. (I gave up on training dogs to sit when people entered our house. Not because the dogs were untrainable, but because the kids were! They looked forward to coming in the door and having multiple dogs clamber over them for attention.)

Odie-the-Puggle, while exuberant like Odie-the-Fox, had no apparent need to be dominant in our happenstance pack. Rascal had not become a drooling mess with Odie-the-Puggle as he'd been when Odie-the-Fox crossed our threshold. We enjoyed eleven days of Odie number two flitting among our resident dogs like he was a best friend at the sleepover. On day twelve of his stay, though, I sensed an air of change in the canine barometer. At first, low rumbles of aggressive thunder reverberated off the walls. Some new conversation was being communicated in dog language; I wasn't privy to its meaning. As metaphorical lightning struck the ground between Odie and Rascal, the mounting and drooling of black poodle and tricolor puggle began. That message I understood well.

Odie transformed from perfect gentleman to challenger. Every walk became a test to see if he could seize Rascal's crown. Rascal would counter the threat by pulling as far ahead of Odie as the leash would allow. Odie would tug with his strong pug shoulders, attempting to overcome Rascal. Rascal would dance to the left. Odie would follow. Rascal would shuffle to the right. Odie kept step. Margo, always a laggard, would drag far behind to keep clear of the commotion. The occasional bustling squirrel or fleeting rabbit would render me buttocks-to-the-pavement if I wasn't paying attention to their swift shifts in effort.

Their canine communication was admirable. There was no passive-aggressive behavior so common in human interaction. Each dog clearly stated his intention and sought to achieve it. It was a clear demonstration of what Temple Grandin referred to in her book, *Animals Make Us Human*, as the blue-ribbon emotion of "seeking." Each dog was actively pursuing his goal. What wasn't praiseworthy was their new game of "who can mark the wall." Odie, taller than Rascal, tested his dominance, and my patience, by revisiting his original behavior of peeing high on the walls in our home. Rascal, who knew better than to mark, couldn't help but challenge once, then surrender. Soon after, Odie stopped marking inside.

Rascal backed down not because he was less than Odie but because his reasoning had become driven by a much greater goal: his commitment to me. He was a canine walking the fine line of wolf in a human world, genetics versus environment, feral versus domesticated.

The end product of his decision to choose human expectation over innate dog behavior was a rapid shift in his demeanor. He'd always been high-strung and sensitive, reacting to the slightest sound, the lightest touch. He was Felix Unger, obsessive-compulsive and neurotic, to Margo's laid-back, Oscar Madison inclination. My once athletic buddy, however, soon became despondent and withdrawn, turning away from me like Mia after her twelfth birthday.

Rascal's capitulation was the segue to my own shift. After many years as a micro-business owner and parent, with my foot firmly fixed to the pedal of my bumper car, fingers in a death grip on the wheel, and sparks zapping loudly like mosquitoes on a light trap, the bruises from the ramming of car against car were the signal I'd had enough.

I'd maxed out on the stress of balancing business needs, shifting marketing approaches created by the rise of social media, the fallout from the Great Recession, raising teens with mental health challenges, and my shrinking foster dog team. The crack in my water glass stretched from top to bottom. No sooner would I refill when I'd near empty. What I thought I needed was that miraculous hole-plugging tape as seen on TV, the kind used by the guy standing ankle-deep in water in a leaking, see-through boat. He'd rip off a piece of magic tape, apply it to the hole through the water, bail his boat, then sail away in his dry vessel towards the sunset. After years of patching my leaky boat, magic tape just wouldn't do. I needed to steer the boat to shore, drain it dry, inspect it for damage beyond the obvious hole, then tend to all the parts in need of repair. It was time for an overhaul.

I'd been a full-time employee at companies outside my own only twice in my professional life, both events leaving a sour taste from coughing up loyalty like a bad flu. I spent two years out of grad school with a small start-up offering marketing services to food companies. One morning, the four employees were summoned to the conference room.

"As you know, I've been working with lawyers to defend myself in a wrongful termination lawsuit with a former employee," began Katherine, squaring her diminutive shoulders and clearing her throat. "This business has been my passion. I don't want to lose it. The building, however, is my investment. I need to do what I can to keep from losing it." Her head dipped slightly with remorse; then her chin snapped up. "I've appreciated your loyalty and commitment to our work, but I'm closing the business as of today and transferring building ownership to my husband. If I lose in court tomorrow, there will be nothing for her to win from me." Just like that, our jobs were gone.

I spent the next two years operating a small food-marketing-support business from the fallout of my former employer. The kitchen in the old bank building, the site of my wallpaper fight with Joe, was a space for my creative endeavors: developing recipes for cookbooks, creating use and care manuals for appliances, and running kitchen appliances through scientific tests to conduct independent comparison studies. The main room where bank tellers used to exchange money with customers had become the collaborative space where I'd prepare and design food for photographers and camera crews to produce food photographs and TV commercials. We'd listen to music, eat catered lunches, and critique each other's work to improve what we'd deliver to clients. My growing portfolio of mouthwatering food images was rewarding. Getting the work in the door? Not so much. A whole lot of pounding the pavement, cold calls, and rejections meant a lot of ebb between the cash flow.

I'd just completed a demonstration of a new microwave product for a client at a national food show when I was approached by the owner of a food product development lab in Minneapolis. He offered me the opportunity to run his program. I jumped at the chance for a steady paycheck, profit sharing, health insurance, and sales commissions on the client projects I'd bring with me. I walked in their door in August and out again that same month two years later when the owner refused to address sexual harassment complaints and failed to honor my commission contract.

I dusted off my food styling portfolio, and I knocked on the door of every food photographer and manufacturer in Minneapolis, of which there were many in the shadows of the world's largest flour mills. I began a successful career as an independent food stylist. This obscure profession of preparing and designing food for cookbooks, advertisements, and TV commercials supported me through the early years with Anna and Mia. The lucrative pay meant I could work part-time for full-time income. The high demand for my design skills and lack of other professionals willing to put their work under the scrutiny of an unforgiving camera meant a reliable income for me when I wanted it. I could easily say I was "booked" and take the kids to the beach, a hike, or play in the fort we'd built in our backyard while the rest of the world worked.

Like the saying "all good things must end," the bustling food industry across the globe began to splinter. A local food manufacturer closed shop, spinning off its brands to two different food companies. One of those companies was snatched up by another out of state. Fifty percent of the marketing-based jobs the original company used to generate were lost, capsizing many local food photographers and small advertising agencies. Many businesses that hired me for gigs were drowning.

Into the melee came the development of digital photography. Its entrance onto the professional food scene was not cause for alarm until the cost of a quality, handheld digital camera became accessible to amateurs. People with writing prowess and decent photography skills flooded the internet with content. Online readers went crazy. Food blogging and pay-per-click advertising soared. Established food companies struggled to keep their large boats afloat in the shifting swells created by these influential writers and their foodie followers.

The work-life balance that Joe and I'd so carefully crafted was at risk. The "pinch me, I must be dreaming" job that paid me to create art in a collaborative setting was in jeopardy. I spent the next two years investigating creative professions that would enable me to work mostly from home. Into my backpack went mechanical pencils and a new laptop. I was off to interior design school at the only local college accommodating adult learners. I designed food by day and studied interior design by night.

In May 2008, I purchased a booth at a large home and garden show to sell the design services of my young company. People flocked the aisles to the frenzy of a construction industry on fire. I left the show with enough design commitments and contract down payments to put my company in the black. I breathed a sigh of relief; my small business had reached the critical milestone of being profitable in five years.

"Cindy, I'm so sorry to break the news," Susan whispered into her clutched hands resting on her lap. We were three-quarters of the way through the design of her kitchen. A contractor had been selected.

"Dave lost his job. I'm afraid we have to put the rest of the work on hold until we're back on our feet." It was October 2008.

"Cindy, we can't continue with our bathroom remodel," Martin uttered over the phone, his voice cracking as he continued. I could hear his hand brush away tears as he choked out, "Both Daryl and I lost our jobs this week."

The shrill of my cell phone made me wince. Like the Bill Murray movie *Groundhog Day*, I'd answer it to client after client choking back tears over jobs lost to the Great Recession. Before long, sixty percent of the architects in our community were laid off and clamoring for the same few employed clients as me. Out-of-work creative types with writing skills and digital cameras began to outpace food bloggers for readership and advertising. Design apps for the do-it-yourself audience flooded the market. I had to wipe away my own tears of loss and frustration.

Anna, concerned about our rising family conversations on collective belt tightening and its impact on horseback riding, caught me in the kitchen on a spring day when horizontal sunbeams illuminated the cat and dog hair scattered over the floor. I was bending over to sweep a pile into the dustpan when she startled me.

"Mom, I know what you can do to make money."

"You do?" I questioned as I gained my composure. Her hopeful voice mingled with the metal clang of dustpan tapping plastic wastebasket.

"You could dust off your food styling kit and go back to the studio part-time. You always said it was easy money." A wide smile resembling mine settled below her deep brown eyes.

It wasn't a bad plan, as self-serving to Anna as it was. I could work several days a month to supplement my design income. It would help me stay afloat while the economy crawled back towards normal. A jagged pothole of attitude, however, stopped me cold. The moment I shook my right hand with the college president as he put my design diploma in my left, I cast off my food styling career. Behind me was the juggling of a day job, night classes, and weekends full of homework. Stepping across the stage I'd felt light and hopeful.

My shoulders drooped at the mere thought of returning to the studio. It felt like defeat. While I knew I'd enjoy the collaborative, creative effort to produce tantalizing food images, I wasn't looking forward to crawling my way up from the bottom. I'd been gone too long to retrieve my top dog status. This old dog would have to settle for scraps.

Those bits of jobs here and there didn't prove enough against a tough recession hell-bent on a take-down of the design and construction industries. Unemployment lines weren't just filled with my homeowner clients but also many staffers from design and construction businesses who'd hired me for jobs in the past.

The need for money was the motivator forcing me to unfurl my tentacles from their commitment to design and stretch them into the depths of "design-related" work. I funneled my technical writing skills into a contract with a housing research team at the university. I wrote design content for other website owners and became a social media maven. Well, not really. I felt I should have been with the amount of blogging, tweeting, posting, and researching of hits and click-through links I was doing for myself and others. I was no longer a single-focused business but a Jill-of-all-trades at all hours of the day and night.

I felt like Rascal, forlorn and dejected, and like Mia when her anxiety overwhelmed her; I wanted to curl up on the sectional and sleep. I left the food industry with hopes of a stable income only to see that belief dissolve as the design world was etched by the acidity of the recession. My desire to be self-employed waned. My energy from juggling spinning plates and flaming batons tumbled. I became easily annoyed with people who told me how lucky I was to be self-employed; I'd achieved the holy grail to happiness. How often I'd heard, "It must be great not to surrender your freedom to an employer," as paychecks were deposited into *their* bank accounts and matching funds were invested in *their* retirement plans by said employer.

I was back to the "what now" mantra I'd chanted when watching the food industry unravel. It was time, once again, to recalibrate. Or not. Sometimes ignoring a problem provided short-term therapeutic value, just like those moments Joe and I went to opposite sides of the ring to cool.

I focused my attention on Rascal instead. Something had to be done with the little body curled like a frazzled ball of yarn, soulful eyes casting pleading glances. What made most sense was to focus my efforts on a new home for Odie. Somewhere with large windows for gazing and an immense yard for exploration.

Much to my amazement, his handsome face caught the eye of an adopter within three days of posting his profile. When I entered Mary's home, it was easy to discern she had a heart for kids and pets. The walls and furniture were adorned in shiny green shamrocks and pastel Easter decorations. A large basket of dog toys sat at the foot of a chair. Odie ran to Mary, greeted her heartily, then sat expectantly at the sliding glass door, tail wagging like a windshield wiper in a driving rain. He bounded out the door, running wildly through the maze of paths formed by raised garden beds and a secure wooden fence. As Mary's grown kids and grandchildren gathered in her backyard, Odie ran from person to person and garden bed to garden bed with the same mischievous grin that greeted me in February. It was all I needed to know he'd found the perfect home.

Rascal took no time reverting to his busy self when I returned without Odie. He rummaged through the toy basket for his favorite bone, then trotted lightly with it to the towel on the floor by the porch door. Joe lounged on the sectional, feet propped on the coffee table, scanning the main floor of the house, jotting notes on where he planned to hide Easter eggs in the morning. The girls and I sat at the kitchen table dipping hard-boiled eggs into colorful cups of dye. We all laughed at the vigorous gnawing and scraping of Rascal's teeth against bone. He had one eye trained on the outside bustle. The other was constantly scanning the floor for scraps. His muscles were primed, waiting to pounce on a tasty treat before Margo could realize something good had fallen to the floor. Rascal's life, like the words on Anna's old blue ball cap, was good. Mine still was unsettled.

SHILOH

Chapter 18

Soul-warming sun in an effortless sky guided us home from campus on Anna's last day of freshman year. Protesting from a cat carrier resting on the console between us in the car meowed Reggie, a Humane Society of Polk County inhabitant who befriended Anna during her volunteer shifts. It seemed like a reasonable request to let Anna adopt the beautiful tuxedoed boy I nicknamed "Mr. Muscles." Brantley, our young cat adopted from Anna's former riding instructor, had died suddenly of heart failure a few months before the end of the school year. Sunny, reclusive and noncommittal to Brantley when he was alive, responded with stretches of yowling in the depths of night. We thought another cat would ease her loneliness and the pangs of sadness her crying stirred in our hearts.

Anna's arrival home brought a flurry of activity when Mia joined us to unpack the car and make room for Reggie. Sunny, ever attuned to change, parked herself at the base of Anna's bedroom door to growl warnings at the newcomer slinking about from corner to corner, sizing up his new environment. I stretched my legs with Margo and Rascal, marveling at the cacophony of red-winged blackbirds ringing like telephones in the marsh. When I returned, Anna laid on the floor by the coat room, letting Rascal and Margo pounce on her. I was looping the dog leashes to their hooks when Anna shrieked in a fit of giggles from two dogs licking her cheeks. Through her laughter, she managed to squeak out, "Mom, what're we having for dinner?" Her laughter warmed my heart but caught my head in a lasso.

Flooding back into memory was Anna's insatiable appetite of an athlete and penchant for healthy food. She'd only been gone one school year, yet it seemed like I hadn't planned a meal in decades. Joe and I had eaten cereal for dinner on more than one occasion since Anna left for college, mostly because we could; social Mia was often out to dinner with friends. I was surprised to find in Anna's absence and Mia's busyness, I'd cast aside my inclination for family meals around the butcher-block table in the kitchen. Anna's request stirred both a longing and despair.

I enjoyed cooking for an appreciative audience. Anna was always the most thankful for a meal prepared to her liking and one served with family. I was looking forward to collaborating with her on menu ideas and to taking her up on her offer to shop or cook so I could garden or work. I'd spun so quickly into old habits of writing a grocery list and checking the shelves that I was blindsided by the knot of an empty money bag.

The string of our budget was already stretched and unwilling to twist to another plea, even one as important as food. The recession had cast many storms which I had weathered, but the constant battering on my business income had taken its toll. I'd done the same things over and over hoping for a different result. Nothing was working as it once had. It was time for real change.

I began consulting with a business coach to investigate ways to remain self-employed with a steady income. I'd been successful before. It seemed logical to believe I could do it again. When the waters grew murky, I lightly tossed out the idea of getting a job. The coach snapped, "Don't count on that option to save you. Employers don't like self-employed people. They feel their independent spirit is difficult to manage." My heart fell to my shoes as I shuffled to my car. As the back of my head hit the head rest, a thought jostled loose. *What kind of coach steers you to a dead end? What a stupid waste of money. I can do better myself.*

I turned the key in the ignition and drove to the library. To wander between the stacks, to wrench my head sideways in search of vertical titles on the spines, to crack open a book to inhale the words and dislodged dust, would be my comfort and inspiration.

A resume-writing book for professionals over forty nearly jumped off the shelf at my feet. The back cover flowed with reviews by individuals who'd followed the format to land the jobs of their dreams. I added the tome to the growing pile of books on resume building and cover letter suggestions guaranteed to land me the same.

As the sun tucked under the horizon, I grabbed an iced tea with lemon and dragged the bulging book bag to the porch. I cracked the cover to the book focused on the over-forty crowd and was startled to realize I'd become "one of those people" in the target audience. While raising a family and juggling a business, my time had been measured by new challenges, deadlines, and successes. Each birthday had been a celebration of life, not the passing of time. The concept of aging had been of little concern to me, until my eyes were drawn to the words on those pages. Like Loree's "I can't unsee what I saw," I couldn't unsee the new label, and its implications for me. It was hard enough illuminating my transferable skills. Making myself seem younger was a challenge for which I wasn't prepared.

That night, and many to follow, I paged through library books and scanned internet pages to discern the best way to massage words into snappy lines. As my contempt for the process expanded and despair at my prospects reached a new low, Lynda called. The need for diversion and the comfort of foster success led me to yes.

Shiloh bounded out from behind the counter at Life Care in hot pursuit of a Shih Tzu entering an adjacent exam room. She was moving so quickly I barely caught a glimpse of wide eyes, alert ears, and red fur. Immediately I thought Shiba Inu. Then I saw the familiar black saddle and feathered tail of Snuka and Sierra. My heart began to melt with the memories of two great dogs.

My wrenched arm tugged against Shiloh's taut leash to slow her down. She pulled equally hard, dragging me in a zigzag pattern to explore every inch of the waiting area. Her exuberance abruptly halted at the front door. She froze in fear; her confidence had apparently reached its limits. It took a lot of pulling and a handful of treats to coax her out of the building. I had to lift her into my car. When we got home, she slunk out of the car door, uninterested in the curious mix of smells in our yard. Shiloh remained aloof, keeping as much distance between us as the leash would allow—until we went inside.

She spied the basket of toys in the family room and dove in. Each ragged toy was quickly sampled and tossed aside like dirt flying when a dog buries a bone, until she reached the bottom of the basket.

Then she tested them all again, tossing them around the family room, watching them crash to the floor. Balls rolled. Squeakers squeaked. Shiloh even brought me rope toys to play a few short games of tug-of-war. Once she spied our cats, she began in earnest to entice them to play until she had them scattered to the basement stairwell. Soon she ran back to the carpet where she flipped on her back and wiggled in delight. She did not act like a dog that had traveled two states, undergone surgery, and was living in a strange home. She settled into ours as if it were hers.

While we knew little about our newcomer resembling a fox, a sled dog, and a stuffed animal rolled into one happy creature, Shiloh quickly became known as a "character," like Crosby. She lived life with gusto. If she were a person, we'd say she had charisma. Each morning began the same way: bolt out from behind Mia's bedroom door, chase the cats, go outside, eat a nibble of food, attempt to eat Rascal and Margo's kibble, chase the cats, and exhume all the toys from every basket. She entertained herself from morning to night. While our dogs napped, she played, she chewed, she invented games. Her favorite was to push a ball down the stairs, bark at it, run after it, bring it to the top and do it over and over and over again. She was like Anna; both were stones gathering no moss.

When she wasn't playing, Shiloh was smiling and following us from room to room. Her affection for us grew. And, with it grew my attachment to a dog with an eerie resemblance to my beloved Snuka. Her rusty face and body weren't a true match to his tan fur, but the black saddle, sweet smile, and feathered, curly tail with long strands of fur kinked into a flow of Zs were. I soon began catching glimpses of the dog we loved decades before, moving about my home in present time.

Shiloh would round a corner or come from a room and my memory would leap to Snuka, tugging my heart down the hall. Some days I wasn't sure if I loved her or hated her for stirring the longing I had for that perfect dog.

Shiloh, however, was nothing like Snuka when outside. She was a one-year-old pup through and through. Whereas Snuka loved to walk, and distance was the goal, walking to Shiloh was a new endeavor and nothing but a game. It was obvious in her former life she had not been acquainted with a leash. She was a dog of circular motion, wrapping around my legs and walking under the belly of Margo to pursue one singular goal—to play tug-of-war with one of the swaying leashes. The other dogs would pull away. Our walks would stop abruptly and frequently, whenever I had to untangle legs and leashes. For a good week, we were the neighborhood entertainment.

Eventually, Shiloh tired of the pursuit when no one engaged in her game. She then began to associate walks with fun. Squirrels chirped. Crows cawed. Her head jerked left and right in pursuit of sounds. Her nose would lead her in the familiar zigzag pattern I'd witnessed at the clinic. Anything she could toss, push, carry, or shove made her happy. In her mouth would be piles of fluffy cottonwood seeds, feathers, abandoned balls, and scraps of food.

Her inquisitiveness was a positive feature for becoming a good citizen. She quickly learned her name, a few key manners, and house training. After two weeks in ours, I knew she was ready to move to a home that would be hers.

Shiloh was all smiles and a big ham, so posing for the camera was no problem. Click, click, click, I captured one picture after another of a ball-loving, people-pleasing whir of beauty.

"Mom! You can't put Shiloh's picture on Petfinder. She'll be snatched up immediately. She'll leave our home before you realize just how much you need to keep her," admonished Anna as I flipped puffed and slightly charred homemade pizza dough over the hot grill. "You can't let her go. She's too special." At the sound of Anna's concerned voice, Shiloh, Margo, and Rascal ran to the screened porch from their lounging positions on the sectional.

Mia, arranging garden basil and fresh mozzarella on a disc of par-baked crust at the kitchen table, followed the dogs to the porch. "What? You're finding a home for Shiloh? You can't do that. I already lost Poet and Crosby. You can't take away Shiloh, too. She's my best friend." She didn't need to say more. 'Bad mom' / 'Mean mom' / 'I hate you, mom' all flashed in my mind like neon at the liquor store.

"I can't keep Shiloh. Not now, anyway." I tried to keep my voice steady as I flipped back my imaginary cape, squared my shoulders, and placed my hands on my hips. This called for the strength of "Resolute Mom."

"I need to focus on my job search. I need time to figure out the next phase of my life. Things are a bit confusing for me. I can't handle a long-term diversion. As much as I love her, I can't keep Shiloh."

"But Dad loves Shiloh. He'll be so mad when she gets adopted," they both countered.

"Yes, sadly, he will. But Dad doesn't like to walk three dogs or feed three dogs or pay the bills for yet another animal. Anna, you'll go back to college in August. Mia, one year from now, you'll leave, too. Who will help with all the pets when you're both gone?"

They had thought my yearning for Snuka and Shiloh's resemblance to him would mean we'd be a three-dog family. When they realized

Resolute Mom wasn't budging, they returned to the task of topping the pizza crusts before their final bake on the grill. The kitchen grew quiet with unsaid words.

I understood their anger, and their sadness. I'd already rationalized putting Shiloh up for adoption. I was ready to get back to me, and she was ready for transition. Keeping her longer would make it harder for her to adjust and for us to grieve. Thinking back to Crosby, I knew there would never be a shortage of dogs in need of a home. When the time would come to find my next great companion, I just needed to open our door.

Within a few days of posting Shiloh's story on the internet, I received a call from Don and Sharon, two people on one phone line eagerly wanting to learn more. I don't exactly remember the details of the conversation, but I do remember leaping for joy as minutes turned to an hour while the three of us talked dogs and kids and life philosophies. We had several more similar conversations to coordinate meeting times around work schedules and family obligations. By the time Shiloh's paperwork was signed, my comfort with this new family was solid; there were no red flags. I was already anticipating the follow-up phone call I would make to their home.

I wasn't disappointed. Don and Sharon excitedly shared story after story of Shiloh's busy personality, love of the neighborhood, and simple transition to their home. Their son, Jeremey, delighted me with his love for his new best friend, the one who plays ball with him in the stairwell. Minutes after the first call, I received a text message with their new family photo: three red-haired, smiling people surrounded by an exuberant, red-haired dog. Over the next few years, we received phone calls and photo texts from a family eager to share the joy Shiloh brought to their life. The thousand unspoken words in those photos were reassuring to the part of my soul that let Shiloh be lost to Logic. Those pictures kept me connected to my biggest foster regret yet.

ISABELLE AND ARISTOTLE

Chapter 19

Twelve-year-old miniature poodle Isabelle was surrendered to a no-kill shelter when her family's home was condemned. Ample care was provided at the shelter. She was spayed, seven rotted teeth were extracted from her pointy nose, her mousy fur was shaved to remove mats, and she was administered antibiotics for a bladder infection. Yet for all the care given, she was doomed. On her kennel hung a sign: "Caution! Snippy! Do Not Adopt."

Lynda watched Isabelle's deteriorating status with increased alarm each time she went to the shelter to pick up other dogs ready for release. One day, she'd had enough. The shelter wasn't doing any more to set Isabelle up for success. Lynda had seen a spark in Isabelle's eyes. She knew Second Chance and Life Care could make it glow. A thorough checkup found Isabelle in need of surgery to remove large bladder stones she could not pass in her urine. Her misery and snippiness were the result of excruciating pain, not of a dog gone bad. Two days later, she was staring into my eyes with the same soul-searching intensity of April the Shih Tzu as we sat side by side on the sectional.

Margo and Rascal seemed unfazed by the new addition that was paying little attention to them. As Isabelle healed, she often slid into deep slumber. During lighter moments of rest, she'd keep one eye open, tracking my every move. If I walked from the family room to the kitchen, she would follow in a flash. Walking from my office to the bathroom, she was sure to be at the door. Oftentimes, I could hear her toenails clicking behind me. In her excitement, the too-big bone she loved to chew would tumble noisily to the wood floor as she scurried to catch up.

Somewhere near the end of her first week, an understanding understood only by dogs occurred. There were no skirmishes, no growls, no baring of the upper lip over canine tooth. No drooling and marking like Odie the Fox and Odie the Puggle. Instead, Rascal was head down. His eyes heavy-lidded. He'd been deposed from his throne of dogdom by Isabelle. The silver-haired gal was wearing the crown.

Isabelle continued to break stereotypes as she recovered. Izzy became a "head up, eyes alert, take-the-stairs-two-steps-at-a-time leader." When I returned home, she'd explode from her crate with a broad smile to race about the house with tiny toenails clicking as they tried to gain traction on the floor. Plenty of raucous barking would engage Margo and Rascal. Soon all three would be running circles around the sectional scattering cats to quieter corners. To restore calm, I would leverage the word "treat." All three dogs would race to the kitchen to sit for a few nibbles. If she wanted more, Queen Isabelle would tip over her empty food bowl, letting it clang against the wood floor.

I grew eager for Isabelle to heal fully so we could walk beyond the back yard. Her need to expend energy was growing. Eleven days after surgery, I hooked her to my two-leash harness system and took her down the road with Margo and Rascal. We went a quarter mile, leaving and returning down the same path to assure her I would bring her home. By week two, we were walking several miles a day, Isabelle pulling and pulling to get ahead of Rascal. Rascal, in turn, was tugging at his longer leash to stay ahead of Isabelle.

One weekend, Joe and I piled the dogs into the car for a weekend retreat at Robyn and Charlie's Wisconsin cabin. The fall color was peaking. A crisp breeze blew through the woods as we let Margo and Rascal off-leash on a hiking trail. Isabelle was attached to four fabric leashes giving her 24 feet to run ahead of me. In what can only be described as a failed experiment, I let the leashes go to give her more freedom, thinking I could easily grab hold of the last loop. What I hadn't considered was the queen's need to maintain power over the former king. Joe and I watched helplessly as Rascal and Isabelle sprinted up and down the hills and around bends out of sight. No amount of yelling "Treat!" drew them from their quest to be number one. It was only when they realized Margo had turned back that they slowed. Gasping for breath in the brisk air, I snagged Isabelle's leash.

As the days marched on, Isabelle easily became another fixture blending with the furniture. She spent more time slumbering belly up, spent less time worrying about my whereabouts, and grew louder in her quest to protect our home from intruders. Her fur, once shaved tightly to her skin, was starting to curl and soften as it grew. On occasion, I would glance her way and her poodle nose would remind me of the cartoon dog Cleo, good friends with Clifford the Big Red Dog.

I would have listed Isabelle on Petfinder had there not been the threat of more bladder stones; a urinalysis at the vet's office indicated her special diet was not helping lower her urine pH. She had to stay in our care until we could find a food that helped. The only way to do it was to adjust her food and monitor her urine for progress. That meant collecting urine samples from a short-legged dog.

I tried standing by Izzy while she sniffed the ground, moving in closer with cup in hand when she positioned herself to go. My effort resulted in nothing more than a sideways glance of quick rebuff. After several failed attempts, I sought help from the internet. I typed "collecting urine from female dog" in the search bar and miraculously got an answer. Before our next trip to the paddock, I grabbed a soup ladle from the blue and white crock next to the cooktop and brought it with me as I led Izzy to the paddock. The long handle gave enough separation of distance from Izzy's bottom that she remained unaware as I slid the ladle under it. Urine in a cup in a flash with no hassle and no mess!

I immediately called Mia to tell her the story. She was an "undeclared" freshman with little idea what she wanted to study or become. Her love of animals had her pointing towards the veterinary profession, but she really wasn't sure. Nevertheless, I knew she'd appreciate my story of Izzy and the soup ladle. No answer. I left a message. No return call. On the third day without a response, I sent a text to her boyfriend. "She's fine," he quickly shot back, alleviating my rising panic. His brevity of text, however, triggered a different concern.

Positive self-talk reminded me Mia was not Anna. Anna, the kid who texted me goodnight without fail, had always been a homebody; two years away and she was still longing to be back. Her texts were a means to inspect the rope, ensuring the line home was still taut.

Mia's need for connection was much like the Colorado River coursing through the Grand Canyon. There were long, languid pools of time where our social butterfly flitted among friends with little need for family. When obstacles appeared in the shallows and water sputtered and frothed, she'd steer her raft to the security of our home shore.

A slight breeze stirred the humid air the August day we brought Mia to college. A group of student athletes assigned to freshman move-in day helped tote Mia's worldly possessions into her dorm. The small room breathed in and out like an iron lung as stuff was added, arranged, rearranged, and removed. Her roommate and parents had come and gone, leaving us to the finishing touches. I opened the tiny dorm refrigerator to chill Mia's favorite flavored water, only to find flat bottles of fancy liqueurs nestled in the wire holder. Red flags started snapping in the gales of my mind.

Alcohol wasn't a worry I'd had when Anna left for college. Once she'd built the ladder leading out of the hole of truancy and trouble-making sophomore year of high school, she reverted to black and white, straight and narrow. She was committed to her goal of being an accomplished equestrian rider. Irresponsibility wasn't going to stand in her way. I often wondered if the hole she fell into in high school was the "bottom" she needed to move forward with recovery.

I worried about Mia, though. When she was young, night terrors and sleepwalking were her way of expending anxious energy straining at the bottleneck. When puberty ushered in ADHD, our extrovert threw in the towel as pressure built. Rather than fight rising tension, she'd acquiesce. She'd snuggle up with the pets on the sectional and check out. It was easy to misconstrue her immobility as laziness.

Like a clock that once ticked must tock, Mia's pendulum, when recharged, would swing in a rush of adrenaline. With laser focus, she'd attend to her homework. She'd tidy her room. She'd complete waiting chores and art projects. She'd pack an overnight bag and spend weekends splitting time between friends. She never returned hung over, but bits of crumbs left behind on her trail often made us wonder what stories her paths could tell.

I recalled the menu of illegal substances available to kids when I went to college. I could only imagine how the options had grown. What concerned me most was substance abuse could become Mia's way to manage her anxiety and low energy associated with ADHD. An internet search had told me I had reason to worry. The clinking bottles chilling in the refrigerator sounded the alarm.

"Mia," I called over my shoulder. "Come look at this. I know you didn't put these here, but I can't help but think about your friend Mike." Mike had been kicked off campus day two of his sophomore year for having alcohol in his room.

"Oh, god. Why did she have to do that?" groaned Mia. "Don't worry Mom, I got this. I'll talk to my roommate about it. There's nothing you need to do."

Mia's sincere sigh of frustration provided calm for the moment. I backed off and completed my task of adding sparkling water to the little refrigerator.

Later, a group of upper-class students attempted to entertain worried freshman and parents with mediocre music on the plaza. Mia clung to Joe and me like Nina when she was separated from Skye. Mia peered at her peers but made no attempt to mingle.

"If this isn't what you want to do, why don't you go find your roommate? You don't need to hang out with Dad and me," I offered.

"I already asked her if she wanted to do something with me. She went to a party with her soccer friends instead." The loneliness sucked her enthusiasm like mud into a sinkhole.

We sat in the diffuse light at the edge of the dark patio, eyeing the other tables of parents and students with huge chasms of silence plunging between them. My thoughts were focused on Dr. Jeff, wondering what conversations between him and Mia led her, an urban girl at heart, to choose this remote school nestled in the bluff. I reflected on the turbulence that led to Anna's bumpy landing at school. The one thing she had to steady her wings was an instant community of riders and a team schedule providing structure. Mia was on her own. Our home, her bedroom, the sectional, the dogs, had all been her rock in the past. Watching her shrink in despair was like watching from shore as a kayaker, trapped against that same rock, struggled against wave after relentless waves threatened to drown her.

The following morning, a breeze replaced the oppressive humidity and whisked in a renewed energy for Mia. She put her arms around Joe and squeezed him tight before turning to me, letting her embrace settle briefly into our mingling tears. She straightened her arms and looked me squarely in the eyes, "Mom, I'm going to be okay, I promise." She quickly gave me one last hug, then raised her hand to flag down a group of kids walking across the plaza. "Hey, wait for me," she called, her voice light and hopeful. Joe and I looked knowingly at each other. Only Mia could make friends in a brief amount of time!

Rascal and Margo greeted us with the usual cacophony of barks and whimpers when we returned home. I immediately readied them for a walk, seeking connection through the leash and a tether to the earth. Our home with no kids made it feel as if I would float into space.

I left two hot dogs in the paddock in hopes the breeze would keep them comfortable. Climbing the stairs to unpack my suitcase, I witnessed the trail of Mia's last moments home, of items discarded while she weighed their importance and things she tried to squeeze, but couldn't, into our car. Like a light wind coaxing the embers of a smoldering fire, my temper began to rise as I assessed the work in a stifling house. And then it hit me. I could wait. There was no immediate need to attend to the mess. No kids would be home to make it grow.

I took a deep breath and turned to my room. My eyes caught sight of an envelope addressed to me and Joe propped against my pillow. I slowly sank to my bed as I removed two folded letters—one white, one yellow.

The white paper was the first when I lifted the flap, so I started there. From top front to lower back, I read two pages of appreciation from a kid grateful to be accepted as herself in our home and thankful for the opportunity to seek new challenges, knowing we'd always have her back. Warmth coursed through me like a hot shower on a cold day. I smiled wide like Odie the Puggle.

The other was a letter written at school before the "mock crash," a solemn theatrical performance of select students, local emergency responders with vehicles, and wrecked cars from actual drunk driving incidents strewn across the football field before an all-student assembly. Mia had been one of the passengers "killed," complete with makeup and torn clothing to enhance the reality.

The letter on yellow-lined paper was written from a "deceased" Mia. I knew she was very much alive, but the words "Dear Mom, today I died" felt very real as a brief thought of a world without her sucked air from my lungs and made my legs feel like lead sinkers.

On the side addressed to me, I read of her admiration of my strength. She spoke of her gratitude for my intervention on her behalf. I learned of the pride she had for herself and who she had become. My Cheshire smile returned. The second side was a thank you to Joe for being the cool dad, the dad who tried to make her smile when she was down, and a dad who taught her to be strong.

Tears welled and fell as I carefully folded the papers and tucked them into the envelope for Joe to read later. I couldn't have been more thankful for the day Mia "died" and for the teachers who provided the means for her to express her gratitude. So many moments through the tumult of her teenage years made me question my parenting decisions, my confidence often in shreds. To understand what Mia felt was a gift. Her letters, along with Anna's, were my most prized possessions.

I moved from my bedroom to the hall to sit amidst Mia's mess where I could easily feel her presence. No sooner had I settled myself against the wall when my cell phone rang. It was Mia. She'd been paging through her college planner and found the letter I wrote to her paperclipped to her first day of class. I smiled as she cried, knowing the string of twinkle lights she'd hung by her bed were illuminating tears of thankfulness.

Mia soon got busy joining committees and clubs. She began to blossom with friendships and experiences, structure and community. On occasion, she'd reply to my texts. On rare occasions, she'd call. We'd talk for hours, each of us grasping for connection. I'd tell her things she knew nothing about. I'd hear quick references to things I knew little about.

"Mom, I went on a hike with a group of friends in the campus bluffs. We made a campfire in the ring near the top. We toasted marshmallows. It was so cool! We could see the lights of the town below reflecting in the river."

Mia, like me, was fond of marshmallows slowly toasted over a fire until puffed and caramel. She'd tuck the molten sugar in between two crisp graham crackers layered with a chocolate chunk. Her thumb and fingers would press gently on the crackers, waiting until the chocolate was melted and oozing before taking her first bite. *How many of these had she made over fire rings on camping trips or with friends in the backyard?*

As soon as that happy memory had played itself out in my mind, a suspicious thought crept in. I imagined a ring of homesick freshman drinking beer, and eating marshmallows, around the campfire made high in the bluffs. A rush to nag, to remind her she was underage, choked in my throat. The referee in my head, however, stepped in. She threw her red card in the air and cried "Foul!" I was sent to the corner to change the subject before I could interfere.

"Mia, Isabelle found a home!"

"Remind me which one is Isabelle."

"She's the miniature Schnoodle like Rascal with a kink in her ear. I sent you her picture. An elderly couple adopted her, giving our old friend a comfortable home. They have a fenced yard. Attached to the garage is a stairway to the attic with a wide landing. The first thing she did when she got in the yard was to climb those stairs and bark into the dark. I think she was telling the other animals to 'look out, the queen is here.'"

"That's funny, Mom. Congratulations on finding her a home. Hey, remember my friend Mara?"

"The one you discovered lives by Grandma?"

"Yeah. We volunteered at the Humane Society. We played for a half hour with the kittens at the end of our shift!"

"What a great way to start your weekend." I let my smile radiate between us while the memory of our three kittens fostered alongside Skip flashed in my mind.

"Guess what, Mia? I found a bus route that stops in front of my new job. I'm now a card-carrying member of the commuter community. The park-n-ride is near the pet store—lucky for our pets!"

"That's great, Mom. It will be less stressful for you at rush hour. How do you like your new job?" My heart skipped with arms swinging gaily at the genuine concern she had for me.

"It's a stepping stone. I'll have to hustle after the holidays to find a long-term job before my contract runs out." I paused momentarily to bottle the sorrow always threatening to escape, hoping Mia wouldn't notice. "For now, a steady income and relief from the chaos of juggling too many hats are good enough."

The more I tried to sugarcoat the loss of the creative freedoms I once enjoyed, the tighter the grip of suffocation. I was that kayaker stranded against the rock of grief, inching closer to the bubbling water. I had little energy to fight the rising pressure, so I quickly changed the subject.

"So...tell me about your classes. What book are you reading in Honors?"

The banter with Mia brought some reassurance I sought about her transition. Her class load was bearable. Her medication, working. Rising to the rim was a resilience I hadn't heard before. Perhaps she was growing stronger roots outside the shadow of her older sister. So much attention had been paid to Anna's hyperactivity. It made sense Mia needed room to grow.

Weeks later my cell phone flashed while my vacuum hummed. I shut off the power and set my chore aside.

"Mommmmmm," Mia choked and sputtered. "I broke up with Luke."

"Why?" was all I could mutter as her sadness pulled me into her chasm of sorrow. There was little I could offer over the distance between us. No arms around her shoulders. No shoulder for her head to rest. Amidst one big hiccup of tears, she paused for a knock on her door. Into that brief silence we both heard the coo of a dove. "Mia, we just heard about the breakup. How ya doing?"

"Ashlie's here with Mara, Mom. I gotta go. Love ya." Silence.

I watched from a distant mountaintop as Mia's new friends poured into the space I once filled. With nothing left to offer from my end, I leashed up the dogs, letting my four-legged friends and an old routine provide comfort. Not far past the osprey nest, a smile began to radiate from the depths of my heart as I recalled the tenacity of Mia to advocate for herself. Luke was a good-hearted young man who wanted more than Mia was ready to give. It pained her to disappoint others, yet she hated to disappoint herself more.

I was reflecting on Mia's self-advocacy two weeks later when the phone in my pocket began a steady *buzz-buzz-buzz* like metal tweezers striking metal body in the game of Operation. I quickly grabbed my phone, anxious to hear how Mia was faring. The desperation in Dan's voice startled me. I'd left my recent foster dog Aristotle with Dan and his elderly mother the night before. The two adults had been beaming like youngsters given a red-bowed pup for their birthdays.

"Please," he begged. "Come get Aristotle. Keep our money. Just get him out of our home!"

He wasn't screaming obscenities like Lizzie's first adopter, but he made it clear Aristotle was no longer welcome. When I arrived a short time later, two adults in tears, bodies propped against each to buoy unspoken weight, apologized profusely. The mother was overcome by the realization she'd grown too old and frail to care for a young dog. The son was overcome with guilt; he'd carefully hidden his crippling anxiety during the screenings and contract signing. Aristotle, caught in their rude awakenings, had been banished to a makeshift crate in a dark corner of their tiny kitchen, not a toy in sight.

Aristotle had been plucked from the streets of St. Paul by Animal Control several weeks earlier. Attached to his collar was a tag bearing his name and a phone number. The woman on the other end of the phone line repeatedly hung up each time Animal Control announced who they were. Aristotle had been dumped.

At first glance, he appeared to be a German Shepherd: erect ears, long, black muzzle, distinctive black and tan markings. Yet at nine pounds and one year, he was fully grown. As he walked around the counter at Life Care, he carried himself on the long legs of a fawn.

I walked him in the neighborhood by the vet clinic before driving home. He never lifted his leg, not even on the fire hydrant. Once home, I walked him in my backyard. He expressed no interesting in marking, not even on Rascal's favorite tree. When I took him into the house to greet Margo and Rascal, he left a puddle on the floor.

I tried as best I could to channel my inner "Jeff" as my exasperation grew with Aristotle's lack of house training. Jeff, of Jeff and Alex—our long-time friends from parenting class—was Joe's hero for being a straight shooter. One day during class when all the parents were in a huff over potty-training our toddlers, Jeff remained calm and unmoved. He looked at the rest of us and said, "Relax, I've been a high school teacher for many years. I've yet to see a kid come to class in diapers." Laughter calmed the group. Jeff's insight reframed our absurd worry.

My fret about Aristotle and house training was for naught anyway. Aris turned to Rascal, not me, for inspiration. He began following Rascal's lead outside, peeing on rocks and tree trunks and clumps of grass. Like Rascal, he became a "budger," nudging hands and arms to secure attention from any human willing to oblige. Much to Rascal's dismay, Aristotle started pushing Rascal away from me to be in prime petting position. As much as I tried to defend Rascal, Aristotle rewrote the rules of our dogdom. He soon rose to king of the pack.

While Rascal was overtly disturbed by Aristotle, Margo was delighted. She loved her little friend who started each day by jumping into the toy baskets to rid them of their contents one by one. Margo's monstrous tail would wag in excitement and send withers wiggling and objects on tables scattering to the floor. Like an old-time prop propeller on a plane, the more Margo's tail wagged, the faster she'd chase Aris around the sectional and over the coffee table until she was flying onto the cushions for a sparring fest. Rascal would bark from his forlorn corner of the room. The cats would scatter.

Aristotle had been with us long enough for me to write and post a truthful profile about his personality and needs. My first attempt to place Aristotle in Dan's home with his elderly mother, however, served as the reminder some people might not always be completely truthful with me.

I met Aristotle's next suitor, twenty-year-old Josh, at a Petco halfway between our homes. As soon as the tall young man bent over to pet Aris, the shaking dog pooped in the Petco aisle. I turned to run from embarrassment, using the need to clean up the mess as my ruse. But Josh made a move first.

"Let me go get the supplies while you calm Aristotle."

Relief washed over me like a gentle wave on a warm beach. As he stooped to clean up the mess, Aris inched close to investigate. Soon he was leaning into Josh's petting. Josh sat on the floor with the little Shepherd in his lap and began to pepper me with questions, the first being "How does he signal his need to go out?"

"I haven't picked up on any signals, but he is listening," I commented. "I walk towards the door and say, 'Aris, go potty,' and he usually sprints to me."

As soon as those words tumbled from my mouth, their absurdity landed in the abyss between me, a mother who raised two daughters, and Josh, a young man. I immediately cringed at the thought of Josh yelling "Aris, go potty" in front of his friends. Without losing a beat, Josh salvaged the awkward moment; he recounted how his family used the same phrase when house training their dogs. With those first impressions, I was confident Aristotle had found his forever home.

Aristotle's adoption and my creative problem-solving with Isabelle served as the wake-up I needed to better frame the changes that'd befallen me. I was not quite settled in my new role as employee rather than employer, but letting go of the throttle let time rush in. It'd been decades since I could close the door of work on a Friday and not open it again until Monday. I now spent weekends fully present when we'd visit Anna and Mia—no social media to write or post, no design proposals to draft. Joe and I vacationed without my computer. My garden blossomed with few weeds to compete. In my honest assessment of self-employed versus traditional employment, the scales of happiness were starting to tip towards a steady income and benefits. A bit more patience and persistence, perhaps a few more trips to the library for more books on resume writing and transferrable skills, and I'd find the right place to land. It was a good theory, and I was sticking with it.

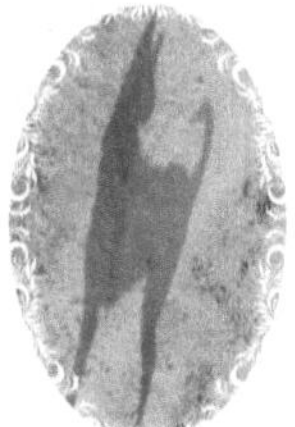

FRANKIE

Chapter 20

I was thirty-six resumes into rejection when Lynda called with a fostering opportunity. I declined her full-scale commitment and asked for a temporary assignment instead. I needed to stay focused. Looking for a job while working eight to five was more time-consuming than I'd planned. I knew from experience fostering a dog from pickup at Life Care to placement in a forever home would require more time than I should devote.

When I opened the crates in the back of Lynda's SUV, the stench of Frankie and Teddy, two young brothers in need of weekend shelter, greeted me before I had the chance to lock eyes. Vomit dripped from their Shih Tzu beards. Panic catapulted them out of the car and into the puddle-ridden parking lot. Wet and stinky, I herded them into my car where they proceeded to vomit more during the short ride home. I let them into the backyard with Margo, Rascal, and Crosby (visiting for the week) to calm their nerves after the passing of a loud and lively summer storm. Five wet dogs, of which two were intact males, altered between grass eating, vomiting, barking, peeing, posturing, and drooling. Once inside, toys flew from baskets, loud barks initiated raucous games of tug-of-war.

After three rowdy days with five dogs, I rose before sunrise eagerly readying Frankie and Teddy for their trip to Life Care. The two brothers would get proper medical care, then go to their designated foster homes. I breathed a sigh of relief. My short-term assignment was nearly complete. It was success on a small scale, and I loved it.

Four days later, Lynda called with another request, involving only Frankie. His foster family had to leave town for a week for a family emergency. Frankie needed a temporary home. I accepted with the belief it would be short-lived. When the foster family returned, their family dog, recently diagnosed with cancer, was in a state of rapid decline. They no longer wished to care for Frankie, choosing instead to focus their attention on their family's needs. Frankie was once again without a home. My vow to take only temporary assignments eroded. We were back to a full-scale commitment.

When Frankie and Teddy first came to my house, I couldn't imagine bonding with Frankie. He was a blur of pacing and whininess. He sought attention, only to draw back when he registered my unfamiliar face. No amount of walking or food calmed him. He slept only at night wound tightly around Teddy. After Frankie returned from Life Care, however, he was a new and improved dog, eagerly nosing himself into every activity in our home with a mischievous personality. He smiled often, his little pink tongue contrasting with his cream-colored beard and dark nose. A faint raccoon mask framed his bright marble eyes. His ink-tipped ears were always damp from dangling in his water dish. It seemed neutering had done him a world of good.

One morning while walking the dogs, I stopped at the lake's edge to let Margo wade belly deep. Frankie trailed Margo into the water with the certainty of a water bird. My eyes immediately went into lifeguard mode like they did when Anna and Mia were young. I had no idea what this dog, abandoned in a city apartment, knew about water. Fifteen minutes later, I had to drag a reluctant Frankie out of the lake. He'd exhausted himself from paddling circles around Margo and herding sticks. From that day forward, anything that held water, held Frankie. He would jump into bathtubs and sneak under shower curtains. I filled large pans and turkey roasters so he could splash in our backyard. He played in the rain when I let him.

That same summer, the businesses of White Bear Lake hosted Dog Days Downtown. People and their pets were invited to stroll along the sidewalks, shop in the stores with dogs in tow, indulge kids and dogs in treats, and visit with rescue agencies to learn about dogs available for adoption. Joe dropped me off in front of Grandma's Bakery after helping to set up our Second Chance table. I hadn't expected much else. Joe had grown quite fond of Frankie and was certain he would get adopted. Joe hated to say goodbye. So he left.

Frankie and I sat on a bench in the cool shade of the bakery awning indulging in homemade treats and ample attention. Mia couldn't make it, but her parade friend, Shelby, came to help. Lynda joined us with two charismatic Shih Tzus in need of a home. The day was one big dog parade after another.

A local resident, Sheryl, had seen the poster of Frankie I'd pinned to the grocery store bulletin board. She'd read about him online. Her dog had died two years earlier. Her heart, now mended, was ready for another.

"Is he house-trained?" She asked. An easy question to launch a discussion.

"He's nearly there," I responded, moving closer to Sheryl so we could hear each other over the growing crowd of chattering people and barking dogs. "He's been a fast learner and an eager pleaser. He hasn't had an accident in over a week. I don't want to give him a 100% rating because I don't know what he'll do under the stress of a new home."

Sheryl stooped to pet a now-panting Frankie. We were still in the shade of the awning, but the summer heat was rising and the breeze from the lake stifled by the throng of people. I turned to pick up a folder from the table to use as a fan when I spotted Joe walking towards us.

"What are you doing here?" I asked, my voice rising with my eyebrows as I tried to reconcile the surprise. "Did I forget something in the truck?"

"No," he casually responded as if it was normal for him to be at an adoption event. "I just came to see what's going on."

I cast aside my suspicion so as not to alarm Sheryl and introduced her to Joe instead.

"Sheryl," Joe jumped in. "Would you like to see Frankie swim? Someone put out wading pools on the sidewalk around the block. I bet he'd like to cool off."

"Come on, Shelby. Take a walk with us," Joe invited.

Joe, Shelby, and Sheryl walked Frankie to the shallow pools filled with cool water. I learned that Frankie spied the floating yellow balls and jumped right in. Sheryl was ecstatic to see such a cute and lively pup filled with joy. Joe was thrilled to see Sheryl delight in Frankie's charm.

When they returned to our table, water dripping from Frankie's black-tipped ears, Joe turned to me, shoulders squared, and said, "If Sheryl wants him, she can adopt Frankie."

It wasn't as easy as that, so Lynda inserted herself into the conversation and began peppering Sheryl with a list of screening questions. Joe's intuition was important, but the adoption process reigned king.

Joe told me later he'd had a good feeling about Sheryl from the moment he met her. The conversations they had on the walk to and from the pool convinced him she was a good fit. His intuition was amply rewarded when I called Sheryl to check up on how Frankie was doing. Happiness bubbled like cheap champagne as she exclaimed, "I can't believe how easy this transition has been. Frankie is already settled into my home. You and Joe did a wonderful job caring for him. Thank you. Thank you. Thank you."

I channeled the confidence I gained with our Frankie success into another personal round of informational meetings and job applications. With nose to the grindstone, I edited and adapted each resume based on keywords I'd scour from job descriptions. I felt like the ball in a game of roulette, my words bouncing around the spinning wheel until settling into some random pocket. I cupped my hands around the ball and whispered good luck each time I threw a resume onto the spinning track. Unfortunately, my good fortune from Frankie had dried up. My hope of finding a new job while still employed fizzled like a dud on the Fourth of July.

I packed a small box with the few pictures adorning my cubicle, the tiny orchid Mia had given me the day she met me downtown for lunch, and my walking shoes for lunchtime diversions through the skyway maze. Weighted by heaviness of heart, I nearly missed the last bus home.

Rascal greeted me at the door, tail wagging and front legs pawing for attention. At nine, he still had plenty of energy but no longer jumped into my arms like a clown. His shrill yapping created the sole ruckus, and he reveled in it; the center of attention was the place he'd longed to be. I lifted him onto my lap, letting his exuberance wash away some of the grief that had multiplied from my last day of employment and the quietness of a home without Margo.

It was not long after Frankie left for Sheryl's that I woke up early one morning to take the dogs out before work. As my feet touched the floor, I immediately noticed Margo was missing from her usual spot by my bed. *No worries.* On warm days, she often slept under the window by Joe. Instead, I found her nose to the corner like a kid wearing a dunce cap, standing still as a statue, refusing to move. Joe and I gently rolled her sixty pounds onto a blanket and carried her to the car. Joe rushed her to the local clinic, sitting by her side until it was determined she needed more advanced diagnostic testing than they could provide.

I met Joe at the same emergency clinic where I'd brought Poet. I found Joe sitting knees to chest on the floor with an unusually quiet Margo lying by his side. Joe, with nerves beyond frayed, left shortly after I arrived. I took over petting Margo's wavy fur, talking quietly to her as the doctor administered the medicine that took her last breath. There were no options to save her. Margo's life had met death quickly when a previously undiagnosed spleen tumor ruptured.

Joe and I took our grief to the patio of a local restaurant, letting early autumn sun-dry the tears we tried to hide from the waitstaff. We'd met in the ring, rather than retreat to opposite corners. We toasted the memory of our sweet dog and the loss of a great hiking buddy. We leaned into each other for solace, knowing the girls had already reached out to friends to help ease their sorrow.

Rascal, who I thought would retreat in grief like Margo after Poet's death, reveled in the attention of a one-dog household. He began sleeping on my lap while I worked at my desk, budging Sunny out of her usual position. He'd snore, with toenails clicking, keeping me entertained while I searched for solutions to my unemployment dilemma.

I startled Rascal from sleep when I opened my email to find a note about unemployment benefits. "I'll be," I said out loud. I'd spent a better part of my working life in self-employment. It'd never crossed my mind to inquire about unemployment benefits. But there on the computer screen was the link to the application and the State benefits page. A day later, an invitation to a benefits orientation awaited my reply.

I sat in a cold, windowless room on the type of summer day I'd rather play hooky than watch anxious people bounce their knees and wipe sweat from their temples. At the head of the classroom, an employment liaison droned on about minimum requirements to receive a weekly check. A few low groans spread like spilled water when she said we were required to attend weekly classes. A collective moan rolled like a wave when she held up the weekly form to track those classes, jobs applied for, and interviews taken. No completed form? Then no check.

To get paid to take free classes seemed like an unfair exchange until I learned just how small my weekly check would be. It was enough to keep us from drowning, but not enough motivation to stay unemployed. The true hope for me lay in the classes and the counseling that could breathe new life into an old routine. I'd been resolute that I could find a job on my own given enough persistence, patience, and research at the library. The growing number of rejections proved I needed to stop doing the same thing while wishing for a different result. It was time to try something new.

Off I went to unemployment centers across the Twin Cities to learn about career change resumes and better ways to flaunt transferable skills. One-to-one meetings with my assigned counselor helped me hone my resumes and cover letters to current trends and specific job descriptions. Role-playing classes provided opportunities to practice the dreaded interview.

Two months later I sat at a new desk looking out an expansive window. The city skyline framed the tree-lined park below. No short-term contract this time, but a full-time job (!) with ample benefits, a bit further from home.

A longer commute and no kids left on the fostering team meant I could only take on short-term fostering assignments. In quick succession came Murphy and Sterling, with white curls and round black noses like Crosby. Zoey and Roscoe, white and caramel terrier mixes, each with a kink in one ear. And Sherlock, a darker version of Aristotle. Each brought a unique energy and inquisitiveness. Some, like Murphy and Zoey, fostered new human relationships tethered by photos and texts shared through the years. Their leaving always brought an audible sigh of relief from Rascal.

I was shifting my car into drive in the parking lot of the park-n-ride at the end of a tiring day when my phone started flashing. It was Lynda. I had a good idea what she wanted; she rarely called for something other than a need for an empty crate in our home. As I slid the car back into park, I steeled myself for the conversation to come.

"Cindy, I have a little Yorkie-mix I'd like to get out of animal impound. There are no open homes but yours. Could you take her on Friday?"

Oh god. My heart felt like a rope had been fastened around it and the heavy stone at the other end falling into deep water. *If I don't take the dog, who will? If I take the dog, how will Rascal fare?* Reason rose from the bottom of the sea, tossing my sense of duty to the wind. After twenty-five fostered dogs, a few of them foster failures, I said no to Lynda. Not because I was done fostering, but because Rascal was growing sicker by the day. We'd been able to manage the symptoms of his Cushing's disease for nearly a year after Margo's death, but the enemy was encroaching. I couldn't add the stress of a new dog to his daily effort to fight.

Rascal got to revel in the joy of being the only dog a few more months before Joe and I gave each other that look: we knew it was time. Rascal had lost a quarter of his body weight. At nine years, he looked elderly and disheveled with sunken eyes and greasy, thinning fur. He shook while standing. His muscles spasmed when he tried to rest. Comfort was no longer something I could give.

The first time I walked to the lake alone, I was amazed how quickly I could get there and back without a dog snuffling through the weeds or stopping to mark each blade of grass. The clarity of the birds conversing in the boughs was unsettling. So was the awareness of being alone. With no other eyes or ears to serve guard, I stopped walking the road.

I upped my walking game at work instead. I'd clock miles by city block with colleagues. We'd cross the Mississippi River at lunch or meander along its shaded edges midafternoon. In winter, we'd strap snowshoes to our boots, stamping skinny ovals into the snow. From my desk at the big window, it would look like a herd of deer had run over the hill in the park.

No dogs at home meant I had more time to putter in my garden. I was leaning over to pull weeds when I felt the familiar buzz of my phone. A smile spread across my face when I saw Sharon's name illuminated on the screen. For three years after she and Don adopted Shiloh, I'd receive regular texts and photos of the smiling, ginger-haired dog we all cherished.

My voice was full of happy. Hers wasn't. Shiloh was fine. Sharon's life was chaotic, forcing her family down a path different from the one they'd forged when they adopted Shiloh. With little time to devote to the still-energetic dog, Sharon asked for my help to find her a new home.

I fought the lump forming in my throat from their loss and my gain. I'd given up that girl when our house was full. I'd let logic steer me down the street with "the right way" sign, always regretting I had not veered left. Shiloh had been the one great dog I'd let go. My great regret was on her way back.

I didn't bring up the idea of adopting Shiloh right away. "We're just fostering," I replied when Joe asked. And I meant it. Joe and I had settled into the rhythm of a relationship unencumbered by kids.

Shiloh was the one to cast the line to hook our hearts. No campaign poster needed. Joe threw a tennis ball into the lake. When Shiloh dove in like Frankie to retrieve it, her adoption was sealed.

I made peace with the winding road outside our home with Shiloh walking beside me. Days turned to passing seasons as ospreys nested, fed, and fledged their young. The oaks, always the last to yield to autumn, would paint their leaves deep hues of red and gold before falling, sometimes onto soft beds of snow. We met new neighbors moving into the homes of old friends.

Anna, the kid we once feared would fail high school, graduated with an advanced degree, got her first job, and moved with her boyfriend, Shaun, to a house with a yard and garden. They rescued a kitten named Chili and adopted a dog named Clyde. Reggie, a.k.a. Mr. Muscles, who'd been spending his days bullying Sunny, went north to live with Anna and Shaun. Sunny purred with Reggie gone.

Mia, the kid who took her first steps before most babies could crawl, continued to seek solace from the dogs, her new kitten, Rambo, our home, and her friends, when her pendulum swung left. She'd use the time to recharge before the starter's gun would signal a swing to the right. With the energy of an Olympic sprinter, she completed her undergraduate degree a semester early, then moved home to work and save money for vet school. She jokingly called Shiloh "sister" while enjoying every moment being the only child.

The world was on pause amidst a global pandemic when Anna brought Clyde home for a visit. Joe and the girls joined me on the screen porch where I'd spread community newspapers over the glass tabletop. I'd scattered tiny pots of paint and paintbrushes between the flat rocks we'd found during a recent trip to Lake Michigan. We talked as we painted the rocks with the names of the pets who'd joined our family since we'd begun to foster. Mia occasionally added a few lines of text to her veterinary school application, open on the computer on her lap. Anna would pause to read a few lines of local news, commenting on people she knew from high school. Two dots were aligned on the strand of sibling DNA.

I brought our binder of foster dog photos to the table when the conversation turned in that direction. Anna and Mia were older and feared reprisal less. Stories of spoiling were abundant. I learned how they fed dogs under the table when I wasn't looking, letting them lick over-easy eggs off their plates. Mia, with a stash of dog treats in her nightstand, would feed them snacks, walk past the crate where they were supposed to sleep, and pat her pillow to invite them to sleep on her bed. At the sight of Rascal's photo, Anna and Mia both exclaimed, "Cuuuuute!" He was sporting a baby blue bandana after his first real haircut.

Then Anna continued, "You know, Mom. Mia and I have Rascal to thank. Because he was so focused on you, you focused your helicopter tendencies on him instead of us! Our friends weren't always so fortunate to have diversions for their parents' control."

I sat dumbfounded as Anna and Mia continued to talk about Rascal, letting sink in the revelation I wasn't the overbearing parent I thought I'd been. Warmth coursed to my toes and into my fingertips as Mia agreed with Anna, both joking about my doting ways with Rascal. As their laughter punctuated the night, Shiloh and Clyde lifted their heads from slumber, then fell back asleep.

We were fortunate during the pandemic. We had our health, our jobs, each other. We could easily escape to the solitude of nature that was right outside our door. I was grateful for the opportunity to work again from home, from my home office, or on the porch, with my eyes over our kingdom of cats and dogs. Others were struggling, but we weren't.

It hadn't been so during the Great Recession nor the early years of ADHD and anxiety. Those days were anything but calm, and yet they were rich because we'd survived it all together. We'd tested our limits and discovered new strengths. We learned to advocate for ourselves and each other, to trust our intuition. We navigated a wide range of character-building moments, including those from the unending parade of dogs. We tended many dogs that'd been abused or neglected. We embraced a few that grew too old or too sick for their families. We cared for the beloved pets of people who themselves grew too old or too sick to care for their pets. Our ringside view of the rescue system connected us directly with the kindness of strangers who adopted our dogs and were equally committed to their care.

When people learn we foster dogs, the number one comment is "I could never do what you do. I would fall too hard in love." We do fall in love. But the pain of separation got easier to navigate as we learned perspective: letting a dog go to live a happy life in a good home was a worthy goal. We got the joy of knowing we saved one life while creating space in our home to save another. Fostering meant we'd continually experience the joy of unwrapping a birthday present; we genuinely didn't know who'd come around the corner at Life Care! Nothing beat the heartfelt thank-yous from adoptive families head over heels in love with their pet.

Most importantly, we learned that grief and growth required tolerance and nurturing. To be a confident leader required patience and calm; control was more a disruptor than a motivator. By letting go of perfection to set reasonable expectations, Joe and I helped Mia and Anna construct ropes of their own, with a yarn or two willingly tethered to home.

For more stories and to stay connected,
visit www.cindyowrites.com

ACKNOWLEDGMENTS

There would be no story without the privilege of being a parent. To my courageous daughters, Anna and Mia, I love you to the moon and back. You continue to be the reason I rise each morning. To my husband who cherishes unfettered quiet, thank you for standing beside me in the noise.

This story would have unfolded on different pages had it not been for the gentle guidance of the physicians, mental health professionals, school counselors, and teachers who believed in us. I'm particularly grateful for Dr. Jeff Steffenson, Dr. Bonnie Carlson-Greene, and Brian Merhar.

My original manuscript on how to foster dogs found new life through generous early readers. Deep gratitude to Rob Salvino and Pik Watson for challenging me to reach into my soul for the tale that would resonate with parents of teens. To Sharon and Joe Soderlund, Kirsten and Mason Olson-Schultz, Val Bourassa, and Laura Justus, your suggestions nourished my words. To Kathe Stanton, those countless meetings amid coffee shop clatter helped clear a pathway to transformation. Marion Wolbers, your editing prowess provided the essential polish.

Lynda Ahlgren, Rebecca Rosenthal, and Marilyn Schroeder of Second Chance Animal Rescue, your commitment to reducing animal suffering continues to inspire me and thousands of supporters. Thank you for your countless sacrifices and for taking precious time to read my manuscript.

Dr. Bonnie said it best: "All you need is one good friend." I'm fortunate to have two whose outstretched hands repeatedly pull me from the muck. Nancy Purdy, your wisdom and eagle eyes mean more than the em dashes you wrangled. Loree Wirtz Odom, your voice through the phone static has kept me afloat for decades.

To Snuka, the first dog I rescued, you transformed my life with your profound love and trust. Caring for you altered the trajectory of my journey. Because of you, my heart opened to helping other animals in need.

To the foster dogs and foster fails who walked beside me, Joe, Anna, and Mia on our winding road, we will carry you with us forever.

DISCUSSION QUESTIONS FOR BOOK CLUBS

PET ADOPTION AND CARE

1. What challenges did the family face when integrating newly adopted dogs into their home, and how did those challenges reflect deeper emotional or relational dynamics?

2. How did the family's routine around feeding, exercise, and housetraining evolve with each new dog, and what did those routines reveal about their capacity for flexibilty and patience?

3. How do the dog's personalities and behaviors mirror the humans caring for them?

4. Which dog would you adopt and why?

PET FOSTERING

1. What are the emotional and logistical challenges of fostering pets, especially in a family with children?

2. How does the concept of "foster failure" evolve in the story, and what does it reveal about the family's values?

3. How does fostering serve as both a healing tool and source of tension within the family?

4. What are the differences between fostering a pet and adopting a pet?

PET LOSS AND GRIEF

1. How does the family's response to Sierra's sudden death set the emotional tone for the rest of the memoir? In what ways does it shape their decisions around fostering and adoption?

2. What parallels can be drawn between the grief of losing a pet and the emotional challenges the family faces with their daughters' mental health?

3. How does the author's approach to grief evolve from Sierra's passing to the later losses of Poet, Margo, and Rascal? What does this say about healing over time?

4. What lessons about letting go—of pets, expectations, or control—are learned through the fostering process?

TEEN MENTAL HEALTH

1. What role do the dogs play in helping Anna and Mia navigate anxiety, ADHD, and emotional upheaval?

2. How does the family's evolving understanding of mental health reflect broader societal shifts in awareness and acceptance?

3. How did the process of diagnosing ADHD in both Anna and Mia unfold, and what emotional or relational challenges did the family face during that journey?

4. What strategies—medical, behavioral, or environmental—proved most helpful in supporting Anna and Mia, and

how did those strategies evolve as the girls few older?

INTUITION AND IMPERFECTION IN PARENTING

1. How does the narrator's reliance on intuition shape her decisions as a mother and foster caregiver?

2. What does the memoir suggest about the value of imperfection in parenting and caregiving?

3. What does the memoir teach us about resilience—not just in children or animals, but in parents themselves?

4. How did the process of learning each dog's unique needs—whether behavioral, emotional, or medical—mirror the family's jouney of learning to care for one another?

LAUNCHING INTO ADULTHOOD

1. How did the transition from high school to college affect the family dynamic, especially between sisters and their parents?

2. In what ways did the dogs serve as emotional anchors during this period of change?

3. What does the memoir suggest about the evolving role of a parent as children grow into young adults? How does one stay connected while giving space?

4. How was the narrator preparing for the profound change of no longer being a fulltime parent?

FOR MORE PEOPLE AND PET STORIES, LET'S CONNECT!

Cindy has been helping people and their pets through stories of **family, friendship, mental wellness, healthy living, pet rescue and fostering**, and more, on Substack and at cindyowrites.com Subscribe to receive her newsletter and get **stories, news, recommendations, and other** updates delivered right to your inbox!
Visit www.cindyowrites.com

***

DID THE STORIES OF RAISING TEENS AND RESCUING PETS RESONATE WITH YOU?

If so, **please** help others find this book by leaving a *rating and/or review*!
Mom Loves the Dogs More on Amazon:

About the Author

Cindy Ojczyk is an award-winning writer, lifelong pet foster, and quiet observer of the threads that bind people to pets. Her work explores the devotion we've shaped in dogs and cats as a reflection of the love and loyalty we yearn to offer—and receive.

She lives near Minneapolis with her husband, a revolving cast of foster animals, and a few eccentric rescues who keep life interesting. Her adult children, raised in a home full of fur, now tend to menageries of their own. Her debut memoir, *Mom Loves the Dogs More*, is a meditation on trust, grief, and second chances. Learn more at cindyowrites.com